Popular Culture and
Political Change
in
Modern America

SUNY Series in Popular Culture and Political Change

Larry Bennett and Ronald Edsforth, Editors

Popular Culture and Political Change in Modern America

edited by

Ronald Edsforth

and

Larry Bennett

State University of New York Press

"Coxey's Army as a Millenial Movement," by Michael Barkun, was originally published in *Religion,* Summer 1989: Copyright 1989, Academic Press Inc. Ltd., London England. Reprinted by permission.

"Encountering Mass Culture at the Grassroots: The Experience of Chicago Workers in the 1920s," by Lizabeth Cohen, was originally published in *American Quarterly,* vol. 41, no. 1, pp. 6–33, Copyright 1989. Reprinted by permission.

Production by Leslie Frank-Hass
Marketing by Terry Swierzowski

Published by
State University of New York Press, Albany

For information, address State University of New York
Press, State University Plaza, Albany, N.Y., 12246

Library of Congress Cataloging in Publication Data

Popular culture and political change in modern America / edited by
    Ronald Edsforth and Larry Bennett.
          p. cm.—(SUNY series in popular culture and political
    change)
      Includes bibliographical references and index.
      ISBN 0-7914-0765-9 (CH : acid-free).—ISBN 0-7914-0766-7 (PB :
    acid-free)
      1. United States—Popular culture—History—20th century.
    2. Politics and culture—United States—History—20th century.
    I. Edsforth, Ronald, 1948–   . II. Bennett, Larry, 1950–
    III. Series.
    E169.1.P5902   1991   # 22381682
    306'.0973—dc20   90-47621
                                                          CIP

10 9 8 7 6 5 4 3 2 1

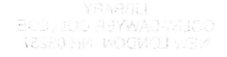

Dedicated to the memory of Howard Abramowitz:

He helped keep us all free.

CONTENTS

PREFACE AND ACKNOWLEDGMENTS

This book has been a long time coming. It began as an idea batted among good friends, and has survived repeated employment difficulties, serious illness, and the deaths of parents and a close colleague. There were many times during the past few years when we questioned the sanity of devoting so much time and mental energy to a project that promised no material rewards or advancement. However, through it all, the two of us believed it was important to develop a way to speak seriously about the history of popular culture and politics that avoided the pitfall of academic obscurantism while at the same time refraining from the excessive enthusiasm so often encountered among those who write about popular culture. We hope the reader will agree that we have been at least partly successful. We also hope that the variety of voices and approaches collected in this volume will encourage others to reach across disciplinary and national boundaries and join us in this important scholarly endeavor.

Many people helped us keep this project on track. We are both deeply grateful for the assistance and support given by Clay Morgan, Peggy Gifford, and Dana Foote of State University of New York Press. Larry Bennett wishes to acknowledge the encouragement of his colleagues Michael Budde, Larry Grossberg, and Harry Wray. Nor would he have risked writing about the things he enjoys so much without the comradeship of fellow enthusiasts Richard DeCordova, Michael Hannon, Lisa Milam, Reece Pendleton, and the singular Gwyn Friend. Ronald Edsforth wishes to thank Robert Asher, Bruce Nelson, Richard Oestreicher, Nelson Lichtenstein, and Maurine Weiner Greenwald for friendship and support, and the History Faculty at MIT for providing the kind of positive work environment he hasn't known since graduate school. He also acknowledges his good friends Ralph Lombreglia and Kate Bernhardt who gave him a home away from home and constant intellectual stimulation during the last year of this project. And, of course, for her sustaining love and encouragement through some very trying times, he thanks Joanne Devine; she is simply the best.

Finally, the editors wish to dedicate this book to Howard Abramowitz, who died before it could be completed. Howard was the kind of activist teacher-scholar that drew so many students of the 1960s into the academic professions. As a young man, he fought the United States Army all the way to the Supreme Court in a case that in 1958 won freedom for all veterans from McCarthyite persecution for political affiliations prior to enlistment. Howard's lively imagination, good humor, and always active sense of justice made him an exemplary colleague. We miss him.

Ronald Edsforth
Larry Bennett

Chapter One

Popular Culture and Politics in Modern America: An Introduction

Ronald Edsforth

This book, *Popular Culture and Political Change in Modern America,* seeks to make a contribution to a rapidly growing field of study. For more than a decade, scholars from various academic professions have been turning in increasing numbers to the historical study of the connections between politics and popular culture.[1] Today, in the United States, historians, sociologists, political scientists, anthropologists, and communications specialists are all working in this truly interdisciplinary field. There are several reasons for the current enthusiasm for this subject, some of them academic, and others directly related to the condition of politics and popular culture in our own time.

The field of study was clearly established when a few brilliant professors attracted bright students who in turn expanded and enriched the scholarly work begun by their mentors. In this particular field, the late Herbert Gutman and Warren Susman were two such founders.[2] The influence of Gutman and Susman was a powerful force on everyone studying American history in the 1970s, and it is still very much felt among a younger generation of scholars, including some of the contributors to this volume. In a sense, all of the essays presented here reveal their debt to Gutman and Susman by analyzing aspects of modern American political history and concurrent developments in popular culture, not separately, but as interdependent and equally important parts of a larger historical reality which must be studied whole.

"History, I am convinced," Warren Susman once wrote, "is not just something to be left to the historians."[3] During the past decade, the historical study of the links between politics and popular culture has expanded as new adherents were attracted from outside the profession of history. By the mid-1980s, a critical mass of newer mentors had emerged from a variety of academic disciplines. Scholars like Stuart Ewen, Neil Postman, T. J. Jackson

Lears, Lary May, Elaine Tyler May, Paul Buhle, and Todd Gitlin write for, and are reviewed in, both specialized academic journals and more widely circulated periodicals. Like a magnet, their work has drawn even more students, academics, and intellectuals into this expanding field of study. This volume, which includes essays by a sociologist, two political scientists, a comparative cultural anthropologist, as well as three historians, offers a selection of some of the newest voices in the field, whose work represents the latest stage of a still developing intellectual project.

Current interest in the historical links between politics and popular culture has also been shaped by the cyclical character of scholarly revision, which seems, in this case at least, to be directly influenced by generational changes. In the half century since World War II, this subject has been the focus of intense intellectual activity at least twice before our own day. During the early Cold War, a deeply pessimistic debate about "mass culture" and its effects on politics and art emerged among a varied group of highly visible intellectuals who had witnessed firsthand the horrors of fascism, stalinism, and global conflict. This debate engaged such diverse thinkers as Hannah Arendt, Edward Shils, H. Stuart Hughes, David Riesman, Dwight MacDonald, and the Frankfort school exiles—M. Leo Lowenthal, Theodor Adorno, and Max Horkheimer. For that generation of publicly prominent intellectuals, it was generally agreed that what they called "mass culture" was degraded and even brutal. As such, mass culture seemed a profound threat to creative expression, individuality, and democracy.[4]

The Frankfort school exiles set the tone for this first postwar round debate about the political significance of popular culture. They had been deeply shocked by the rise of National Socialism in Germany, an event they saw as uncovering the insidious potential of modern mass media. Using their distinctive critical theory, a blend of Marxism and Freudian psychology, to analyze modern capitalism and its communications technology, these thinkers came to the unambiguous conclusion that mass consumer-oriented culture was proto-fascist. In their seminal essay, "The Culture Industry: Enlightenment as Self-Deception," first published in 1944, Adorno and Horkheimer attacked the star system of Hollywood and popular jazz as evidence of the way mass consumer-oriented capitalism corrupted individualism by producing "the deceitful substitution of the stereotype for the individual." In such a society, Adorno and Horkheimer argued, a "pseudo-individuality" is mass-produced, which mesmerizes the population, destroying their own critical self-awareness, and opening the way for the anti-democratic politics of demagogues and dictators.[5]

The Frankfort school's extremely negative description of the political impact of mass culture has remained a staple of cultural commentary in the United States. Although its radical implications were never embraced by the more conservative intellectual mainstream, it still profoundly influenced the attitudes of whole generation of scholars who entered the academy in the late 1940s and the 1950s. This first postwar generation of intellectuals generally conceived of "mass," or "popular" culture as it is called here, as without redeeming value. In the tradition of Matthew Arnold, this mainstream bemoaned the debilitated state of so-called "high culture" in this country, contrasting its weaknesses with the vitality of the "lower" mass culture. In 1959, for example, at a symposium on the mass media, the prominent sociologist Edward Shils explicitly rejected the political implications of the Frankfort school analysis of mass culture in his keynote address. Nevertheless, in the same speech, Shils repeatedly derided what he saw as "the cascade of mediocre and brutal culture which pours out over the mass media."[6] Such sentiments were *de rigeur* in higher education and intellectual circles at the time. Thus, during the early Cold War era, becoming a professor included learning how to dismiss popular culture, and how to discourage students from taking it seriously.

The second round of postwar debate over the relationship between politics and popular culture emerged in the mid-1960s as part of the student generation's rebellion against the values of their professors and parents. The failure of higher education to actually insulate students from the influences of popular culture was revealed by this stage of the debate. It also rejected the basic premise of the original debate, the idea that popular culture was necessarily debased and degraded.

Ironically, the origins of this newer debate can be traced to the publication of Herbert Marcuse's *One-Dimensional Man: Studies in the Ideology of Advanced Industrial Societies* in 1964. Perhaps the most convincing of the Frankfort school's "mass culture" critiques, *One-Dimensional Man* seemed deliberately designed to depress and politically immobilize its readers. Relentlessly pessimistic in its analysis of the "pattern of one-dimensional thought and behavior" which Marcuse saw as a product of modern industrial capitalism, the book might have been read as an obituary for any hopes that something positive could come out of popular culture. "One dimensional thought is systematically promoted by the makers of politics and the purveyors of mass information," he proclaimed.[7] Yet, Marcuse was not read that way by the new generation of students, even when he was introduced to them by teachers who had learned to scorn and dismiss popular culture.

Instead, Marcuse's *One-Dimensional Man* became the touchstone of a new round of debate about the political character of popular culture because the most popular aspects of the youth culture of the day—like the music of Bob Dylan and the Beatles and the films of Stanley Kubrick and Arthur Penn—seemed to both confirm and contradict Marcuse's pessimistic analysis. Like Marcuse, the cultural heroes and heroines of this new music-based youth culture (Dylan, John Lennon, Mick Jagger, Jimi Hendrix, and Janis Joplin for example) recognized the sterility, conformism, and lack of passion in the lives of the dominant suburban-based middle class. At the same time, the youth culture's heroes and heroines (like the young Marlon Brando, James Dean, and Elvis Presley of the previous decade) projected the possibility of resistance and rebellion. Indeed, the lives of rock music stars as presented in song, on stage, and in films were an inspiration for the so-called "counterculture" of the era. That counterculture, with its insistence on the democratic, equalitarian, and oppositional potential of the production and consumption of popular culture, distinguished the New Left from the Old Left in the United States and Europe. Marcuse himself became a hero to this younger generation of rebellious students because he embraced, especially in his *An Essay on Liberation* (1969), what seemed to be the revolutionary potential of a popular youth culture that could promote in 1968 a Paris uprising, a Prague spring, and rebellions on American and Mexican university campuses.

In the mid-1960s, Marshall McLuhan and Susan Sontag also generated positive, widely discussed interpretations of the political-popular culture connection that transcended the earlier "mass culture" debate and offered more hope than Marcuse's *One-Dimensional Man*. Their work celebrated the use and integration of new mass media technology and techniques in art and politics. McLuhan, a Canadian literary critic famed for the slogan "the medium is the message," promoted acceptance of the same mass media technology which had been so feared by the Frankfort school and their followers. In his book, *Understanding Media: The Extensions of Man* (1964), McLuhan predicted a new era of human understanding would result from the establishment of a media-based "global village." Not surprisingly, this prediction was enthusiastically endorsed in the mass media, and derided as hopelessly naive by older radical critics. However, the eruption of worldwide youth protest in 1968, which shared ideas and styles clearly promoted by the mass media, made McLuhan look like a true prophet to many in the New Left and the counterculture.[8]

For her part, Susan Sontag rejected the dichotomy between the "high" culture of true art and the "low" culture of the technology-based mass media that had been a foundation of the mass-culture critique of the previous decade. Indeed, in a series of brilliant critical essays published in the mid-1960s, including "One Culture and the New Sensibility," Sontag endeared herself to artists, musicians, and student intellectuals by celebrating the artistic vitality and liberating potential of pop art, "happenings," and rock music.[9]

The cultural criticism of Marshall McLuhan and Susan Sontag revealed what was truly "counter" in the counterculture of the 1960s. Far from assuming that popular culture was proto-fascist, these leading intellectuals saw mass media technique and technology as aesthetically valid and potentially liberating. They gave credence to the belief that producing and consuming popular culture could mobilize political opposition to the war in Vietnam, the military-industrial complex, racism, sexism, and even mass-consumerism. Hence, a principal intellectual legacy of the New Left and the counterculture was the tendency to see popular culture as an anti-hierarchical, critical political force.

The way television news seemed to bring world events home in the 1960s heightened this conviction. Student strikes at foreign universities and international protests against dictatorial regimes and the Vietnam War were frequently shown to network news audiences. These broadcasts made American students more aware of their similarities with students in the rest of the world, and this, in turn, stimulated a greater interest in societies where the historical connections between politics and popular culture were already being studied systematically. By the 1970s, graduate students studying American society and culture eagerly read British historians like Eric Hobsbawn and E. P. Thompson, as well as French scholars like Roland Barthes and Michel Foucault. These developments finally opened the way for serious sustained study of the political role of popular culture in earlier periods of American life.

Herbert Gutman's extremely influential essay, "Work, Culture, and Society in Industrializing America," which appeared in the *American Historical Review* in 1973, explicitly acknowledged its debt to European scholars. It showed how previously unstudied aspects of American everyday life, such as the working class celebrations of secular holidays, could be presented as evidence of resistance to dominant corporate industrial capitalist development. Gutman's inclination to treat popular culture as a multi-faceted political resource, instead of a monolithic oppressive force, grew more widespread as many of the generation of 1960s undergraduates entered the academic professions. By the early 1980s, a core of younger professors had established this "new" American social history by making every aspect of everyday life and popular culture a valid subject for political analysis.

In the most optimistic of the new social histories, a book like Lewis Erenberg's *Steppin' Out: New York Night Life and the Transformation of American Culture, 1890–1930* (1981), the development of a mass-based popular culture phenomena is presented as a powerful creative and liberating force that resolves some of the problems of modern urban life. Summarizing the significance of the emergence of the nightclub, Erenberg exclaims:

> This pursuit of a release transformed American popular culture, opened up a vision of an expanded and deeper home life, and helped develop personalities more capable of self-development, self-gratification, and self-adjustment.[10]

Such an extremely positive assessment of popular music and dance fads would not have been possible in the 1950s, yet by the 1980s it had become a familiar interpretation in academic circles. This new view of the political character of popular culture was perhaps the most dramatic aspect of the New Left's break with the mass-culture critics. As the Reagan era dawned, it was becoming firmly entrenched in several academic disciplines because so many veterans of the New Left had established careers in higher education. Certainly, in the 1980s, the belief that popular culture is a contested political terrain and a potential source of rebellion was sustained, even as evidence of its hegemonic character mounted.

Of course, academic trends alone did not stimulate the current round of debate in this field. The foregoing account neglects a crucial development of the 1980s, which more than any other, highlighted the need for sustained systematic reflection on the relationship between what we call "popular culture" and what we call "political culture." This development was Ronald Reagan's mastery of the Presidency, and ultimately of the whole America political arena. Reagan's domination of the American political landscape in the 1980s necessarily focused academic attention on this subject because the President's career was so clearly a product of the popular culture.

Ronald Reagan was born in Illinois, but his real home was Hollywood. He served in the American armed forces in World War II, but as a non-combatant narrator of training films. His career as a film actor fizzled in the 1950s, but following a second career as a corporate spokesperson and his national television speech on behalf of Barry Goldwater in October 1964, Reagan emerged as a conservative political hero. Elected governor of California in 1966, he immediately set his sights on the White House. Ronald Reagan spent fourteen years as a professional Presidential candidate before he finally triumphed at the GOP convention and the polls in 1980.

In his eight years in the White House, Reagan certainly showed he was more than a product of the popular culture. The President and his team of advisors were also skilled producers of popular culture. Great extravaganzas like the First Inaugural Weekend and the Statue of Liberty Celebration were the equivalent of his administration's big-budget pictures. Press conferences and frequent appearances on the White House lawn were its daily network television fare.

The fact that Reagan was both a product and a producer of popular culture was self-evident. Yet the news media and most political analysts hardly knew what to make of it. They gave us the sobriquets "Teflon man" and the more ubiquitous "Great Communicator," but these terms, even when elaborated with descriptive details, hardly served to illuminate political developments. Instead, these terms were themselves popular cultural artifacts that actually blocked our view of the priority-setting, decision-making Ronald Reagan who stood behind them safe from the political criticisms he so richly deserved. By invoking the term "Great Communicator," the news media and political analysts repeatedly directed us to judge his performance and its immediate impact, but not the actual policies for which he was responsible.

"An actor, he's just an actor," my New Deal Democrat father would shout at television screen images of the President during a press conference or a campaign debate. This was a basic and immutable fact, and yet the commentators and analysts, who were supposed to make sense of the President's obfuscations, his apparent lapses of memory, his trivial and often inaccurate anecdotes, did not use this fact to break down the act and expose his administration's policies to critical scrutiny. Indeed, the commentators and analysts were part of the performance, convincing us to suspend our disbelief so as to get on with the show that Reagan made of politics. Whether Reagan was "on" or "off" was as far as most mainstream new media criticism ever went. As a result, we seldom discussed whether he was truthful or untruthful, right or wrong, wise or misguided in the policies he established.

During the years of Ronald Reagan's ascendancy, national political campaigns became completely submerged in popular culture. Reagan made acting "Presidential" the principal prerequisite for the Presidency. Acting Presidential, as popularized by Reagan, is not an easy task. It requires the ability to project the right masculine warrior-hero image and the ability to make yourself the apparent embodiment of national myths (especially the rags-to-riches, conquest of the West, and hard-boiled detective myths), while at the same time maintaining the fiction that you are really no different than the guy down the block. Fortuitous circumstances undoubtedly helped Reagan achieve this seemingly impossible theatrical balance.

In 1980 Ronald Reagan, who had seldom had roles in first-rate Hollywood westerns, rode like John Wayne to the rescue when America was, in the endlessly repeated words of ABC's "Nightline," "held hostage." Having saved us from the evil Ayatollah and his savage Muslim tribe, Reagan further endeared himself to the media by surviving, with good spirits still blazing, a mad assassin's bullet, the kind of bullet that could strike down any of us any day of the week. After Reagan recovered from his wounds, as our warrior-hero king and our everyman, he could do no wrong in the eyes of most reporters. Indeed, it seemed as if the facts of every subsequent breaking story were framed to confirm the popular images of the President that had been presented in 1980–1981. The hero had his bad days—like the death of 230 Marines in the Beirut barracks bombing in October 1983, or his first pathetic debate against Walter Mondale in 1984. Such "off" performances made us again recognize him as human like us, but they also built up great anticipation for his inevitable recovery and triumph. The "real hero" always triumphs after setbacks when his real heroic nature resurfaces—just as Reagan's seemed to do in the conquest of Grenada only forty-eight hours after the Beirut bombing, and in the second television debate of 1984.

In 1988, Vice President George Bush had to overcome the handicap of having played for eights years "the wimp" to Reagan's heroic President. To do this, Bush quickly appropriated Clint Eastwood's cowboy-turned-detective "read my lips" as the keynote of his campaign. He was also greatly assisted by Reagan's willing ness to transfer his mantle, and even more so by Michael Dukakis' failure to act sufficiently "Presidential." As we all probably remember, Dukakis' moment to seize center stage in the campaign came in yet another televised debate when he was asked right off what he would do to someone who had raped and killed his wife. The question itself is a benchmark in modern political history because it was absolutely irrelevant to the substance of politics and policy making, and to the condition of the country; yet it was completely grounded in the popular culture. Dukakis responded without emotion, using the question as an opening to explain his views on capital punishment.

Clearly, the Massachusetts governor was no fan of Charles Bronson's incredibly popular revenge films. Nor had he seemed to learn anything from the public's enthusiastic endorsement of Reagan's use of bombers in Libya to attempt to kill Momar Khadafy. Instead of playing to, or at least trying to defuse, the public's much-cultivated revenge response, Dukakis failed to even acknowledge it. Thus, he failed to be recognized as either a warrior hero or another everyman. In 1988, Dukakis showed little understanding of his national audience, something that had been carefully constructed during the Reagan years. That failure cost him any chance he had to win the general election.

Playing to a preconstructed audience—the essence of mass media entertainment—became the essence of effective national campaigning in the Reagan era.[11] In 1976, as this trend was emerging, poet-songwriter Gil Scott Heron wrote,

> Acted like an actor,
> Acted like governor of California,
> And now he acts like someone is going to vote for him
>   for President of the United States.[12]

That year, such sarcastic skepticism seemed justified as Ronald Reagan tried and failed for the third time to get the nomination of his party. But just four years later, nearly forty-four million Americans cast their ballots for Ronald Reagan for President; and in 1984, over fifty-four million Americans voted to keep him in the White House.

This remarkable electoral performance, by a man who headed an administration that was from the beginning plagued by unprecedented corruption and the largest budget deficits in American history, created a real crisis for intellectuals who tried to take politics seriously. That crisis was compounded by the landslide election of Reagan's Vice President to succeed him in 1988. The intellectual difficulty has been especially acute for those aging members of the New Left and the counterculture, including the editors of this volume, who had once seen popular culture as a liberating and democratizing force. Now faced with overwhelming evidence of the way popular culture had served, and been shaped by, the most conservative political groups in America, our faith in its oppositional potential has been shaken. Indeed, for some of us, Reaganism completely shattered that faith, while restoring lost confidence in the mass culture critique.

For example, Herbert Schiller and Neil Postman have recently forthrightly revived and up-dated the one-dimensional-man theme of an earlier period. For Schiller and Postman, the developments of the Reagan era have revalidated the critics' extremely pessimistic evaluation of popular culture and its impact on politics and individual expression during the early Cold War. From their point of view, the corporate media that dominate popular culture are seen as ideologically motivated and powerful enough to manipulate their mass audiences to get desired political responses. Dismissing what he calls the "active audience thesis," which is portrayed as an outdated remnant of the New Left's optimism, Schiller writes in his *CULTURE, Inc.,*

> Audiences do, in fact, interpret messages variously. They may also transform them to correspond with their individual experiences and tastes. But when they are confronted with a message incessantly repeated in all cultural conduits, issuing from the commanders of the social order, their capacities are overwhelmed.[13]

Postman is equally ominous. In his *Amusing Ourselves to Death,* he rejects Schiller's kind of Orwellian imagery, relying instead on Huxley's *Brave New World* for his model of the relationship between popular culture and politics. "Big Brother does not watch us, by his choice," says Postman. "We watch him, by ours." He continues,

> When a population becomes distracted by trivia, when cultural life is redefined as a perpetual round of entertainments, when serious public conversation becomes a form of baby-talk, when, in short, a people become an audience, and their public business, a vaudeville act, then a nation finds itself at risk; culture-death is a clear possibility.[14]

Do we have to be so pessimistic? Is there no alternative to a return to a variant of the mass culture critique of the early Cold

War years? Other intellectuals have tried to temper the pessimism brought on by the collapse of the New Left and the counterculture, and by the triumph of Reaganism, by introducing the concept of "hegemony," derived from the writings of Italian Marxist Antonio Gramsci, into the debate over the relationship between popular culture and politics. Stuart Ewen, in his studies of advertising and style, and Todd Gitlin, in his work on the news media and television, have done much to popularize the hegemony model.[15] These scholars accept the idea that the corporate purveyors of popular culture have an ideological agenda, and the fact that particular products of the popular culture convey political meaning. But they also recognize that the power to impose particular political values in specific situations is imperfect and challenged by other groups in society who have commitments different from the dominant corporations. Thus, as now presented by the proponents of hegemony, what frequently occurs in the popular culture is not the simple inculcation of ideology, but an expression of underlying political tensions which are uncovered when attempts to maintain and extend corporate power encounter popular resistance.

In this sense, the updated concept of "hegemony" mediates between the pessimism of the mass culture critique and the original optimism of the New Left and the counterculture. It forces us to recognize the exercise of political power in the production and consumption of popular culture, while at the same time recognizing that not all people are simply audiences, that resistance to, and subversive use of, popular culture media and products is possible. If hegemony is described in this way, to borrow Leslie Good's words, as "an ever-changing, imperfect, contradictory . . . process,"[16] then analysis of the political character of popular culture in modern America becomes, at best, problematic. That is to say, the relationship between popular culture and politics remains something requiring, not large generalizations, but more careful study of discrete popular cultural developments and productions.

The essays in this book generally advance this trend in the field. However, as a collection, this book insists on no single political viewpoint or methodology. It seeks rather to present a range of possibilities that reflect the dimensions of the current debate and practice in the field. The editors had no ideological litmus test for the contributors, and this may upset some readers. Here, popular culture is treated as categorically neither good nor bad, in either political or aesthetic terms. Instead, the collected essays reflect the editors' convictions that popular culture is simply too important to be ignored by those academics who treat politics and its history seriously; and that everything that comes out of the popular should not be condemned in an ideologically reflexive manner.

This collection also reflects the editors' conviction that studying popular or mass culture in a historical way illuminates a variety of possible relationships between popular culture and politics. American popular culture has a history dating back to at least the nineteenth century. In other words, popular culture and mass media are not synonymous with television. Television has certainly become an important part of popular culture and the mass media of modern America, but both preceded the widespread distribution of electronic video equipment and programs. Discussion of the impact of television enters several of the essays presented here, but it does not dominate them, as it often dominates discussion of contemporary popular culture and politics. Nor are models of the relationship between popular culture and politics that are derived from the study of television imposed on other popular media in other eras.

The essays collected here reveal popular culture to be a realm of history where power is always being used and contested. Thus, as these essays present it, popular culture is inherently political. And, since it is a political realm, the balance of power in the popular culture is often uncertain and likely to change over time. Consequently, the specific political character of American popular culture at any point can be fixed only upon careful examination of specific phenomena.

Some products of popular culture may reflect widely held values and beliefs, and thus be in a sense democratic, as their distributors so often argue. The increasing convergence of popular culture and politics may be just another stage in the evolution of democracy. However, the essays in this volume raise profound doubts about these widely disseminated views. At a minimum, they show that neither the political intent nor the political efficacy of popular culture can be confidently predicted.

Still, there seems no getting around the fact that popular culture has frequently functioned to advance the political agendas of powerful groups and ambitious individuals. As the late Howard Abramowitz' case study of press coverage of the Red Scare of 1919–1921 argues, there are theoretical insights of the "mass culture" critique which should be maintained. Among these, Abramowitz especially emphasized the importance of the class interests of the owners of the institutions that purvey popular culture, as a factor determining its political meaning. For Abramowitz, an Old Left scholar, the Red Scare was something manipulated from above by newspaper publishers to thwart a movement for democracy from below among workers. Yet, as a participant in the contemporary debate, Abramowitz also recognized the problematic character of consumption. Thus he was forced to the conclusion that we may never know whether or not the anti-communist panic that swept the nation after World War I was really popular.

More overt efforts to control the meaning of popular cultural products via censorship are the subject of two other essays in this collection. Nancy Rosenbloom's essay on reformers and censorship of the movie industry in the early twentieth century, and Pamela Steinle's innovative inquiry into grassroots attempts to censor J. D. Salinger's Novel, *The Catcher in the Rye,* in the 1950s, examine the most direct kind of attempt to politically control popular culture. This kind of activity is what often comes to mind when politics and popular culture are discussed together. Yet each of these essays offers new insights. In both cases, the intentions and the results of censors' efforts are found to be more complex and ambiguous than might be assumed. These findings enable each author to open up a discussion of wider political/cultural questions—specifically, the meaning progressive reformers gave to democratic education for Rosenbloom, and the impact of the atomic arms race on the middle class for Steinle.

Popular culture may also function as a gathering ground for opponents of the economic and social status quo. Michael Barkun's essay on Coxey's Army and Larry Bennett's essay on rock and roll explore two popular culture phenomena of intentional opposition that failed to lead to the political changes desired by their creators. In each case, the authors find the sources of political failure in a combination of the creators' ideology (which is itself a popular cultural inheritance) and the process by which the ideas of individuals are made available to a mass audience. Moreover, each of these essays suggests that the purveying institutions of popular culture may be able to defuse the oppositional power of particular movements, like Coxey's Army and rock and roll music, by converting them into readily available myths and archetypes which can be understood, and even presented again and again, as performances that vent oppositional emotions without ever establishing an institutional basis for effective political opposition.

Liz Cohen's important exploration of consumerism among Chicago workers in the 1920s probably goes further than the other essays in making the case for the active-audience thesis and the oppositional potential of popular culture products. Here, she demonstrates how developing a "bottom up" perspective on a new popular culture development—mass consumerism and leisure in her case—can force revisions in the theory of mass culture. Instead of mass markets and mass audiences, Cohen describes how working people in Chicago with distinctive ethnic subcultures responded to, and transformed, the mass consumer culture of the 1920s. Surely, it will be difficult for anyone reading her essay to maintain the universality of the unrevised one-dimensional-man thesis of Marcuse and the Frankfort school. As Cohen demonstrates, in modern America's popular culture, repressive and homogenizing political intent does not necessarily determine political outcome.

My own essay on "consumer-oriented Americanism" among postwar automobile workers describes a more successful, although still politically ambiguous, process of cultural homogenization. By combining elements of the popular culture and the political culture—mass consumerism and anti-communism—Walter Reuther was able to fashion a political program for the United Automobile Workers that channeled workers' rebelliousness into liberalism during the 1940s and 1950s. At the same time, and somewhat in the manner of Liz Cohen's Chicago workers of the 1920s, postwar auto workers used the promise of mass consumerism to challenge major corporations and improve their living standards.

The juxtaposition of Cohen's essay on Chicago workers in the 1920s and my own essay on auto workers in the post-World-War-II era highlights the unpredictable, contingent political character of modern American popular culture. Although the intent of the producers of mass-consumerism was the same in each period, different economic, social, and political circumstances contributed to distinctive political outcomes. In addition, read together these essays confirm the definition of hegemony as a process, not a static state of affairs. American corporations seek to establish and maintain their economic and political power through the popular culture, but this power is never completely secured because people retain the ability to think and act in ways that cannot be completely controlled by either popular cultural or political institutions.

Finally, the chronological ordering of these essays does suggest that there has been a pattern in the way the relationship between politics and popular culture has developed over the last century. Increasingly, since the emergence of a truly national daily press in the days of Coxey's Army, politics and popular culture have become intertwined. Today, they seemed to be virtually fused. In the twentieth century, the language of popular culture has displaced an older language of political analysis, and popular culture media have displaced political parties as the principal link between the people and the politicians who run their government. Indeed, this long-term development, seen emerging in the essays that follow, is one of the defining characteristics of the modern era in American history.

Chapter Two

Coxey's Army as a Millennial Movement

Michael Barkun

I.

Until at least the end of the First World War, reference to "Coxey's Army" was synonymous with "rabble" or at least an "unorganized group." For Canadian soldiers, it meant "a carelessly happy-go-lucky army."[1] In fact, it was none of these, not a rabble, despite the shabby dress of the marchers; not unorganized, indeed divided into units with a command structure; and certainly not "happy-go-lucky," either in its origins or in its quixotic journey.

"Coxey's Army" was a march of unemployed workers in 1894, very likely the first protest march on Washington and certainly the first such march to receive national media coverage. As such, it has customarily garnered a sentence or two in most histories of the period. To some scholars, it stands more broadly as the best known of a series of so-called "industrial armies"—bands of workers meandering toward Washington from all over the United States. Most of the other "armies" originated in the West, where Jack London briefly attached himself to one of them; some of those that came after Coxey had never heard of him, and none ever reached its destination.[2] For others, "Coxey's Army" was simply a picturesque episode in the chronicles of Populism, a movement so richly endowed with vivid personalities and eccentric ideas that "Coxey's Army" did not appear particularly unusual. Richard Hofstadter mentions the "Army" only in passing, along with Populism and the Homestead and Pullman strikes, as a basis for the fear of revolution that gripped the middle class in the 1890s.[3]

These characterizations are all correct, as far as they go. "Coxey's Army" certainly looked like an unorganized rabble as it tramped through the Middle Atlantic states. There were indeed numerous "industrial armies," some substantially larger than Coxey's, and the leadership of the "Army" was staunchly Populist. Thus, "Coxey's Army" can serve as a useful symbol of the political consequences of the Panic of 1893 and the ensuing depression, which increased both the numbers of the unemployed and the

depth of their misery. Nonetheless, to categorize and thus in a
sense dismiss "Coxey's Army" as merely a dramatic protest during
a period of economic contraction is to miss one of its central elements, for Coxey's Army was at least as much a religious movement as it was an economic one.

Indeed, its religious character was evident in its very name,
for while "Coxey's Army" was the name given it by the press, it
was in fact officially the "Commonweal of Christ." Its religiosity
was an idiosyncratic amalgam of millennialism and reincarnation-
ism, fused with a radical critique of the distribution of wealth in
America. Although this religious character was widely remarked
upon at the time, it was scarcely mentioned in later years, and
has plainly been considered an embarrassment by authors sympathetic to Coxey. To reconstruct "Coxey's Army" as the millenarian
movement it was—as indeed the "Commonweal of Christ"—does
not, however, diminish its dignity or denigrate the sufferings of the
unemployed; rather, it recaptures a remarkable fusion of millenarian religion and social protest.

In addition to the light "Coxey's Army" sheds on patterns of
protest at the turn of the century, it also illuminates more contemporary concerns. The "march" anticipated events of the late 1960s,
'70s, and '80s. On the level of action, it prefigured the much larger
marches on behalf of civil rights and an end to the war in Vietnam. At the level of belief, its intertwining of religion and politics
was replicated both in recent "cult" movements and in the political
activation of Fundamentalists. If the March lapsed into obscurity
after World War I, as the rapid decline in the literature about it
attests, that was because it was more easily defined in later years
as an exercise in public eccentricity. While elements of it seem no
less bizarre now than they did then, much of it speaks to us with
unusual directness, suggesting that the time may have come to
re-examine the March of "Coxey's Army."

II.

The story of the March has already been well told. For present
purposes it suffices only to provide the outlines of its journey. The
March began on March 25, 1894, in Massillon, Ohio, the hometown
of Jacob Sechler Coxey, an affluent businessman of strong Populist
views. There were fewer than a hundred marchers at the beginning and never more than two or three hundred until near the
very end. The route lay through the industrial communities of
eastern Ohio and western Pennsylvania, where popular support

for workers' causes struggled against official hostility. From there the March entered the forbidding terrain of the Cumberland Mountains, an area so insular it seemed scarcely changed since the eighteenth century. The primitive roads, the absence of local Populist support, and a Spring blizzard turned the mountain crossing into an ordeal that very nearly ended the journey. But new supporters were waiting in the lowlands near Washington, so that when the Army entered the city May 1, 1894, it consisted of between five hundred and a thousand. All the while its progress had been tracked by a press corps that sometimes numbered over forty reporters together with linemen and telegraphers who moved like advancemen a day or two ahead to set up communications.[4]

The March came to a grotesque end. Coxey wished to conclude with an address from the Capitol steps. The vacillating administration of Grover Cleveland, wishing both to ignore the March and to suppress it, left matters in the hands of the District of Columbia authorities. Under the Capitol Grounds Act, Coxey and two associates were arrested and sentenced to twenty days in jail for displaying banners, while Coxey and his chief lieutenant, the "Marshall" of the Commonweal, Carl Browne, were fined an additional five dollars for walking on the grass. The Marchers retreated to a suburban campsite, where the humid Washington heat dispersed them more effectively than any police.

Jacob Coxey, an Episcopalian, was not conspicuously religious. His interests instead centered on a set of legislative proposals he had devised to simultaneously cure the unemployment problem and provide the nation with a much-needed transportation infrastructure.[5] Roads and other public works to provide jobs for the unemployed were to be financed by non-interest bearing bonds issued by local governments and deposited with the federal Treasury. The Treasury in turn would use the bonds as security to issue additional currency as an economic stimulus.[6] While Coxey was constantly in search of new ways to place these proposals before Congress, the idea for the March was apparently not his. He lent the project his stature as a local notable, he financed it out of his small fortune, and he used his Populist connections to give it visibility and support. He also served as an articulate and respectable spokesperson for the interests of the unemployed. But he not only did not conceive the March, he did not organize it and only rarely led it.

The March was conceived, organized, and led by a much more obscure figure, Carl Browne—a Populist orator, a crude but powerful political cartoonist, and a patent medicine salesman. He also thought of himself as a kind of prophet, and it was he who saw in a march on Washington not merely a vehicle for the dramatization of political and economic ideas, but as a sacred event which would tap extraordinary sources of spiritual energy, indeed, as an event which might bring the millennium itself.

Coxey was a "mild-looking [man] with rounding shoulders . . . and gold-bowed spectacles," who did not impress the journalist Ray Stannard Baker "as a great leader of a revolutionary movement." Carl Browne, on the other hand, was larger than life. To Baker, one of the most distinguished reporters of his time, Browne was simply "too good to be true": "He reminded me," Baker later wrote, "of some of the soap-box orators and vendors of Kickapoo Indian remedies I had seen on the Lake front in Chicago."[7] Indeed, Browne was both.

His physical appearance seemed calculated to draw crowds and reporters. He wore a fringed leather coat of the kind identified with Buffalo Bill Cody, with silver dollars for buttons. Although others ascribed his flamboyant clothes to a desire for self-dramatization, Browne himself claimed the wardrobe originated when the San Francisco newspaper that employed him, sent him to the Chicago World's Fair in 1893 as both artist-correspondent and part of a Fair exhibit called the "Wild and Wooly West."[8] In any case, he continued to affect the Cody style long after the Fair ended.

Like Cody, Browne had long hair, a heavy moustache, and a beard. Significantly, his hair and beard did not lead others to note a resemblance to Cody. Instead, they suggested that Browne wanted to look like Jesus Christ. That Christ rather than Cody might be his role model stemmed principally from a picture Browne had painted of Christ, which subsequently appeared on the "Army's" banner. Observers were divided about the reason for the resemblance. Some suggested, perhaps uncharitably, that Browne painted Christ to resemble himself, while others suggested that the picture had come first, and that Browne decided to trim his hair and beard as a way of expressing self-identification with Christ.[9]

The plausibility of both views was the result of the belief system for which Browne claimed to speak. What he called his "theosophy" was only distantly related to the organized Theosophical Society, then at its height in Britain and America.[10] Although he claimed to have been a "Theosophist (of my thinking)" for many years prior to his first meeting with Coxey, their initial contacts apparently did not expose any of Browne's religious commitments.

Rather, the two initially came together as a result of shared Populist views.[11]

They first met in Chicago in the late summer of 1893 at a meeting of the American Bimetallic League. Browne, in addition to whatever journalistic activities he was involved in, was also offering a kind of Populist medicine show on the lake front, utilizing the patent-medicine staple of a wagon turned into a makeshift stage. The wagon was covered with Browne's cartoons about the evils of the "money power." His discussions of financial policy with Coxey continued on a subsequent visit Browne made to Coxey in Massillon, Ohio, in the fall. In later years, the two men remembered the origins of the March quite differently. In Coxey's version, the two were driving in the country near Massillon in November 1893: While Browne was reminiscing about his participation in a march of the unemployed in San Francisco, Coxey said, "Browne, we will get up a March to Washington."[12] Browne's version differs in every particular: time, place, occasion, and speaker. While visiting a soup kitchen in the Chicago City Hall on December 18, 1893, with a group of reporters, "the idea came to me to organize these idle men into a 'petition with boots on,' and march to Washington as an object lesson to Congress and country as well," an idea he fired off at once to Coxey. Despite Coxey's claim, journalists at the time were unanimous in ascribing the original idea to Browne, and it was completely consistent with his theatrical approach to politics.[13]

There is no indication that Browne had discussed religious issues with Coxey in their conversations and correspondence during the latter months of 1893. Coxey agreed to support the March during January 1894, lending it his financial resources and associating it with his lobbying organization, the Good Roads Association. A formal announcement of the proposed march appeared in the Association's *Bulletin* on January 31, 1894.[14] The next issue of the *Bulletin* reprinted an article from the Massillon *Independent* of February 20, presenting Browne's religious views and by implication associating Coxey with them. Coxey spoke little about Browne's peculiar ideas, but made no effort to disassociate himself from them until much later.

Donald McMurry, in one of the earliest scholarly treatments of the March, written decades after the event, says bluntly, "Browne converted Coxey."[15] Observers at the time were less sure. Shirley Plumer Austin, a writer hostile to the entire enterprise, who called the March's footsoldiers "the worst specimens of the worst types of the American tramp," portrayed Coxey as unreflective and acquiescent:

> Coxey's religious views did not prevent his ready conver
> sion to Browne's abortive theosophy. He does not claim
> any supernatural wisdom as Browne does, but modestly
> poses as the living representative of Christ because
> Browne says so.[16]

According to Henry Vincent, the Populist editor whom Browne commissioned to write the "Army's" official history, Browne gradually indoctrinated a Coxey "who leaned toward theosophy, without comprehension of its theory. Since that time the latter has fully unbound the doctrines of Browne, and professes to believe with him. . . . "[17] Ray Stannard Baker certainly had no doubts about the sincerity of Coxey's belief. Both Browne and Coxey, he wrote, "seemed to me to be living in an unreal world of their own feverish enthusiasm."[18] When the Massillon *Independent* asked Coxey about the banner of Christ that Browne had painted, Coxey was unperturbed about the association: "He [Christ] was simply a great reformer. He went about like Browne, here, doing all the good he could, and as he preached against those who live upon interest and profit, they controlled the masses as they do now, and so they encompassed His death on the cross."[19] If Browne had simply recast Jesus as an advocate of the oppressed, it would have been unexceptional, but in fact he did much more.

Browne, whose manner was that of the carnival pitchman rather than the theologian, was never much concerned to set his ideas down in a formal and systematic manner. Except for the memoir of the March he wrote in 1912, two years before his death, his writings were rarely longer than brief newspaper articles. Nonetheless, from these a reasonably clear account of his beliefs can be reconstructed. Browne's cosmos included three main elements: his "theosophy," which was in fact his version of a doctrine of reincarnation; a closely related concept of the Second Coming; and a conception of the Apocalypse.

Browne believed that the soul, upon a person's death, passed into a universal reservoir of "soul matter," where it became intermixed with the souls of all those who had already died. This may have been related to his analogous belief about the physical body, whose "chemical elements . . . go back into their various reservoirs of nature at the death of a person. . . . "[20] This idea of recycled elements took an even more bizarre form when, after the March, Browne advertised his miraculous medical discovery, "Carl's

California Cure," which promised to "PROLONG LIFE INDEFI-
NITELY." It was well known, Browne said, "that the animal system of Man is renewed entire . . . every seven years," so that "no
man is ever more than seven years old physically, if he can but
keep his system free from *microbes, insects, that cause all diseases
known to man & beast!*"[21] Just as the elements of the body return
to nature for recycling, so the soul itself was recycled by moving
from the individual to the universal reservoir and then to the
newly born.

The implication Browne drew from this recycling was that
each individual might possess some fractional part of the souls of
those who had previously died. In his own and Coxey's case, he
decided that the accident of soul redistribution had given to each
of them part of the soul of Christ.[22] That accounted both for their
affinity and for the power they might wield together. Browne
asked a reporter,

> Do you not see anything singular in the coming together
> of Brother Coxey and myself? I believe that a part of the
> soul of Christ happened to come into my being by re-
> incarnation. I believe also that another part of Christ's
> soul is in Brother Coxey by the same process, and that
> is what has brought us together, closer than brothers.
> That prevents all jealousies between us; that strikes
> down all rivalry.[23]

In a bizarre metaphor, Browne sometimes referred to Coxey as the
"cerebrum of Christ" and himself as the "cerebellum of Christ."[24]

This concept of migrating and fractionalized souls led Browne
to an equally novel idea of the Second Coming. The Second Coming would be brought about by a kind of critical mass of "soul-
matter," for although he and Coxey presumably were endowed with
particularly significant segments of Christ's soul, others had portions as well, and if these components could be brought together,
the Second Coming would result. "The remainder of the soul of
Christ has been fully re-incarnated in thousands of people
throughout the United States today, and that accounts for the tremendous response to the call of ours, to try to bring about peace
and plenty, to take the place of panic and poverty."[25]

It was not always clear in Browne's thinking what was cause
and what was effect. Would the March succeed because the Christ-
segment of thousands of souls would be drawn together in a
common enterprise, or was the drawing together the essential pre-
condition for something grander, the Second Coming itself? The

notion of soul attraction may explain Coxey' and Browne's penchant for extravagantly overestimating the size of their following in the days just before the March. Twenty thousand, Coxey thought. "There'll be nearer one hundred thousand," Browne responded.[26] When only a scant hundred appeared, however, Browne was unfazed. It was, after all, his and Coxey's soul contribution that mattered most; others would come.

What kind of Second Coming the March was meant to produce was cloaked in Browne's typical ambiguity. He devised the movement's official name—"Commonweal of Christ."[27] He also painted the famous banner carried at the head of the procession, dominated by his own painting of Christ. The banner bore the following legend:

> PEACE ON EARTH
> GOOD WILL TO MEN!
> HE HATH RISEN!!!
> BUT
> DEATH
> TO *INTEREST* ON BONDS!!
> HIS SECOND COMING
> THE BANNER OF
> The J. S. Coxey Good Roads
> Association's on to Washington[28]

However, the Second Coming that Browne had in mind was not the Second Advent of such traditional premillennialists as William Miller, who expected Christ to physically descend and inaugurate the millennial kingdom.

Instead, Browne had in mind a collective Second Coming, in which the multitude of marchers was to be both the symbol and the soul of Christ. As Browne put it in early 1894, "I believe in the prophecy that He is to come, not in any single form, but in the whole people."[29] In a public statement, unsigned but surely by Browne since it refers to Coxey as "Brother Coxey," the March's Marshall elaborated upon the linkage between reincarnated souls and the Second Advent:

> His coming is not in the flesh of any one being, but reincarnated in the souls of all those who wish to establish a co-operative government through such legislation as this [march] proposes, to take the place of the cut-throat competitive system that keeps alive the crucifixion. . . . [30]

Confusion between cause and effect are present here, too, for one is left not knowing whether possessors of part of Christ's soul instinctively abhor the "money power" or whether those opposed to "the cut-throat competitive system" must naturally be presumed to harbor part of Christ's soul. Yet another version appears in Browne's 1912 recollections, this time emphasizing the predominance of Christ's soul in himself and Coxey, and at the same time demoting a physical Second Coming to the realm of fancies:

> No matter if the Christ DOES ever come, as many mortals believe He will some time, that ere He does there must prevail HIS spirit—of the "Sermon on the Mount," and I give it out that there was incarnated in Mr. Coxey and myself so much of that spirit that if the people would cooperate with us, Christ's "SECOND COMING" was at hand—at least the John the Baptist of it.[31]

The confusion derives in part from Browne's penchant for expressing subtle distinctions in fuzzy language. Beyond the problems of idiom, however, both his reincarnationist views and his ideas about the Second Coming were tied to a millennialism that was equally dependent upon both the traditional imagery of the Book of Revelation and upon the financial conspiracies of Populism.

His ambiguous fusion of economic radicalism and millennial expectation parallels that of the seventeenth-century Puritan sectarian, Gerard Winstanley, who at the end of the 1640s spoke for the agrarian radicalism of the Digger movement. The Diggers, who sought "to occupy the common lands and form collective farms," frontally attacked the inequities of a society that measured wealth in land.[32] Around the example of their spontaneous seizures and their cultivation of untended waste areas, Winstanley constructed an eloquent and elegant theology—at once more sophisticated and artful than Browne's, but curiously similar in some respects. Winstanley's immanent God placed Christ inside each individual: "This is the excellency of the work, when a man shall be made to see Christ in other creatures as well as in himself."[33] He drew from this a Second Coming that, like Browne's, was in the form of an awakened consciousness rather than a supernatural event, when realization of a Christ within would take the place of a physical Second Coming.[34]

Like most millenarians, Browne was vague about the character of the world to come, clearer about what it would not be than about its positive characteristics. Like many chiliasts, before and since, he was drawn to the Book of Revelation, both for its vivid scenario of the last days and for the extraordinary plasticity of its imagery, limited only by the ingenuity of the interpreter.

Browne's sermon on Revelation was apparently a set-piece which he delivered numerous times. He sermonized regularly on the March, where Sunday services open to the community provided not only a platform for Browne but a device for convincing the locals that the March was more than a gathering of tramps.[35] A full text of "Revelations Rightly Revealed" survives, and although it comes from 1896 when Browne delivered it during the People's Party presidential campaign, comparing it with descriptions of the 1894 sermons indicates that it is fundamentally the same, save for some concluding reflections on the coming election.

The special twist Browne gave to the text lay in the symbolic associations of the beast with seven heads, ten horns, and ten crowns (Revelation 13:1). The beast itself was the idea of a national bank. The seven heads were the pieces of financial legislation long hated by advocates of cheap money, and involved the contraction in the supply of "greenbacks," the demonetization of silver, and the resumption of the gold standard.[36] For the listing of acts of Congress, Browne freely confessed his reliance on Mrs. S. E. V. Emery's Populist tract, *Seven Financial Conspiracies Which Have Enslaved the American People*. Mrs. Emery's book, which first appeared in 1887, claimed to expose a conspiracy of English and American financiers who enriched themselves while they "squeezed the industry of the country like a hoop of steel."[37] The ten horns "represent the ten great trusts": railroads, land, sugar, oil, coal, meatpacking, provisions, iron and steel, department stores, and utilities; the crowns were the plutocratic Rockefellers, Vanderbilts, and their ilk who controlled the trusts and lived, Browne said, with the splendor of potentates.

All this St. John of Patmos had presumably seen in his vision but "so veiled in allegory that he could escape the martyrdom, if possible, of the usurers of his time. . . . " The world St. John foresaw when the climactic battles of the latter days had ended was "a new heaven and a new earth," "when it was possible for the people of the earth to become so intelligent as to overthrow kings and usury. . . . " In this version of the sermon, Browne ended by explicitly linking the attainment of the "new heaven and new earth" with not only a victory for William Jennings Bryan in the election then approaching but also the eventual triumph of Coxey's monetary theories. He was not, he said, certain that McKinley would be defeated. But even if McKinley won,

the final victory will certainly come soon, anyway . . . for
Revelations plainly show that the old Satan—usury—
will be chained, and if it ever is, it will be through the
plan of the Coxey non-interest bearing bond bills, for
which the Commonweal made the march to Washington.
It may come through Bryan; it may come through the
next congress, without his election; it may come through
another, greater, grander, more glorious march to Washington . . . but come it will, for the everlasting God,
through St. John, hath ordained it.[38]

This peroration faithfully carries through the linkage of apocalyptic vision with financial reform that Browne had first declared in a
statement issued before the 1894 March in his twin capacities as
Secretary of Coxey's Good Roads Association and Marshall of the
"Commonweal of Christ":

We firmly believe now, in view of the surrounding circumstances, that the time for the fulfillment of prophecy is near at hand, and that all those who go in this
procession to Washington will be the humble instruments through which the second Babylon—the MONEY
POWER OF USURY—is to fall. . . . [39]

Even the failure of the "Army" to place its proposals before
Congress at the Capitol was only a passing episode in a struggle
whose outcome was predestined. The dispirited remnants retreated to a Maryland campsite, from which Browne issued a
newspaper on the Fourth of July, 1894, dated: "TRANSITION PE-
RIOD *NEW DISPENSATION.*" "The battle of Armageddon is now
on," it proclaimed.[40] It was scarcely any wonder that the English
journalist and reformer W. T. Stead characterized Browne as a
Fifth Monarchist speaking "with a modern accent."[41] Insofar as
Browne had anything specific to say about the coming new order, it
was to be a society free of "usury," with "government furnishing
money direct to the people. . . . "[42] This "kingdom of heaven" was
for the most part describable only in negative attributes: the absence of poverty, oppression, degrading labor, and so on. Its social
structure and political system could presumably be left to the be-
liever's imagination.

A millennium defined in terms of opposition—the elimination
of that which is evil—assumes the existence of some malevolent
force whose defeat is required before the great day can arrive, and
indeed much of Browne's rhetoric was couched in terms of a call to

battle. He wrote the lyrics for a "Commonweal Rallying Song" filled with the imagery of struggle:

> See our stars and stripes are streaming
>   See our banner glow;
> In Christ's Second Coming Triumph
>   O'er our usury foe.[43]

Who in fact was the "usury foe"? It was not simply all who charged interest for the use of money. More concretely, it was a cabal of international bankers who had conspired to deprive the American laboring man of his just rewards. More concretely still, it was the Rothschilds, who stood at once as symbols of the conspiracy and as its leading members.

Browne and, it appears, Coxey himself explicitly identified bankers and the Rothschilds as Jews, not simply as individuals who were among other things Jewish. The judgment of one modern scholar that the "Army" was free of explicit anti-Semitism is not supported by the evidence.[44] Thus, the first verse of Browne's "Rallying Song" concludes:

> 'Tis the glorious non-interest legions,
>   Foes of Shenee [sic] gold.[45]

"Sheenee" or "sheeny," a word of uncertain origin, was an invariably derogatory term for a Jew and first appeared in English about 1880, often carrying the implication of greed and untrustworthiness.[46] Although in subsequent versions of the song "Shenee" is omitted, anti-Semitic motifs remained in other forms, particularly pictorial.[47]

Browne always thought of himself as an artist, apparently had some training, and had worked as a panorama painter before his political activities began.[48] His cartoons, however, betray a crudity even judged against the work of the time. One cartoon from 1895 shows a group of seven bankers, with "Rothschilds" at the head. All are in the standard form of the anti-Semitic caricature—bald, with bulbous hooked noses, and bushy black beards. Dollar signs serve as eyes. Each has his mouth open and is in the process of swallowing, head first, an American workingman.[49] Beginning in 1895, Coxey began to publish a newspaper, *Sound Money,* which chronicled his and Browne's activities. A favorite illustration in it, a cartoon by Watson Heston entitled "Crucified Between Two Thieves," shows a crucified Uncle Sam whose pockets are being emptied by two plutocrats labeled "Republicanism" and "Democracy," while two Jewish caricature figures prick the dying American with a "Gold Standard" spear while offering a debt-soaked sponge marked "Interest on Bonds." Surmounting the cross is a sign: "This is U.S. in the Hands of the Jews." The cartoon was reprinted many times.[50]

Browne consequently constructed a full-blown millennarian system, where the forces of good confronted the forces of evil on a battlefield of world finance. Notwithstanding occasional defeats, the result would be—would have to be—the Second Coming, and the ensuing millennium.

III.

From what sources did Browne's system spring? Some elements can readily be identified as part of the common discourse of late nineteenth-century American radicalism, the fixation upon financial conspiracies, for example, and the demonization of the Jew. "[It] was chiefly Populist writers," observes Richard Hofstadter, "who expressed that identification of the Jew with the usurer and the 'international gold ring' which was the central theme of the American anti-Semitism of the age."[51] While controversy continues on the question of how intrinsic to Populism such anti-Semitism was, it was clearly the source from which Browne and Coxey derived their verbal and pictorial stereotypes of the Jew.[52]

Other components of the system are less typical, hence more difficult to trace, and none more so than Browne's concept of reincarnation and the link between it and the Second Coming. Browne called himself a "theosophist." On the one hand, that designation seems to have been accepted without quarrel by W. T. Stead, who should have known a theosophist when he met one. It was, after all, Stead who had inadvertently launched the career of the most famous theosophist of the time, Annie Besant, by securing an introduction for her to the movement's founder, Mme. Blavatsky.[53] On the other hand, Browne's "theosophy" bore little resemblance to Annie Besant's or to that of any other recognized spokesperson of the movement. Theosophy sought to systematically link religion with doctrines of a spirit world, and reincarnation was a significant element in the synthesis. The function of reincarnation, however, was to give the soul the opportunity to perfect itself through successive lives. The greater the evil committed in past lives, the longer the sequence of rebirths before a soul achieved union with the divine essence. Those who escaped reincarnation, ranging from saviors such as Jesus or Buddha to less exalted sages, might voluntarily return to earth or prolong their lives to help those less fortunate cast off the consequences of past misdeeds.[54] Absent from theosophical thinking was Browne's notion of the fractionalization of souls, which had allowed him and Coxey, together presumably with many others, to partake of segments of the soul of Christ.

In addition to these doctrinal differences, there are circumstantial grounds for doubting that Browne had anything to do with organized Theosophy. In the first place, that movement was staunchly middle class, with a large number of professional people as members.[55] Browne, born in a log smokehouse near Springfield, Illinois, was an itinerant popular artist and political journalist, and while neither background nor occupation disqualified him from participation in Theosophical circles, his daily contacts were unlikely to bring him in touch with them.[56] Second, Browne eagerly shared his views on theosophy with anyone willing to listen, but oddly said nothing about the organized Theosophical movement itself—despite the fact that in 1894 Theosophy was in the throes of a struggle for leadership that threatened to split the organization.[57]

Where, then, did his idiosyncratic views come from? It will not do simply to attribute them, as Stead did, to an innate American predisposition to mysticism.[58] Instead, a far more likely explanation lies in the swirl of ideas in the Chicago of 1893. Motivated by a desire to see the Columbian Exposition, participate in the bimetallism convention, and in general peddle his political wares, Browne came to Chicago in the spring and apparently remained, with perhaps some brief interruptions, until the late fall.[59] The Exposition and the bimetallism meeting were not, however, the only notable events in Chicago that year, for the city also hosted the World Parliament of Religions. The Parliament not only provided an unprecedented opportunity for the presentation of historic Asian religions to Western audiences, but also became a major occasion for the presentation of Theosophy. In September, Annie Besant took the Parliament by storm, speaking to three thousand on one evening, and thirty-five hundred the following day. Her appearances made front-page news in the next day's *Tribune*.[60] Given the sensation Mrs. Besant created and the extraordinary press coverage of her lectures, it is inconceivable that Browne, the self-appointed religious thinker, was unaware of her presence. Although there is no reason to believe he heard Mrs. Besant speak, it is entirely likely that he had gotten some notion of

Theosophy secondhand, either through word of mouth or through newspaper articles, which would account for both his sudden interest in reincarnation and for the differences between his and orthodox theosophical doctrine.

Coxey's own relationship to Browne's metaphysical speculation seems problematic. During the planning phase and the March itself, he had only supportive things to say about his colleague, although in fact Coxey tended to avoid being drawn into discussions of religion. He preferred to concentrate on specific legislative proposals. He may well have felt flattered to think that the economic views he held somehow meshed with transcendent cosmic forces, proof both of their validity and of their ultimate triumph. In a sense the two were also in a relationship that could be viewed, depending on how charitably one regards it, as either symbiotic or mutually exploitative. Coxey's money and connections suddenly gave Browne the opportunity to lead a movement of national visibility instead of lecturing to the curious and scoffing on the Chicago lakefront. Coxey, unable to secure a respectful hearing for his measures in Washington, saw in Browne someone whose gifts for organization and promotion would allow him to appeal to Congress in the name of the American people and make his proposals impossible to ignore or sidetrack.

After the March, Coxey and Browne temporarily drew apart. At one level, the breach was occasioned by purely personal factors. Mamie Coxey, Jacob Coxey's stunning blonde daughter, eloped with Browne in 1895, against her father's express wishes. Coxey, a Populist but also a prudent businessman, doubted Browne's ability to support his daughter, a reasonable consideration in light of the fact that Browne was already living off of Coxey in his capacity as Marshall of the "Army" and Secretary of the Good Roads Association. It did not help that the domestic tiff was almost as widely reported as the March itself.[61] By the time of the Populist Convention in July 1896, the relationship was still sufficiently distant for the St. Louis *Chronicle* to describe a meeting between Browne and Coxey as "very frosty."[62] But the relationship seems to have warmed sufficiently by the fall so that the Brownes could return to Ohio where Carl campaigned vigorously for the Populist ticket on Coxey's home territory, and on the day before the Presidential election, Browne drove his "campaign panorama wagon" in a Coxey-led parade through Massillon.[63]

Beyond the soap opera of Coxey domesticity, Coxey was clearly edging away from Browne's religious vision of Populism. The earliest indication came on August 15, 1894, only three and a half

months after the "Army" arrived in Washington, when Coxey renamed the "Commonweal"—or what was left of it. As a Coxey publication delicately put the matter, "The word Christ was dropped
out of deference to the misunderstanding existing in the minds of
many good people in regard to its use and the words United States
of America put in place."[64] This secularization by decree was
linked to Coxey's belief that Browne's religious views exposed the
cause to unnecessary ridicule.[65] Yet the irony of Coxey's retreat
into a more secular brand of economic radicalism lay in the fact
that the more he distanced himself from Browne, the less attention he received. He lived on like some museum exhibit until 1951,
when he died at age 97, until the very end wearing the high cellu-
loid collar of a proper Edwardian gentleman. Yet he never regained
the national stature he had achieved in 1894, not even during the
Great Depression when his views once again found an audience.
For Coxey's economic panaceas had been carried to prominence by
precisely the eccentric millennialism of his colleague which in
later years he found so painful an embarrassment.

IV.

"Coxey's Army" is still a good story today for the same reason
journalists found it good copy at the time. It had precisely the
right mixture of personal eccentricity, deviant religion, moral out-
rage, and quixotic heroism. Yet the "Army," its March, and its
leaders were more than merely picturesque, and I will touch
briefly on their larger significance, and in particular on two sets of
implications. The first concern the manner in which "Coxey's
Army" prefigures social movements of the last twenty-five years,
for much in the events of 1894 strikingly anticipates those of the
late 1960s, 1970s, and 1980s. Second, the March, particularly in
its millennial aspects, must be seen as a response to an evil that
was in the 1890s still relatively novel, the evil of large-scale economic dislocation. As to the anticipatory aspects of "Coxey's
Army," these lie in three main areas: its relationship with the
communications media; the search for a dramatic and potent public act; and the elaborately syncretic character of its doctrine.

Although both Browne and Coxey expected to lead a mass
movement numbering at the least in the tens of thousands, in the
end they had to settle for a few hundred. Yet the failure of numbers did not translate into obscurity; far from it. The tiny band of
marchers transfixed the nation and its political leadership be-

cause of the magnifying effects of press coverage. The combination of telegraphy and mass circulation newspapers allowed the progress of the March to be followed all over the country, and for national importance to be accorded it as a function not of its size per se but of news value as judged by reporters and their editors. When Coxey told Ray Stannard Baker that his Chicago *Record* article had generated "a large gunnysack half full of mail and telegrams," Baker reflected with sudden awareness that "I was helping to launch this crazy enterprise!"[66] Browne quickly recognized that what the "Army" lacked in marchers it could gain in press attention if only he could provide a steady supply of the dramatic and picturesque. Thus the March increasingly approximated what Daniel Boorstin calls a "pseudo-event," an event held for the express purpose of being reported.[67]

The pseudo-event, by blurring the boundary between the authentic and the counterfeit, has become a cliche in modern life, but it was only beginning to intrude on the country's consciousness in 1894. In our last quarter century in particular, national visibility has been accorded to many groups and causes whose adherents have sometimes been fewer than Browne's and Coxey's. Consequently, although the "Army" was not truly a mass movement, it was treated as though it were by authorities along the way, as well as by the national administration. Officials of municipalities, the District of Columbia, and the national administration treated the March as though it were the onslaught of thousands. Conditioned by the amplifying affects of newspaper coverage, they allowed Browne and Coxey to behave as if their movement were vast and politically powerful. In light of Browne's histrionic impulses, he required little prompting to fit his behavior to the interlocking expectations of public officials and journalists.

The amplifying effect of reportage was closely related to another of the March's prefigurative characteristics: The "Commonweal of Christ" was an act-centered organization. At one level, of course, its behavior was avowedly instrumental. Public manifestation of the misery of the unemployed would provide Coxey with the opportunity to present his proposals in a manner that would assure Congressional attention, and once such attention was given, he felt their inherent rightness would become so clear as to make adoption inevitable. At the same time, the March was expressive, to the extent that it bonded together into an intense although temporary community a collection of individuals who had no secure place in society. But the March also existed on a plane which was neither clearly instrumental nor demonstrably expressive, a plane of what may be called "sacramental politics," in which particular actions themselves are believed to unlock cosmic forces, irrespective of one's own beliefs or the responses of others.

Browne, for example, seems never to have been troubled by the fact that the "Army's" foot soldiers seemed neither to understand nor care about his theology of the Second Advent and reincarnation. Whether they cared or understood was irrelevant to the outcome of the March. As we have seen, Browne's sacramental side included a variety of theories. According to one, the March brought together a critical mass of the "soul matter" of Christ. According to another, the Second Coming would be a collective phenomenon, in which the gathered people would be, as it were, the body of Christ. There seems little point in trying to extract a consistent position from the meanderings of Browne's mind. But there does appear to be a consistent belief that the very occurrence of the March placed American society in closer touch with a transcendent reality. Just as Browne was not unduly disturbed by the small number of marchers or by their low level of awareness, so he does not seem to have been greatly disheartened by the fiasco at the Capitol steps. Unlike Coxey, he was not result-oriented, in the conventional political sense of the term. Since the March was a magical or sacramental event, its mere occurrence was sufficient, for it brought in closer touch the realms of the sacred and the mundane, whatever the immediate political consequences.

Act-centered politics have recurred in varied ideological contexts since the days of "Coxey's Army," and while the range of variation is broad enough to make clear that the "Army" could scarcely have by itself given birth to so many offspring, it did significantly prefigure an increasingly important strain of political activity. During the 1960s, it was conspicuously in evidence among some members of the "New Left," for whom acts of violence and protest were often assumed to have an intrinsic significance. It was sufficient merely to engage in acts of confrontation without the necessity of calculating their consequences.

Finally, "Coxey's Army" is set apart, at least from most of the movements of its own time, by a strikingly syncretic system of beliefs, interweaving religious and secular strands. Here, once again, the movement's character owed far more to Browne than to Coxey, for Browne synthesized his beliefs out of at least three principal sources.

First, he appears to have had at least some familiarity with Protestant millennialism. Browne's millennialism drew on both the premillennial and postmillennial strains of American eschato-

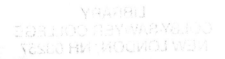

logical thought, the former expecting Christ's return to precede the millennium, the latter expecting it to follow. On the one hand, Browne's commitment to monetary reform—present long before his first meeting with Coxey—suggests postmillennial gradualism and an associated confidence in the potency of human action. Indeed, at one level the March itself could be construed as a dramatic reformist endeavor. The phrase often employed by Coxey and Browne—a "petition in boots"—sounds the postmillennial, reformist theme.

Nonetheless, in important ways, Browne was at least as much a premillennialist, and his commitment to reform managed to coexist with apocalyptic expectation. As he made unmistakably clear, he viewed his own time as ripe for the climactic battle between good and evil. Coxey's economic proposals offered the vehicle by which the forces of good could secure total, permanent victory over their adversaries. The elaborate revisioning of Revelation in Populist terms unmistakably linked changes in the economic system with an imminent and definitive break in mundane history.

Browne's seemingly effortless shift between pre- and postmillennialism might be regarded simply as the inconsistencies of a mind little given to systematic and disciplined thought. Yet while Browne did leap disconcertingly from one idea to the next, his hybrid millennialism had deeper roots. Premillennialism had reached its peak of influence in the early 1840s, when the self-taught preacher William Miller predicted that the Second Coming would occur in 1843–44. Miller's mass movement collapsed in disillusionment and sent premillennialism into disrepute. But the distinction between pre- and postmillennialism, so sharply drawn in the early decades of the nineteenth century, became increasingly blurred by the second half of the 1800s. A number of factors seem responsible for the convergence: First, premillennial readings of Biblical texts were once more acquiring intellectual respectability. Yet, confidence in gradual human improvement had become a virtual article of faith among Americans of all religious persuasions. Finally, and ironically, pessimism in intellectual and artistic circles made cataclysmic visions both commonplace and fashionable.[68] Browne was consequently not alone in simultaneously holding to ideas of activism and of fatalism, robust optimism and expectations of terrifying calamity.

Browne also had, albeit probably at second-hand, some acquaintance with Asian spirituality as his second principal source of ideas. This included, of course, his "theosophy," with its concept of reincarnation. Americans were just beginning to develop their

belief in the superiority of Indian spiritual attainment, an infatu-
ation demonstrated not only by Annie Besant's appearance at the
World Parliament of Religions in Chicago but by the equally dramatic appearance there of Swami Vivekananda.

Finally, Browne, a committed Populist, had an easy familiarity
with its doctrines of economic protest and financial conspiracy, the
third of his sources. The purity and indeed the very survival of
American society was threatened by a "money power" of unimag-
inable resources and guile. Richard Hofstadter categorizes this
vein of Populist thought as an example of the "paranoid political
style," which combines an overheated concern for conspiracies with
a belief that the ultimate battle between good and evil is at
hand.[69] While elements of the "paranoid style" surely shine
through in Browne, and indeed in Coxey himself, neither betray
the suppressed pessimism so often found in its representatives,
the fear that in the coming final battle, evil rather than good will
triumph. By contrast, Coxey and especially Browne remained convinced of the imminence of a millennial triumph. America would
not only regain its former virtue, but would extend it to create a
new society of unprecedented justice and equality.

Browne's tripartite synthesis of Protestant millennialism,
Asian spirituality, and Populist conspiracy theory had an extraordinary cohesiveness. The world, he said, was ruled by unseen
forces, the malevolent forces of the financial cabal and the redemp-
tive forces of reincarnated souls. The struggle between them
played out the ancient script in the Book of Revelation, giving
both contemporary meaning and imminence to its ambiguous
predictions. By implication, Christians who took eschatological
prophecies seriously needed Populism in order to understand
their present meaning, and "theosophy" in order to bring them
to fruition.

This curious fusion of religious fundamentalism, a modish
concern for the occult, and radical politics reappears in the movements of the 1960s, 1970s, and 1980s. An entire genre of contemporary religious literature now seeks to transform the Book of
Revelation into a political tract, as, for example, in the work of Hal
Lindsey.[70] Eastern conceptions of religion, filtered through Western sensibilities, appear in so-called "cult movements," such as
that of Hare Krishna, and in the more diffuse "New Age" fascination with "channeling," in which mediums serve as the literal
mouthpieces of long-dead "ascended masters." The contemporary
appetite for conspiracies has found dramatic expression among
right-wing groups, which combine notions of a Jewish conspiracy

with millennialism and radical economics in ways that eerily echo the Populist era.

The current outburst of right-wing activity recapitulates many motifs present in the 1890s, albeit with some novel elements. The present political milieu includes organizations such as the Aryan Nations, committed to the creation of an independent "Aryan" state; survivalist communities, such as Covenant, Sword, and Arm of the Lord, which withdraw in anticipation of massive social chaos and race warfare; Klan organizations that seek a white-dominated social order; and a variety of groups such as The Posse Comitatus groups hostile to elements of the economic order, including the state taxing power and the Federal Reserve System. This diverse array of groups shares overlapping memberships and common core beliefs.[71]

These common beliefs differentiate contemporary white supremacists from "mainstream" American conservatives and from right-wing movements of the past. While similarities exist between present groups and such earlier organizations as George Lincoln Rockwell's American Nazi Party in the 1960s, Klan groups of the 1920s and 1950s, and Fascist organizations of the 1930s, the differences are dramatic. The most significant lie at the intersection of political and religious beliefs. White supremacist groups seek to advance a political agenda that includes the subordination of Blacks, the subordination or destruction of Jews, and the dissolution of financial institutions that they believe to be controlled by Jews. These are not novel themes; indeed, we have already seen the emphasis on a Jewish financial conspiracy in the views of Coxey and Browne. However, contemporary white supremacists, unlike their predecessors, have linked this economic and political agenda with the theology of "British-Israelism."

"British-Israelism," a product of late Victorian religious speculation, asserts that the "Ten Lost Tribes" of the Bible survived intact, migrated northwestward, and eventually populated the British Isles.[72] Almost from the beginning of British-Israelism, a division developed between champions of British-Celtic descent from the Biblical tribes and so-called "Teutonists," who argued for the Israelite origins of all Germanic peoples. Although those holding the more narrowly British view prevailed within "British-Israel" organizations, the "Teutonists" were never wholly displaced. Both groups accepted the Israelite origins of contemporary Jews, but like other Protestants asserted that the Jews' failure to accept Christ had deprived them of a central role in the economy of salvation.

This so-called "Identity" theology created by "British-Israel" writers passed in time to the United States, both because of America's English origins and because political changes created in the United States a situation similar to that earlier in Great Britain. The trans-Atlantic transposition of the ideology sometimes amounted to a virtual duplication of the original, save that America now occupied the place of Britain, as, for example, in Herbert W. Armstrong's Worldwide Church of God.[73] However, a more complex process brought together "British-Israel" theology, anti-Semitism, and white supremacist politics. Beginning in the 1920s, "British-Israel" views began to appear in the United States as a vehicle for anti-Semitism, through writers associated with both the *Dearborn Independent* and Gerald L. K. Smith.[74] Not surprisingly, it was the "Teutonist" variant that found acceptance in these circles.

In addition to identifying Germanic peoples with the "Lost Tribes," "Identity" writers on the political right added a concept of Jewish demonization wholly absent from original "British-Israel" thought. Thus Jews are now said in "Identity" texts to have descended not from Israelites but from a literal biological union between Eve and Satan in the Garden, and to have usurped the place of "true Aryan" Israelites. "British-Israelites" commonly asserted that "while all Jews are Israelites, not all Israelites are Jews"; American white supremacists now insist that no Jews are Israelites but that all "Aryans" are.

This strange amalgam has produced an American right-radicalism in which older concepts of racial and religious subordination are grounded neither in self-interest nor in community custom but in immutable divine command. Although this ideology is closely related to a reading of Biblical texts, essential to it is an elaborately spurious erudition that purports to read Biblical associations into European languages and place names, to reveal their putative Israelite origins.

Like Browne's homegrown "theosophy," in which each individual inherited a quantum of Christ's soul, the myth that the "Ten Lost Tribes" are the ancestors of contemporary Europeans and Americans is a gratifying and unfalsifiable fantasy for believers. Like Browne's belief system, it too melds together a traditional millenarian scenario with deviant beliefs that lie outside both major denominations and fundamentalist sects. The deviant beliefs serve the catalytic functioning of demonstrating to believers that the final, millenarian times are near; that the movement's political aims are God's aims, too; and that in a world polarized between good and evil, a Jewish conspiracy is the ultimate adversary.

In short, while the mental universe of Carl Browne may have been eccentric, it was isolated neither from intellectual currents of its own time nor from future directions of religious and political thought. Indeed, although Coxey was sufficiently embarrassed to try to purge the movement of Browne's eccentric notions, in the end it was the long-lived Coxey who seemed like the historical relic, increasingly out of touch with a changing world; while Browne, with his countercultural buckskin costume, would scarcely have been out of place in the 1960s.

Part of the continuity may be ascribed to the nature of the moral world Browne saw himself confronting. He was responding both to the pervasive inequalities of Gilded Age America and to the accentuated form they took under the pressure of the 1893–94 depression. Economic depression lay outside the traditional apparatus of signs and portents that had governed millenarian thought in the West since at least the seventeenth century. Millennialism looked for signals, on the one hand, in instabilities in nature, in the form of either natural disasters or anomalies; and, on the other, in instabilities in politics, signaled by warfare and sudden changes in rulership. Depressions counted as neither the one nor the other.

The Millerites had failed in part because they remained embedded in the old millenarian calculus, in which man-made disasters had little place and economic depressions none at all. Browne, on the other hand, although he retained the traditional symbolism of the Book of Revelation, explicitly expanded it in order to enfold the novel catastrophes of an urban-industrial society. The fusion of millenarian religion with political radicalism extended to the March to the Capitol itself, a journey which was both a pilgrimage to a shrine and an act of confrontation with the authority that the shrine symbolized. In keeping with Browne's battle cry, "He is risen!" the March began on Easter Sunday, but it was carefully timed to arrive on May Day.

Browne's religio-political synthesis therefore addressed weaknesses of both economic radicalism and millenarian religion. The former, preoccupied with conspiratorial machinations, sometimes lapsed into the negativism of the "paranoid political style." In its Manichean vision, the forces of evil were always on the verge of victory, while the virtuous managed to survive only by dint of extraordinary heroism or temporary reprieves. In this precariously balanced moral universe, the triumph of the good could never be taken for granted. Thus Mrs. Emery had dedicated *Seven Finan-cial Conspiracies* to "the enslaved people of a dying republic."[75] If economic radicalism could perish in its own dark visions, millenarian religion, as we have seen, approached the world with a frame of reference more suited to the problems of the traditional agrarian past than to the industrialized present. Unable to speak directly to the ills of modern societies, its vision of a perfected world seemed increasingly irrelevant. Where earthquakes, storms, and dynastic changes were no longer the great symbolic fears, the scenario of millenarian fulfillment appeared increasingly irrelevant.

Browne, cobbling together bits and pieces of economic conspiratorialism and millenarian religion, linked by occult-Eastern conceptions of the soul, lifted the conspiracies beyond the paranoid style to become part of a larger world-redemptive process. At the same time, the millenarian vision was severed from the old and outdated categories of portents, and instead explicitly linked to the most fearful plague of modernity, economic collapse. He and "Coxey's Army," therefore, pointed simultaneously back to the symbols of earlier ages and forward to the hybrid millenarian visions of our own times.

Chapter Three

Progressive Reform, Censorship, and the Motion Picture Industry, 1909–1917

Nancy Rosenbloom

Nowhere is the relationship between film and the society that produced it more tantalizing and perhaps less understood than in the Progressive Era. During the decade preceding America's entry into World War I, reform captured the political imagination of an entire generation of Americans. Lacking confidence in the ability of the traditional two-party system to address the human costs of economic progress, self-styled reformers from John Dewey to Jane Addams jumped on the band wagon of Progressivism and turned their attention to exploring how the culture as a whole could meet the demands of an emerging urban-industrial society. As writers, academics, businessmen, and settlement workers began to grapple with America's problems, the potential of the moving picture to reach deep into the hearts of the cities across ethnic, class, and, on occasion, racial lines to touch the daily lives of hundreds of thousands of people could only have filled them with a sense of wonder and a tinge of envy. Awakened to the social potential of moving pictures, some reformers sought an effective means "to harness [its] force to the chariot of social ideals."[1]

While the power of the moving picture appealed to many, it also threatened the sense and sensibility of others, particularly entrenched public officials—mayors and police chiefs—as in New York and Chicago.[2] When the closing of motion picture houses in New York City in 1908 raised the spectre of censorship, it became apparent to exhibitors and film manufacturers alike that, if the business was to grow, an accommodation with the political establishment was imperative. Between 1909 and 1917, the motion picture industry, itself experiencing the strains of its rapidly changing structure, sought to free itself from the threat of censorship. With a momentum of its own, the struggle over censorship politicized the moving picture industry as no other issue of the day. As the film industry became increasingly aware that only an organized and aggressive political campaign could protect it from

the costly impact of hostile municipal, state, and federal legislation, it redefined its relationship with those reformers who had
originally championed its cause and came to rely on them far less
to mediate the political and social problems the industry faced.

Although the relationship between film and Progressivism has
been addressed most notably by Lary May, Garth Jowett, and Robert Sklar, the precise nature of the relationship between Progressivism, censorship, and the motion picture industry has not been
adequately explored.[3] Any explanation of this relationship is complicated by a lack of consensus on the meaning of "Progressivism."
Still, Progressivism remains a historically significant concept for
understanding not only the achievements of twentieth-century reform but the ideological component of the debates surrounding the
reformers' specific goals.

Characterized by an increased reliance on administrative
agencies and trained experts, Progressivism answered a number of
the political and social needs of America in the early twentieth
century.[4] As a middle class reform movement, it drew its impulse
from the basic values of nineteenth-century liberalism, with its
emphasis on the development of the individual, its confidence in
education as the proper way to develop the rational and tame
the irrational in the human animal, and its concern for achieving
the proper balance, not only between individual and social welfare,
but also between municipal, state, and national governments. Not
the least of the values that lay at the heart of Progressivism was
its commitment to the free exchange of ideas and a reliance on
exposure and discussion to motivate change from within. From
this perspective, moving pictures were welcomed as a means to develop a new cultural consensus, mediate between social classes,
and thereby blunt social conflict. Since Progressives promoted
moving pictures out of their commitment to free speech and to improving the lives of the masses, it would be around the principle of
free speech—or, conversely, the question of censorship—that the
relationship between the motion picture industry and Progressivism evolved.

Between 1909 and 1917, the relationship between the motion
picture industry and Progressivism underwent a major transformation. The Motion Picture Patents Company, in 1909 the most
powerful single element in the industry, cooperated fully in creat-
ing a scheme of voluntary censorship under the auspices of the
National Board of Censorship. Both the Patents Company and the
National Board agreed that "uplift" was desirable—their alliance
grew out of a sense of enlightened self-interest. The first shift in

the relationship between the film industry and Progressivism came in 1912 when Frederic Howe assumed the chairmanship of the National Board. Howe radicalized the environment at the Board by his commitment to free speech. Not only did his defense of free speech for the moving pictures complement the series of court cases which the Mutual Film Corporation had initiated first in Kansas in 1913, and then in Ohio, but his reform activities also provided an important link between the activities of the Board, its orchestration of a battle against legal censorship, and the types of moving pictures produced by Hollywood as well as by companies affiliated with the Patents Company.

By 1915, however, the industry had reached a significant turning point in its strategy for fighting legal censorship. The Patents Company was no longer in control of the American film industry, the Supreme Court had affirmed the rights of the state to protect its citizens by passing censorship laws, and the phenomenal growth of Hollywood had created an entirely new set of circumstances that made it difficult for the film industry to respond in a concerted way to pressure for legal censorship. While the National Board tried its hand at organizing a response to state censorship on behalf of the principle of free speech, it was unable to avert criticism that it was acting more as an advocate for the industry than as a champion of the public interest when it professed to be representing public opinion.

Under these circumstances, the film industry began to organize its own trade associations—first the unsuccessful and short-lived Motion Picture Board of Trade and then the National Association of the Motion Picture Industry—for the ostensible purpose of fighting legal censorship. The tactics they pursued differed substantially from those of the National Board in that they were willing to try partisan politics to defend themselves and to exert peer pressure against exhibitors. Although the industry continued to cooperate with the National Board and established a joint committee on censorship, for all intents and purposes the Board was powerless to prevent hostile legislation. Clinging tightly to the principle of voluntary censorship, the National Board cooperated in the struggle against legal censorship but departed from Howe's political legacy by maintaining that the best defense against legal censorship was to produce educational and entertaining pictures that met standards of middle class taste. These circumstances vitiated the alliance between Progressivism and the motion picture industry after 1915. At the time the United States entered World War I in 1917, the question of motion picture censorship had become bound up with the demands for mobilization. By that time, however, the ties between Progressivism and the motion picture industry had helped to shape, indelibly, the development of commercial film.

The courtship between Progressivism and the motion picture industry dated from the spring of 1908, when a Joint Committee from the Women's Municipal League and the People's Institute, a reform-minded association that promoted a Progressive agenda, initiated an investigation into cheap amusements in Manhattan. Since its founding in 1897, the People's Institute had elicited solutions to the social and industrial problems of modern America through presenting many varied speakers and by applying social scientific theories to community building.[5] The Institute provided a non-partisan forum for free discussion of proposals for good government, social cooperation, and peaceful social evolution. While the speakers represented all points of view, the audience was predominantly composed of immigrant and working class men and women from the Lower East Side. In addition to its lecture series, the Institute also organized educational and social activities, as well as civic clubs whose members were "after Tammany with a club and unsightly streets with a broom."[6]

The most articulate member of the Joint Committee was John Collier, a field investigator for the People's Institute, who reported favorably on the nickelodeon. His criticism of the conditions of some local showhouses notwithstanding, he believed in the potential of the moving pictures to become a "true theater of the people, and an instrument whose power can only be realized when social workers begin to use it."[7] Concerned with raising the standards of the pictures being shown, the Committee believed that this could be best accomplished in cooperation with the moving picture business. It would take two major developments in the second half of 1908, however, before Collier and his associates could realize their goals. The first of these was the incorporation of the Motion Picture Patents Company in September; the second was the decision of New York Mayor George McClellan to close down all the moving picture theaters in Manhattan at Christmas. Though completely unrelated, these two events created the organizational structure and the sense of urgency that led to the establishment in New York City of the Board of Censorship of Motion Picture Shows early in March 1909.[8] By June this local agency would transform itself into the National Board of Censorship.

Since February 1908, negotiations had been under way between the Edison Manufacturing Company and its licensed manufacturers on the one side and Biograph and George Kleine on the other, to bring an end to years of fighting over patents on motion picture cameras, projectors and other cinematographic equipment. These discussions culminated in the incorporation of the Motion Picture Patents Company in September 1908. The Motion Picture Patents Company represented ten firms including Armat, Biograph, Edison, Essay, Kalem, Kleine, Lubin, Pathé Frere, Selig, and Vitagraph. A number of unlicensed producers and independent exchanges competed with the Patents Company.[9] There is little doubt that from the outset the members of the Patents Company intended to exert control over the production, distribution, and exhibition of their films. To what extent and at what point these efforts to rationalize a seemingly chaotic industry led to the formation of a trust acting in restraint of trade were questions that invited investigation from the federal government little more than a year later. The creation of the General Film Company in 1910 by the same men who formed the Patents Company to distribute the films produced by these members of the Patents Company would be challenged under the Sherman Anti-Trust Act in lengthy court proceedings beginning in 1912. In the interregnum, however, the Patents Company attained recognition both in the United States and in Europe as the respectable and legitimate standard-bearer in the American film industry. To improve its chances of dominating what appeared to be a lucrative and fast-growing enterprise, the Patents Company sought to minimize competition at home by making it difficult for independent producers to make films and, when they succeeded, from finding outlets for their exhibition. Even more important than upstart American producers was the problem of foreign—and particularly French—competition. In an attempt to control the flood of foreign pictures, Pathé and Melies joined in the negotiations over the Patents Company, as did film importer George Kleine. As a result, American companies, including the members of the Patents Company, operated in the shadow of popular French films made either abroad or in the American studios of Pathé company until the onset of war in Europe in 1914.[10]

What on the surface appeared to be mechanisms aimed at improving the national distribution and exhibition of films produced by members of the Patents Company therefore were also efforts to intimidate those outside the system that had been created by the Patents Company. Even so, the long-term failures of the Patents Company to persevere against the independent producers, the anti-trust case, and the reorganization of the industry prompted by the war should not obscure their self-professed goals to introduce greater efficiency and order into the industry. Above all, the managing officers of the Patents Company believed that their plan would be most effective if moving pictures could be made to appeal to a larger audience drawn from the American middle class as well as from the ethnic and working class enclaves where the nickelodeons had already achieved considerable popularity.

Shortly after its formation, the Patents Company sent an announcement of its objectives to the exhibitors. In this circular the Patents Company explained that the manufacturer needed to insure "a fair and reasonable price for his film so as to enable him to maintain and improve the quality of his pictures." It further clarified that the Company aimed to "eliminate the cheap and inferior foreign films which have been forced upon the market, and to so educate the public taste that only high class and attractive films will be accepted as reaching the American Standard."[11] To accomplish this goal, the Patents Company initiated an in-house review of films they were releasing and more importantly offered to supply certain exhibitors with "licensed service," that would guarantee a variety of high quality, "first-class" subjects.[12]

When the Patents Company agreed to impose a form of voluntary censorship on moving pictures in March 1909, the managing officers justified this step by pointing out that they had already announced their intention to promote an "American Standard" of "high quality" film and first-class subjects.[13] This coincided with efforts on the part of motion picture exhibitors to gain relief from city officials whose increasing complaints threatened them with theater closings.

Among the most vulnerable exhibitors were those in New York City. On December 24, 1908, Mayor George McClellan had closed down on the grounds of danger and immorality all the city's nickelodeons, which were operating under common show licenses. McClellan was responding to a variety of pressures, in part from those who wanted the theaters closed on Sunday.[14] Not all who advocated Sunday closings were pure-minded; the motion picture theaters had enemies among those whose investments in vaudeville, saloons, and dance halls were suffering from too much competition. Colored by anti-Jewish feelings directed against both the owners and patrons of the picture shows, the conflict over Sunday closings thus drew to a stormy climax on Christmas Eve.

McClellan's actions proved to be a turning point for New York exhibitors. At the same time that the newly formed Association of Motion Picture Exhibitors of New York obtained court injunctions against these closings, exhibitors also realized the need for more long-term protection. Considering the extent of hostility from City Hall and from the powerful Tammany machine that determined so much of political life in New York City, the exhibitors sought help from those already battling Tammany Hall, the men and women at the People's Institute.

The opportunity to enter the fray on the side of the exhibitors, if not on behalf of New York's working class families, presented precisely the sort of challenge the People's Institute sought. Charles Sprague Smith, the founder and managing director of the Institute between 1897 and 1910, had long focused his attention on why those who lived "downtown"—that is, in the working class and ethnic neighborhoods—assented to and supported corrupt governments. The Forum, in many ways the center of intellectual life at the Institute, conceived of itself as an alternative to the existing party structure by providing, together with the civic clubs, an "extra-political organization where men of all parties and of no party could join hands."[15] Confident that the Institute had a significant role to play in redefining the social fabric so tautly stretched by divergent class interests, Smith thought that government should not be bound by the traditional two-party system nor indeed by partisan politics at all.[16] To this end, the Institute reached out to the working class and ethnic populations, and considered itself the political voice of the people it served. Thus, the more partisan the attack on the motion picture theaters appeared, the more eager was the Institute to come to their defense.

Even before Mayor McClellan's announced decision to close the moving picture showhouses for Christmas 1908, the Institute had expressed an interest in improving them instead. Set against a background of social unrest, industrial dislocation, and massive immigration, unemployment had emerged as the most compelling problem in 1908 and, to Smith, threatened open class warfare. He warned that he had never experienced "anything approaching the unrest, the ferment, that there is to-day, the bitterness."[17] Stymied in his efforts to force civic authorities to address this problem, Smith focused much of his own concern on the daily lives of New York's working men and their families. This concern led him in 1908 to hire John Collier as a trouble-shooter who would help identify special projects for the Institute.

Among Collier's first assignments was the investigation of moving picture shows. As Smith's co-worker at the Institute, Collier vigorously pursued the goal of improving the quality of cheap, popular amusements. Both men recognized that the moving picture offered tremendous possibilities for improving the leisure of industrial workers and their families. By transforming the moving picture shows into cleaner, safer social centers and by encouraging the production of quality entertainment, Smith and Collier hoped to create better alternatives to saloons, dance halls and the streets. The possibility of using the moving pictures to help invigorate community life piqued Collier's imagination. Upon completion of his first investigation, Collier noted the broad popularity of moving pictures and their significance in neighborhood life. The vulnerability of the exhibitors played perfectly into Collier's plans.

The Institute's willingness to come to the help of the New York Exhibitors was a natural consequence of the interest it had already shown in the moving picture as a new medium of popular entertainment and education. For their part, the exhibitors agreed to abide by the recommendations of the joint committee for cleaner, safer theaters. At the end of its investigation, the Joint Committee had framed a bill for the New York State Assembly that sought to raise license fees for moving picture shows from twenty-five dollars to one hundred and fifty dollars, and transfer licensing from the jurisdiction of the police to the city's license bureau. Moreover, the bill recommended that school children be excluded from the showhouses during school hours and after 8 o'clock in the evening unless accompanied by an adult.[18] Raising the license fee was a small price to pay for exhibitors like Marcus Loew and William Fox, whose theaters served an upwardly mobile ethnic community.

However, as theaters moved into new neighborhoods and began to attract more middle class audiences, the question was no longer merely one of safe conditions but was complicated by differing standards of taste.[19] To be sure, moving picture standards had also concerned Collier and the Joint Committee but they had refrained from suggesting a legislative response to this problem. Collier believed that moving picture standards could be improved most effectively by cooperation with the moving picture business rather than by legislation, and he suggested that the Institute had a significant role to play, first by offering to endorse the best of the shows in exchange for the right to regulate their programs, and secondly by establishing one or more model nickelodeons.[20]

In rapid succession these events—the joint investigation, the formation of the Patents Company, the closing of the theaters, the Patents Company's announcement to the exhibitors that better quality pictures were to be offered—created the basis for a consensus between movie exhibitors, the Filmmakers, and the People's Institute that the time was right to improve the standards of moving pictures. "Uplift" became the password for transforming the moving picture shows into cleaner, safer social centers and for encouraging the production of quality entertainment. The word "uplift" resonated for both reformers and the leaders of the industry. Together they agreed to the creation of the National Board of Censorship under the auspices of the People's Institute.

No single person was as influential in the formation and development of the National Board of Censorship as John Collier. Collier believed in the viability of an informed public which,"not confined to any dogma or party," would form the "true culture of the nation," and "the soul of American democracy."[21] From the time the Board began operating in March 1909 until 1917, Collier remained a significant force at the Institute and on the National Board, although after 1914 much of his interest shifted more and more toward other projects. Collier fit the mold of so many of the bright young men and women college graduates whose intellectual grounding in the new social sciences, especially psychology, sociology, and anthropology, was joined to their commitment to reform society.[22] At this point in his life Collier was especially interested in the problems of adolescence and of leisure pursuits. Strongly influenced by John Dewey and Lester Gulick, Collier summed up his ideas about the role of motion pictures in a letter he scrawled to a co-worker at the National Board:

> Our present object is to make motion pictures a center of gravity of the whole leisure time problem.... In emphasizing Leisure Time we are trying to force civilization to change the focus of its attention from production to happiness. The economic revolution, making possible such a change of focus is taking place rapidly. Ours is it to help that some human nature, some social richness, some life-exuberance, survives the present famine and the impending revolution.[23]

Inspired by his philosophical concerns about the relationship between the individual and society, Collier served as a chief administrator at the National Board. As general secretary, Collier insisted that the principle of voluntary censorship was to be the essence of operations at the National Board. On March 15, 1909, Collier informed the motion picture companies that the Board of Censorship was operating, and he soon boasted that it was previewing 70 percent of the pictures shown in the nation.[24] Organized by committees—there were an Executive Committee, a General Committee, and a Censoring Committee, and before long an Advisory Committee—the actual review of individual films was the responsibility of the unpaid volunteers who composed the

Censoring Committee. They met at the Patents Company offices
on Fifth Avenue in Manhattan, where they were provided a viewing room with the appropriate equipment and a technician. This
allowed the Board to save on overhead expenses, although it also
invited criticism that it was merely acting as an extension of the
Patents Company.

During the first few months of operation, the Executive Committee established a number of precedents for the Censoring Committee to follow.[25] The Executive Committee decided to prepare
ballots for each picture which gave members the option of approving, rejecting, or questioning each film previewed. Only if the committee unanimously approved the film could it inform the moving
picture companies' representative immediately of its decision. In
all other cases, committee members waited until after they had
viewed all the day's pictures before discussing individual problems.
The committee passed most films, although on occasion it recommended specific changes. A decision could be appealed by producers to the General Committee of the National Board. Since not all
movie manufacturers accepted the Board's decisions graciously,
the Board decided to pursue a "firm but tactful" policy in cases of
those who refused to submit their pictures, and to call violations
either to the attention of the Society for the Prevention of Crime
or directly to the city authorities.[26]

If the picture did not pass the Censoring Committee it was
returned to the production studios for alterations. This caused
only mild frustration for Edison and Biograph, since their studios
were nearby, but greater problems for the other members of the
Patents Company, including Lubin whose studios were in Philadelphia, and Selig, in Chicago. In general, the Board refrained from
dictating too closely to the trade and, after an altercation with
Biograph, never interfered on matters considered to be artistic.
The companies complied with the requests of the Board because
the managing officers of the Patents Company were confident
that it could help improve the status of the motion picture
business. Beside, the main consideration of the Board was to "preserve the dignity of the committee" and not to "antagonize the
manufacturers."[27]

Between the spring of 1909 and the spring of 1912 there would
be little variation in this basic pattern. By that time, however, the
Censoring Committee had expanded to a pool of well over a hundred members from which smaller groups were created. The com-
position of these subcommittees constantly changed in order to encourage the generation of fresh opinions by averting the formation

of a powerful faction or the domination of discussion by any single individual. To preview the large numbers of pictures being produced by both the Patents Company and the independent producers, the subcommittees met four or five days a week. The subcommittees continued to preview films in viewing rooms provided either by the Patents Company or one of the two large exchanges handling pictures for the independents, Mutual and Universal.

The Censoring Committee reviewed films on an ad hoc basis according to what Collier labeled "empirical standards."[28] The Board defined its moral mission broadly, as promoting dramatic entertainment and the depiction of the human condition while at the same time discouraging sensationalism and exploitation. At the beginning, the Board targeted especially "obscene pictures and pictures of crime for crime's sake."[29] One of the first reports that the Board sent to the Patents Company singled out five films for failing to meet approval. The reasons varied from showing "a succession of criminal acts," "excessive and gratuitous use of whiskey," and "women's legs as they [the women] fell over backwards," to being "offensive to good taste." On this last point the committee made clear that it thought manufacturers responsible for improving artistic standards, which included matters judged in bad taste.[30]

The committee also commended certain films and scenes. One of the best films in the committee's opinion during its first month of operation was a Vitagraph release, "The Shepard's Daughter." Suggesting that a clarification be made by inserting a subtitle to "disarm public prejudice" against what many of the audience might believe to be "a sheer and sinful seduction," the committee commented that, "We wouldn't object to the film even if it *did* portray seduction, because the treatment is earnest and artistic and the effect on the mind is pleasing and moral."[31]

In addition to concern about standards for moving pictures, the National Board worked towards achieving a model municipal ordinance.[32] This legislation addressed such questions as how to create optimal lighting and ventilation, how to secure adequate and well-located fire exits, and how to provide sufficient standing room. Sonya Levien, educational secretary at the National Board, was trained as a lawyer and was instrumental in designing the model ordinance. Both Collier and Levien were careful to separate their support for legislation regulating safer theaters from their opposition to legal—or official—prior censorship of the moving pictures. Collier rejected legal censorship as having no place in America. The only precedent was a "royal anachronism," the Master of Revels, who had censored plays in seventeenth-century England for Royal "edification."[33]

If the principle of voluntary censorship made it possible for the National Board to gain the confidence of the manufacturers, then it also left the Board vulnerable to charges that it had no legal authority to enforce its recommendations and was therefore ineffectual. Opposition to voluntary censorship began to surface as early as 1911 and developed into an especially bitter controversy in New York City, where the most damaging challenge to its authority manifested itself in an attempt by the Board of Alderman to impose pre-publicity censorship by legislation. Collier and the Board refused to support the proposed ordinance even though it also mandated badly needed improvements in the showhouses in order to make the Board's opposition to legal pre-publicity censorship abundantly clear.

On this point, the Board had the support of Mayor William J. Gaynor, who had replaced McClellan in 1909. Prior to his election, Gaynor, as an appellate judge, had granted an injunction preventing the closing of all the motion picture theaters late in 1908. An eloquent jurist, if not always a savvy politician, Mayor Gaynor vetoed one version of the Ordinance that had a censorship proviso attached, and used the occasion to expound on his theory of the constitutional protection of free speech and free press. Gaynor interpreted the state constitution to mean that

> publications, whether oral, or printed to by writing, or by pictures, shall not be restrained in advance, but that everyone shall be free to speak or publish what he sees fit, subject to being prosecuted afterward for libel, immorality, obscenity or indecency therefor.

Furthermore, Gaynor addressed the class bias underlying the whole question. In recognizing that moving picture shows were "attended by the great bulk of the people, many of whom cannot afford to pay the prices charged by the [legitimate] theaters," he defended the moving picture shows and questioned why they be regarded "as subjects necessary to be protected by a censorship?" as compared to uncensored legitimate theaters. Incensed, Gaynor wrote: "Are they any more in need of protection by censorship than the rest of the community? Are they better than the rest of us, or worse?"[34]

Collier applauded Gaynor's decision, and so too did Frederic Howe, who had been appointed managing director of the People's Institute in April 1912 and subsequently chair of the National

Board of Censorship. During Howe's tenure as chair of the Board—he requested a leave of absence in May 1914 and officially resigned in April 1915—the work of the National Board of Censorship became the main activity at the People's Institute. At the time of his appointment, Howe presented an impeccably Progressive profile and had a national reputation. Howe had recently moved to New York City and found the intellectual life in Greenwich Village stimulating. He enjoyed inviting friends such as W. E. B. DuBois and Max Eastman to address the Institute. An outspoken advocate of direct primaries, municipal ownership, labor legislation, and women's suffrage, Howe politicized the National Board.

During Howe's tenure as chairman of the National Board of Censorship, the Board reaffirmed its public stance that official prior censorship was unconstitutional. While Howe stressed the necessity of a free exchange of ideas in a democratic society, he also offered new justification for the work of the National Board. Rather than represent the interests of the trade or of reformers, the Board now identified itself with the moving picture audience and adopted the position that it tried to "reflect what the people of the United States would think about any given picture were they sitting *en masse* to view it." Moreover, Howe insisted that the Board operated from the premise that "the general conscience believes in free speech on religious and political matters; in the right of people to live and enjoy themselves in the way they see fit, so long as fundamental morality is not injured."[35]

Howe realized that the censorship question was complicated, and he was particularly concerned about the difficulty of applying general standards to the criticism of specific films. Taking as an example the depiction of vice and crime and the dramatization of street life in New York, Howe cautioned that in one audience it might encourage the desire for reform while in another the desire to imitate. Howe believed that any censorship, whether voluntary or vested in federal and state officials, contained dangers to a free society. Keenly sensitive not only to the importance of the medium in the formation of public opinion but also to the role of public opinion in a democracy, Howe understood the political implications of legalized censorship—in fact, of any censorship—as well as any man of his day. On this point Howe frankly admitted:

> Aside from the question of the constitutionality of such [official] censorship is the question of the ultimate effect of the assumption by the State of the right of regulating this most important avenue of expression [the motion picture]. Should the State pass upon the desirability of

the portrayal of labor questions, of Socialism, the Industrial Workers of the World, and the other insistent
issues crowding to the fore? . . . If such [official] censorship be provided for, will not this great field of dramatic
expression be subjected to the fear of suppression, so
that only the safe and sane, the purely conventional, the
uncontroversial film will be produced? . . . Then the control of this official board would be a prize worth struggling for—a prize comparable to the control of the
Associated Press, and almost as dangerous to the freedom of the country.[36]

Howe feared official censorship because it was even more vulnerable, both to government and to narrowly individualistic
biases, if not outright graft, than voluntary censorship. The mis-
takes that the National Board made in judging particular films
might pose temporary problems, Howe admitted to his critics, but
this paled in comparison to the dangers posed by legal censorship.
Howe feared that legal censorship would

stifle, or threaten to stifle, the freedom of the [motion
picture] industry as a mirror of the everyday life, hopes
and aspirations of the people. The motion picture show
is not only democracy's theatre. It is a great educational
agency, and it is likely to become a propagandistic
agency of unmeasured possibilities.[37]

Howe's appointment as executive chairman of the National
Board of Censorship had assured the Board of greater legitimacy
for its work. But the moving picture interests, preoccupied with
commercial and artistic problems in the quickly expanding industry, did not realize how far short of its goal the National Board
would fall by 1915. Between the Board's formation in 1909 and
Howe's resignation six years later, the National Board offered the
motion picture industry an alliance with Progressivism. Yet in
spite of their successful campaigns to uplift the industry, increase
the size of middle class audiences, introduce moving pictures into
schools, and generally improve the public image of the industry,
their joint efforts to allay the anxieties of those who favored legalized censorship met with strong and organized opposition. As interest groups such as the Motion Picture Board of Trade and the
National Association of Motion Picture Industry (NAMPI) formed
after 1915 for the specific purpose of combating censorship, the alliance between the National Board and the motion picture industry faltered.

The events of 1908 had led to confidence that an alliance with Progressivism promised to benefit the motion picture industry. A trio of events in 1915 turned that promise sour. The first of these was the failure of the industry's campaign against official prior censorship. Since 1911, when Pennsylvania initiated state censorship of motion pictures, the industry had fought to protect itself not only against excising scissors, but also against having to pay inspection fees in states across the country. Ohio and Kansas passed censorship laws in 1913, while Maryland, New York, and Massachusetts threatened similar legislation.

To thwart further action of this sort, the Mutual Film Company brought two test cases challenging the states' right to censor moving pictures in federal district court in Kansas and Ohio. When unfavorable decisions resulted there, it appealed the decisions to the Supreme Court. When the Supreme Court rendered its decision in 1915 that the states had a right to censor films before exhibition, the motion picture industry had suffered a devastating blow. Not only did the decision disappoint the industry and the National Board, but the Court's refusal to consider the argument that motion pictures were entitled to constitutional protection under the first amendment deeply shocked free speech advocates like Collier and Howe. The industry doubted that the National Board could effectively avert disaster if state after state began to impose official prior censorship.

Shortly after the court decision was announced, Frederic Howe resigned as chair of the National Board, which now found itself thrown into turmoil by a leadership void. Although Howe had angrily opposed the Board's decision to pass D. W. Griffith's *The Birth of a Nation,* he insisted that this did not cause his resignation. In fact, Howe had been confirmed as Commissioner of Immigration at Ellis Island months before and had already assumed his new responsibilities. Moreover, he had already resigned as managing director of the Institute while maintaining some ties to the Board by serving on its advisory committee. For years, Howe's co-workers had been complaining about his lack of efficiency as an administrator. But none had questioned his political commitment or his social vision. Now the effects of his resignation were immediately apparent.

Throughout the spring and summer of 1915, Collier fought with members of the Executive Committee about the future direction of the Board. Dedicated to fighting legal censorship and securing constitutional protection for film, Collier lost patience with the day-to-day activities of the Board as it assumed a low profile in the political fight. The executive secretary, W. G. McGuire, and the new chair of the Board, Cranston Brenton, reassessed how the Board could fill its mission. Although they did not waver in their philosophic objections to legal censorship, they tried to redirect the energy of the Board away from politics toward the task of establishing lengthy and specific guidelines for film producers to follow.[38] Reasoning that they could best protect the film industry from legal censorship and the public from offensive films through carefully defined standards, the National Board renamed itself the National Board of Review. At the end of 1915 Collier began to dissociate himself more and more from the Board, until he finally broke completely with the Executive Committee in 1917.

If the lack of consensus on the Board weakened its relationship with the industry, then the dissolution of the Patents Company in October 1915 only amplified its problems. Since its founding in 1908 the Motion Pictures Patents Company had been the most powerful single force within the moving picture trade, and had done much to help establish the legitimacy of the National Board. Moreover, not only had the Patents Company loyally supported the Board and provided its financial backbone, but it had also centralized much of film production and distribution. The anti-trust case that the United States government initiated against the Patents Company in 1912, however, brought the relationship between the Company and the Board under intense scrutiny. Although Collier in his testimony before the Court steadfastly denied that the National Board had ever acted in collusion with the Patents Company to eliminate competition, the Board's relationship with the Patents Company placed Progressive reformers who in other sectors of the economy had spearheaded the crusade against trusts and monopolies in an embarrassing situation. While Collier publicly welcomed the court's decision, as a leader of the National Board he could only have deplored the demise of the Patents Company, since the dissolution of the trust diminished what little leverage the Board had in making the producers comply with voluntary submission. By exerting pressure on film production firms, the officers of the Patents Company had been able to assure their cooperation with the Board. With the dissolution of the trust, that was no longer possible.

In exploring the relationship between Progressivism and the motion picture industry, the impact of the National Board on the development of commercial film is the most intriguing question. The impact of the National Board on commercial film was strongest between 1909 and 1915, while the industry relied on the

Board as its political ally in the fight for the constitutional protection of free speech. This led film producers to make films that reflected the moral vision of Progressive America, its ambivalence towards modern urban society notwithstanding. If D. W. Griffith's *A Drunkard's Reformation* was a film the Board held up as an example for the trade to follow, then it was only one of the first of many films that took reform themes seriously. Even with the heavy loss of films from this period, a cursory examination reveals the significance of reform themes as film subjects. Stories about the effects of alcohol and drug abuse, the evils of child labor and prostitution, the exploitation of labor by greedy factory owners, abuses in politics ranging from bribery to bossism, inequities in medical and social services between the rich and poor, the violence of urban gangs and of crowded tenements, the woman's question—all of these issues were dealt with on the screen. Designed to capture a larger share of the middle class audience without losing those already hooked by "nickel madness," these film subjects served to illuminate, if not expose, the main social and political problems of the day. Although produced by different studios, these films shared a moral sensibility in which good triumphed over evil.

If some manufacturers, like the Edison Company, with its studios in the Bronx, self-consciously ordered production for reform audiences such as the Red Cross or the Kindergarten Association, then others, especially those with West Coast studios, adapted their film output to suit the tastes of the National Board. When the National Board sent an emissary to Hollywood in 1914 to discuss their goals with studio directors, he reported back that while they all deplored legal censorship, they also appreciated the constructive role the National Board was defining for itself in advising, if not supervising, the moving pictures. Interviews with Griffith and Thomas H. Ince, both of whom favored the production of feature-length dramatic films, and with Macklyn Sennett and Charles Chaplin in comedy reassured the Board that directors shared their goals to produce "bigger and better" pictures and cleaner comedies. Ironically, the Board's representative reported that artistically weak pictures were being made at Universal City where they adhered most strictly to the Board's standards. The report concluded that for the most part the moving picture public wanted longer pictures and that the best of the directors were willing to oblige.[39]

If the dynamic situation on the West Coast gave the National Board hope for improved pictures, then the standards which the

Board formulated under Howe and Collier reflected this optimism.[40] The Board refrained from censoring matters of taste and accuracy, and defined the audience in the broadest possible terms, so that all filmmakers were not required to cater to one particular audience such as children. Prior to 1915, the Board judged the details in each film by what they contributed to the overall story, and it tried to be sensitive to the integrity of the film as a whole. Generally, the influence of the National Board manifested itself in the encouragement of feature films that portrayed real life dilemmas complex enough to sustain audience interest but not necessarily duplicating life itself.

Ironically, the most vigorous battles the National Board fought were aimed not so much against the studios as against local and state censorship boards whose detailed criteria for judging films showed peculiaristic tendencies and threatened a nightmare for the dream machine makers. The challenge from censoring boards forced the National Board to define the boundary between desirable and undesirable films more rigidly, straining relations with the industry in the process.

The legacy of Progressivism to the moving picture industry must be measured not only in scenes cut from controversial films, but also in how far the National Board of Censorship went in challenging the industry to see itself as a vehicle for the expression of ideas. Never was the relationship between Progressivism and the motion picture industry more vital than during the six years when the National Board of Censorship operated under the leadership of John Collier and Frederic Howe. A self-styled Nietzschean, greatly influenced by contemporary psychology, Collier wanted to exploit the social potential of moving pictures to liberate the play instinct and encourage the development of personality.[41] In Howe's advocacy of free speech, on the other hand, there lay a commitment to liberal values that informed his belief that film could both entertain and enlighten as it brought the community together and helped create social harmony and class interaction.

After 1915, however, these values seemed to antagonize other social reformers. As the alliance between Progressivism and the motion picture industry faltered, arguments about the protection of children's morals and sexual taboos effectively emasculated the Progressive impulse at the National Board. Since the National Board of Censorship had represented an alliance between Progressivism and the motion picture industry that was based on mutual enlightened self-interest, that alliance began to dissolve when the industry lost confidence in the National Board. The National

Board could not deliver what the industry needed in order to protect itself from a crazy quilt of state and municipal censorship laws. By taking a more narrow view of their role and issuing dozens of rules and regulations of their own, the Board tried to defend its usefulness to the industry on new grounds.

When the Board failed as an effective ally in the political world and ceased to define for itself an aggressive role in the struggle against censorship, the industry responded to the challenge by lobbying directly on its own behalf through the creation of trade associations. The film industry had gained political experience through years of fighting on both sides of the anti-trust case, testifying at federal hearings, and organizing in its own defense. The newly organized National Association of the Motion Picture Industry immediately assumed a prominent role in campaigning against censorship. NAMPI differed from the National Board in three specific ways. First, it directly represented the interests of the industry. Second, it resorted to partisan politics to advance anti-censorship legislation. And finally, it lacked the social and political conscience that had motivated men like John Collier and Frederic Howe to advocate constitutional protection for the moving picture industry. In nearly a decade of struggle on the question of censorship the industry had tried to "stay out of politics." By 1917 the industry welcomed, albeit reluctantly, the fight.

The spring of 1917 promised to bring a showdown between those who supported and those who opposed censorship. Censorship legislation had been introduced in seventeen states. Then, in April, the United States entered World War I. The formation of the Committee on Public Information under George Creel to mobilize public opinion behind the war effort recognized the power of motion pictures to serve the government's purpose. Progressivism had originally focused its energies on domestic reform, but by 1917 the task of making the whole world "safe for democracy" seemed a noble goal. The Creel Committee offered the motion picture industry a new basis, however transient, for an alliance with Progressivism.

Chapter Four

The Press and the Red Scare, 1919–1921

Howard Abramowitz

By 1919, in the United States anti-communism was a well established, widely employed device for dealing with threats to the
existing order, especially those that arose in the industrial workplace. As early as the railroad strikes of 1877, red-baiting had
been used by businessmen, the clergy, and newspaper editorial
writers to rally middle class support for violent repression of dissident workers. The Haymarket affair of the mid-1880s intensified
anti-labor red-baiting, and can be considered the nation's first
true Red Scare. Anti-communism flourished again in the decade
before World War I, when it was used repeatedly to justify the
suppression of IWW and other militant labor unions.

The Red Scare of 1919–1921, however, marked a new and qual-
itatively different stage in the public use of anti-communism.
In that postwar period, when organized labor once again shocked
the middle class with its widespread use of the strike, anti-
communism was adopted by the federal government as its central
theme for dealing with labor radicals, alleged internal subversion,
and external enemies. During this most important red scare, anti-
communism shaped systematic policies of federal repression. J.
Edgar Hoover took command of the Justic Department's Alien
Radical Division. Deportation was used extensively as a political
weapon. Radical political parties had their offices raided according
to coordinated national plans. Throughout the period, undercover
agents employed by the federal govenment acted as political spies
and agents provocateur.

Viewed in this way, these and the other events that constitute
the Red Scare of 1919–1921 appear as a political process through
which the American government simultaneously eliminated radical political parties and developed anti-communism as its official
ideology. In 1919–1921, the federal government first promulgated,
and mobilized support for, the ideological core of what would become its mid-twentieth century foreign and domestic politics. By
means of red-baiting, overt repression, and covert activities, anti-
communism was transformed from a domestic anti-labor device

into the pivotal organizing principle shaping counter-revolutionary policies abroad and political conformity at home. The Red Scare of 1919–1921 narrowed the politcal spectrum of the United States. After the Red Scare, anti-communism became a clear-cut litmus test of legitimacy within the electoral system. Thus, the Red Scare of 1919–1920 has defined the practical limits of dissent and political tolerance right down to our own time.

The Political Power of the Press

The federal government did not transform American politics during the Red Scare of 1919–1921 without assistance. Veterans groups and patriotic societies, manufacturers' associations, chambers of commerce, and even the Boy Scouts and the YMCAs and YWCAs all played a role in this anti-communist drama. But more than any other institution, the daily press legitimized the government's anti-communist ideology among the wider public. As the chief sources of news about world, national, and regional events and as major sources of political ideas mass-circulation newspapers were in a key position to mobilize public support for the specific policies of the Red Scare. To say this is to invite dispute over whether or not a "free" press really existed. The prominence of the press in the Red Scare also raises questions about who controlled the press, and whether or not it worked, either consciously or subconsciously, in concert with the federal program. Thus, to understand the role of the press in the Red Scare, it is necessary to consider the structural relationship of the mass-circulation press to the public and other institutions in early twentieth-century America.

"By 1914," writes one authority on the history of the press, "the modern newspaper had emerged with the characteristics which were to characterize it for the next few decades."[1] These characteristics may be summarized as the quest for mass circulation, a shift from entrepreneurial to corporate ownership, the need for costly new production technologies, the rise of the wire services, greater concentration of ownership, and finally, a great increase in advertising revenue.

The quest for mass readership reflected changes in the American economy and in the city itself. Between 1879 and 1919, the gross national product had grown six-fold, led by a seven hundred percent increase in manufacturing output. By 1920, the United States was an urban nation, with three times as many industrial workers as it had employed four decades earlier. Fifty-four million people lived in urban places in 1920. Rapid urbanization boosted daily newspaper circulation from three million copies in 1880 to twenty-eight million copies in 1920. In the same period, the number of places with daily newspapers rose from 398 to 1,295. Some big city dailies saw phenomenal increases in circulation. For example, Joseph Pulitzer's *World* experienced a two thousand percent increase in daily readership over these years.[2]

Price reductions to a penny, and the addition of sections designed to appeal to women were two ways that newspapers built circulation. But key technological innovations—like high-speed presses and the linotype machine, as well as the electric light bulb which made reading easier—were the underpinning of mass-circulation journals. Of course, many of these innovations were expensive.

The higher capital requirements of mass-circulation dailies encouraged the shift from entrepreneurial to corporate ownership in this era. As the cost of presses and other technology rose, so did the entry costs of the industry. In 1835, James Gordon Bennett had used just $500 to start his *Herald;* and William Randolph Hearst had paid only $180,000 for the *Journal* in 1885. According to *Editor and Publisher* magazine, it would have taken at least a million dollars to start another daily newspaper in New York City in 1901. By 1920, big city newspapers were in fact selling for anywhere from $6 million to $18 million.[3]

The growth of mass-circulation dailies was also facilitated by the development of the wire services. The Associated Press (AP), controlled by a small number of large publishers, was the most important wire service in the period under consideration. The AP's agglomeration of news sources assured some degree of editorial variety, but this was drawn from the narrow range of the few large publishers it represented. Nor was there much objectivity. Oliver Grambling wrote in his study of the AP that a handful of men controlled the monopoly and "continued to take liberties with the news whenever it dealt with politics, economics, or other controversial issues."[4] Upton Sinclair was highly critical of the AP in his scathing study of the press, *The Brass Check*. Sinclair produced abundant evidence that the wire service was clearly biased against organized labor and political radicals while consistently favoring employers. In its reports on the great steel strike of 1919, Sinclair found AP had lied, failed to correct inaccuracies after they were brought its attention, and used reporters from steel company-owned newspapers as correspondents.[5]

The growth of newspaper chains and the concentration of newspaper ownership complemented wire service growth. While circulation of dailies increased continuously up to 1920, the number of newspapers declined between 1910 and 1920. At the same time, the number of one-daily cities and non-competitive newspaper markets increased. Chains were responsible for much of this shift away from competition. Between 1910 and 1923, the number of newspaper chains in the United States increased from 13 to 31, and the number of chain-controlled dailies rose from 62 to 153. The growth of newspaper chains actually accelerated greatly after World War II, but in the early 1920s, eight percent of American daily newspapers had already been combined in this manner.

The quest for circulation also spurred the growth of newspaper advertising. In 1880, advertising still accounted for less than half of all newspaper revenues, but it was growing rapidly in importance. By 1900, fifty-five percent of all newspaper revenues were derived from advertising; by 1910, it probably exceeded sixty percent. In dollar terms advertisers were spending about a quarter of a billion dollars a year on newspaper space by 1914. And since advertising revenues were growing far faster than circulation, profits were increasing rapidly too.[6] The investments required for mass-circulation newspapers were substantial, but so were the returns.

Given their large circulation and the great number of advertisers, it might appear at first glance that the big-city newspapers of the early twentieth century were independent of outside control. No single political party could command the loyalties of all the people in a mass-circulation market, and thus the strict identification between particular parties and particular newspapers had already been broken in the pursuit of mass circulation. Moreover, as Robert Park noted, since the newspaper purchasers were not organized and did not act as a unit independent of political parties, successful dailies could not simply tailor the news for a specific public.[7]

Still, the growing importance of advertising revenue did put advertisers in a postion to exercise at least indirect influence over news and editorial content. This was especially true because mass circulation was generally not sought as a goal in itself. Edward Herman and Noam Chomsky have noted that most big city dailies wanted not simple increases in circulation, but were "interested in attracting audiences with buying power."[8] This business strategy put the radical and labor press at a disadvantage, not only because they targeted a small segment of the newspaper buying public, but also because they failed to attract the better advertisers who could finance the expansion of circulation. Of course, the pursuit of more and better advertising by the big city dailies did not mean advertisers controlled the news, only that publishers' awareness of their concerns was, to use Herman and Chomsky's term, one of the "filters" used to determine "the news fit to print."[9]

The early twentieth-century press played a pivotal role in shaping the world view of the general public. At the time of the Red Scare, newspapers did not have to compete with television, radio, or newsreels. However, there were certainly other sources of news which influenced public perceptions of political reality. The institutions within ethnic communities included their foreign-language newspapers, as well as a great variety of labor and radical organizations and their publications, which provided alternative viewpoints for millions of Americans. Churches and their publications were also influential. However, on a national scale, only the mass-circulation daily press and the wire service reporters spoke to the whole polity by 1919–1920.

There is much debate in academic circles over exactly how the public responds to the news media. Do people attribute a degree of importance to particular issues consistent with the news coverage they read? In recent years, despite the significant differences among them, most media scholars, including Maxwell McCombs, Donald Shaw, Doris Graber, and W. Phillips Davison, have agreed that, at a minimum, news journalism has an important "agenda-setting" impact on the public. McCombs and Shaw have defined this function as one of determining the important public issues, issues salient in pubic debate. In other words, this more recent scholarship has confirmed Bernard Cohen's now classic statement, "The press . . . may not be successful much of the time in telling people what to think, but it is stunningly successful in telling its readers what to think about."[10] In 1919–1920, the influence of mass-circulation newspapers was undoubtedly at least this great.

Other recent scholarly studies of the way the news media function when setting the public agenda raise the distinct possibility that the now traditional understanding of the Red Scare as a national panic misrepresents a much more complex and problematic event. This historical image of the Red Scare was established, in large part, by writers and scholars who used contemporary newspapers as their primary source. As Frederick Lewis Allen wrote in his still-popular, *Only Yesterday,* "Those were the days when column after column of the front pages of the newspapers shouted news of strikes and anti-Bolshevik riots."[11] The concept of the "media frame" developed by media scholars like Erving Goffman, Todd Gitlin, and Mark Fishman provides students of the Red Scare a way to critically assess the role these newspapers played in making anti-communism the top national priority in 1919–1920 without having to resort to crude conspiracy theories.

As originally formulated by Erving Goffman, "frames" are principles of organization used by news media to govern subjective involvement in events. Todd Gitlin had defined them well:

> Media frames ... organize the world for both the journalists who report it and ... for us. Media frames are persistent patterns of cognition, interpretation, and presentation, of selection, emphasis. ... [They are] composed of little theories about what exists, what happens, and what matters.[12]

Obviously, newspapers never report all that has happened, even in the smallest city on any given day. The media frame, as defined above, is what enables reporters and editors to select the sample of events to be included in the daily newspaper. And as Gitlin indicates, the media frame also imparts pattern and meaning to the discrete events selected for inclusion.

Mark Fishman's study of a New York City crime wave provides a model for applying dynamic media frame analysis to phenomena that appear very similar to a political panic like the Red Scare of 1919–1920. Fishman and a group of assistants spent six months at a television station and a newspaper working with, observing, and interviewing editors and journalists. In the book that resulted, *Manufacturing the News,* Fishman found:

> New York's crime wave was a public event produced through newswork. ... News organizations created the wave, not in the sense that they invented the crimes, but in the sense they gave a determinant form and content to all the incidents they reported. Out of newswork arose a phenomenon transcending the individual happenings which were its constituent parts.[13]

It is not a question of there having been no crimes—there were in fact many incidents. But these had to be, and were, shaped and given meaning by the news media. In New York City, journalists supplied the frame, the concept of "crime wave," that made sense of the many crime incidents they chose to report.

Fishman's conclusions about his crime wave study were published in the journal *Social Problems* in 1978. They provide keys to exploring the role of the press in the Red Scare of 1919–1920. By substituting the words "red scare" for "crime wave" and anti-radical themes" for "crime theme" in the excerpts from those conclusions that follow, the reader will find a model for studying newspaper coverage of the Red Scare of 1919–1920. Fishman stated:

> Crime waves [red scares] begin as crime themes [anti-radical themes] that journalists perceive in the process of organizing and selecting news to be presented to the public. . . . They learn to use it [the crime wave/red scare frame] in their news.

He continued, "for the crime wave [red scare] dynamic to occur, journalists must be able to associate a crime [anti-radical] theme with a continuous supply of incidents." At this point, with the frame firmly established in the minds of editors, reporters, and presumably a large segment of the public, the power of the press is in a sense coopted by government. Turning to Fishman again, he found, "once the crime [anti-radical] theme receives heavy coverage in the media, authorities can use their power to make news in an attempt to augment, modify, or deny a burgeoning crime wave [red scare]."[14]

This media frame model should enlarge our understanding of the role of the press in the Red Scare of 1919–1920. The standardization of news coverage introduced by the AP wire service, the common pursuit of mass circulation and quality advertising, and the role of the federal government as a newsmaker made it possible for a national media frame to be developed as reporters covered the crackdown on radical political parties and organized labor after World War I. In fact, just a cursory reading of the 1919 issues of newspapers as geographically separated as the *New York Times* and the *Los Angeles Times* lends credence to the idea that a common national media frame had emerged by 1919. A media frame analysis of a single newspaper's coverage of the Red Scare is presented here as a demonstration of the model's explanatory powers.

The Los Angeles Times and the Red Scare

The start of 1919 could have ushered in a new era of peace and tranquility. The Great War was over, and the nativist attacks on Americans of German descent had subsided. However, new battles, both foreign and domestic, erupted. In the new Soviet Union, Red Russians fought White Russians and their foreign allies, including contingents from the United States. In Central Europe, revolutions convulsed Germany and Hungary. In fact, throughout the world, in China, in Mexico, and many of the still colonial countries, revolutionary movements and radical politics seemed to be on the rise.

At home, returning veterans found a nation torn by major and sometimes violent strikes: in the steel industry and the coal fields, in Seattle and Boston and hundreds of other places. The year 1919 was a year of record-setting strike activity. The front pages of the daily newspapers were filled with reports about the uprising of organized labor, and stories about radical activity, including terrorist plots. Homes were allegedly bombed by radicals; other bombs were intercepted in post offices. Radicals and alleged radicals were arrested in a series of spectacular government raids, and many of those arrested were deported.

These developments were not presented to the public as a series of discrete events with diverse local causes—a strike here, a bombing there. Rather, they were shaped and given meaning by the theory of the "communist menace." This theory was the dominant frame used by the newspapers to present and combine in a meaningful way all the news about revolutions and threats of revolution overseas and strikes and bombings at home. In the newspapers of the day, all of these widely separated events were framed by repeated references to Bolshevism, Reds, communist plots and threats, agents of Moscow, and the like. The newspapers of 1919–1920 made the communist threat the number one item on the public agenda. This frame contained within it an implicit policy orientation. Either the American people and their government did something quickly to stop the tide of communsim, or it would rise to overwhelm even the United States.

An analysis of the headlines in the *Los Angeles Times* from January 1919 to January 1920 illustrates the efficacy of using Fishman's crime wave model to enhace our understanding of the Red Scare. Specifically, this analysis focuses on the *Times'* treatment of the Russian revolution, revolutions and the threat of revolution elsewhere, and domestic labor conflict. It also covers antiradical statements and actions by politicians and other community leaders. Here, a distinction is made between two types of headlines: (1) "event statements," like "FRENCH ADVANCE" (January 1), which are straightforward reports of events; and (2) "mobilizing statements," such as "PRIEST TELLS OF RED TERRORISM" (May 4), which give readers strong cues on how to respond to the news. All dates are 1919 unless otherwise indicated.

Headlines about the Bolshevik revolution in Russia and Hungary, and threatened revolutions elsewhere in the world reveal the foundation of the media frame on the communist threat. As reported in the daily newspaper, these developments overseas consisted of plots, coups, systematic terror, random violence, and a generalized breakdown of all social order and morality. In varying combinations, these conditions were reported as both the substance and the result of communist revolution.

During the thirteen months under study, the *Los Angeles Times* carried 71 stories about these overseas events. Only 14 of the headlines on these stories could be read as "event statements"; the remaining 57 were "mobilizing statements." Fear was the predominant emotion evoked by the mobilizing statements. For example, the threat of terrorism and conquest were repeatedly reported: "RED TERROR GRIPS SIBERIA," "AMERICANS IN RUSSIA HOLDING BACK RED TERROR," and "POLES PLAN WAR ON BOLSHEVIKI TO CRUSH RED TERRORISM SWEEPING WESTWARD" (all from January 1); "BERLIN FACING BLACK BEASTS" (January 5); "AIM OF BOLSHEVIKI . . . WORLD CONQUEST" (April 24); and "SOVIETS WOULD ENGULF THE WORLD" (January 5, 1920).

Headlines also coveyed more specific ideas about the nature of the threat. Nothing less than civilization and its moral values appeared to be at stake. How else could one read headlines like these: "BOLSHEVIKI DESTROY SCHOOLS IN SIBERA," and "REDS KILL OFF PEASANTS" (both January 1); "REDS GRIP BUDAPEST. RIOTS AND MURDER ON INCREASE" (January 5); "ECONOMIC CHAOS IN RUSSIA" (February 12); and "BOLSHEVIKI PREVENT PEACE IN THE WORLD" (February 13).

These headlines highlighted the dire consequences for Western civilization—terror, chaos, moral anarchy—that resulted from Bolshevik activity. They ran concurrently in the newspaper along with stories about domestic labor unrest, bombings, and radical political activity. Indeed, stories about revolution and Bolshevism abroad established the underlying framework for organizing, reporting, and imparting meaning to these events within the United States.

In Los Angeles, the tremendous volume of news about domestic labor unrest in 1919–1920 was also colored by recent local history. Since the turn of the century, while San Francisco had become a generally closed-shop city, Los Angeles' employers sought to maintain their competitive advantage in the California labor market by preserving the city's open-ship reputation. Harrison

Gray Otis, the publisher of the *Times,* was a leading figure in the adamantly anti-labor Merchants' and Manufacturers' Association. In 1910, after the newspaper's offices had been bombed during a labor dispute, he said about union organizers, "Their instincts are criminal, and they are ready for arson, riot, robbery and murder."[15] With Otis' *Times* leading the fight, local employers had kept up a united front against unions that frustrated organizers and intimidated potential members during the years immediately preceding the Great War. In fact, historian John Caughey has concluded, "It was largely because of the truculence of the *Times* that Los Angeles became a battle front" between the open and closed shop movements.[16]

The employers' united front against organized labor weakened during the war years. High profits and federal policies that encouraged unionization enabled local unions to make unprecedented membership gains. The Industrial Workers of the World (IWW or Wobblies) were especially active in Southern California in this period. During and after the war, the IWW became the target of systematic public vilification and legal attack. Criminal syndicalism statues were enacted to outlaw the union, and it suffered strike defeats. By 1920, the collapse of the Wobblies had weakened the entire Southern California labor movement.

Throughout 1919–1920, the *Times* demonstrated a hostile preoccupation with the IWW. During one thirteen-week period it carried 28 stories devoted to the radical union. All of the headlines on these stories were mobilizing statements. As 1919 opened, the *Times* generally presented the Wobblies as a desperate threat to society in their own right, as it had done for over a decade. However, during the Red Scare the newspaper altered the frame so that the IWW became just a part of a larger worldwide communist threat.

This identification of the IWW with the larger communist threat was highlighted by the hysterical headlines the *Times* ran following the pitched battle between Wobblies and American Legionnaires in Centralia, Washington, on Armistice Day 1919. Readers of the November 15 issue saw "ALL FORCES OF LAW AND ORDER HERE FOR SMASHING WAR ON IWWS, BOLSHEVIKS, AND OTHER ENEMIES OF GOVERNMENT," "ACTIVITY OF IWW LEADS AMERICAN LEGION TO WAR ON REDS," "URGE NATIONAL GUARD TO FIGHT [IWW]," and "WRECK HEADQUARTERS OF IWW HERE." "LEGION'S MEN SWORN INTO WAR ON RADICALS" and "POSSE HUNTS DOWN IWW" (both November 18), and "URGE WAR UPON IWW"

(November 20) followed. Similar formulations headlined the *Times* coverage of other events where the IWW had either a proven or alleged involvement including the Seattle general strike, the Butte copper strike, and most bombings. In 1919, the *Times* made the IWW an important item on the public agenda by shaping all news of the union to fit the communist menace frame. Only a highly critical local reader with access to low-circulation alternative news media would have been able to discover the concrete issues for which the Wobblies organized and struck that year.

According to the Bureau of Labor Statistics, more workers went out on strike in 1919 than in any year prior to the end of World War II (in terms of both absolute numbers and as a percentage of the labor force). The Seattle general strike, Boston police strike, and national walkouts in the steel and coal industries have long been the considered the most significant of the more than thirty-five hundred postwar labor disputes. At the time the mass circulation press presented these four strikes as self-evidently radical and violent, and as posing the greatest danger to society. News of these labor disputes was given priority and meaning by the communist menace media frame. When framed as a part of the global Red threat, these admittedly major strikes loomed extremely large on the public agenda of the time, far larger, it seems fair to say, than they would have if contemporary newspaper accounts stuck to the specific details of each particular labor dispute.

The Seattle general strike of February 1919 was an extraordinary event. Though it remained primarily a local labor dispute, the strike seemed to open up a wide range of radical possibilities. As the General Strike Committee itself declared at the beginning of the strike, "We are starting on a road that leads—NO ONE KNOWS WHERE."[17] In this respect, the Seattle General strike, coming as it did at the start of 1919 when the counter-revolution against the Bolshevik regime in Russia was at its height, appears tailor-made for igniting what is usually described as the public hysteria of the Red Scare. Moreover, since it was extraordinary, the Seattle general strike was difficult to understand, particularly for those not on the scene. The communist menace media frame already being used daily by the newspapers in their reports from abroad provided both reporters and readers with a way to picture and make a meaningful response to this unexpected event.

The general strike was set in motion by the Seattle Central Labor Union. It was made up of representatives from all the local trades unions, and it contained a significant number of radicals.

The Central Labor Union called on the city's working class to support shipyard workers who were engaged in a long strike over management's refusal to negotiate any wage raises. Approximately sixty thousand Seattle workers answered the call for a general strike on February 3. Most of them stayed away from their jobs for five days, while a General Strike Committee tried to maintain order and provide essential services.

There was considerable local confusion about the true nature and purpose of the strike. In the days preceding the citywide walkout, local business leaders and major dailies expressed unwavering hostility to the Central Labor Unions' plans. For example, on January 30, the Seattle *Times* ran a scare story predicting mass starvation under the headline "SEATTLE WOULD BE DESTITUTE IN 48 HOURS." Edward Selvin, publisher of the *Business Chronicle,* placed a series of full-page advertisements in the city's three other non-labor newspapers charging that Seattle was "overrun by red-flag agitators in the guise of labor leaders," and that those same labor leaders were using the strike "to loot the union treasuries."[18] Such pronouncements were clearly designed to shape expectations and mobilize middle class support for repression.

Once the strike began, Seattle's radicals added to the confusion and class tensions by distributing handbills and leaflets that stressed the radical potential of the strike, and in a few cases equated the General Strike Committee with a Soviet worker's council. Harvy O'Connor, a young radical, published a pamphlet titled "Russia Did It" that exclaimed:

> The Russians have shown you the way out. What are
> you going to do about it? You are doomed to wage slav-
> ery till you die unless you wake up and realize that you
> and the boss have not one thing in common.[19]

The strike committee went to great lengths to disavow "Russia Did It," but opponents of the strike seized upon this document to make their case that for the existence of a great Red conspiracy. Seattle's Mayor Ole Hanson was particularly adept at leveling charges of Bolshevik plots and IWW terrorism, charges the press quickly picked up and amplified. Even though the strike collapsed, after just five days, failing to attain its stated goals, the Seattle story had a much longer run as a national news item.

In Los Angeles, readers of the Los Angeles *Times* saw a total of 24 strike-related items over a thirteen-day period. Only three of the accompanying headlines, like "GENERAL STRIKE CALLED" (February 4), could be classified as event statements. The remain-

der were clearly mobilizing statements that revealed and emphasized the underlying communist menace frame.

Variants on the term "Bolshevik" were used repeatedly by the
Times in ways that were designed to stir up both anti-radical and
nativist passions. For example, "STRIKE LED BY BOLSHEVIKS"
the *Times* proclaimed on February 8. In this same issue, readers
were told "SEATTLE BELIEVED A BOLSHEVIK EFFORT TO
START A REVOLUTION." The term "Red" was also used frequently to indiscriminately comdemn the leaders of the Seattle labor movement. "REDS DIRECTING SEATTLE STRIKE" the
Times announced on February 8. An editorial that condemned the
strike in extremely hostile language on February 12 was simply
titled "RED." As late as February 15, the *Times* carried a story
about the anarchism of the strike leadership under the headline
"SEATTLE LABOR CRIMINALS."

The *Times*'s use of communist menace themes in its extensive
coverage of events in Russia and Central Europe added credibility
to the emphasis the newspapers placed on the role of Bolsheviks
and other Reds in the Seattle general strike. In both places, what
appeared to be a breakdown of order could be explained by the
same evil force, Bolshevism. Thus, the way the newspaper framed
its reporting of the general strike also lent credibility to the way
it reported on revolutions and counter-revolutions abroad. Moreover, when news of the Seattle strike was presented as a Bolshevik
plot, the idea of a global communist conspiracy come home to
roost no longer seemed impossible. As historian Robert Friedheim
has written,

> For one week in February 1919, the newspaper head-
> lines throughout the country screamed, "Revolution in
> Seattle!" The theme was familiar—Americans were be-
> coming accustomed to reading about upheavals, revolu-
> tions, putsches—but the location was an ominous
> novelty. The Seattle general strike seemed to signify it
> *could* happen here.[20]

The Seattle general strike was the first of the major strikes of
1919. It was also, especially when framed as part of the communist menace, a very important news item. Mayor Hanson recog-
inzed this fact, and continued to stump the country making
hundreds of speeches about the Red threat in an effort to establish
himself as a Republican presidential candidate. On April 28, he
received a crude bomb in the mail that was discovered before it
exploded. The next day a similar bomb blew off the hands of a

maid at the home of ex-Senator Thomas Hardwick of Georgia. These bombs led frantic investigators to the discovery of thirty-four similar devices addressed and mailed to prominent political figures all over the United States. Here, it seemed, was conclusive proof that Hanson and the press were right: There was a real communist conspiracy in the United States and the Seattle strike had been the first demonstration of it.

The April bombing attempts came at the very moment strike activity was on the rise all across the United States. This coincidence, and the way the bombs were linked to the Seattle strike by Hanson's prominence as a news item and a newsmaker, firmly established the communist frame for reporting the remaining major strikes of 1919 in the mass circulation press. News of the long, disruptive general strike in Winnipeg, Canada, which stretched over six weeks in May and June, reinforced this inclination to use the communist menace frame in the selection, presentation, and interpretation of labor strife in the United States. Thus when major strikes in Boston, the steel industry, and the coal fields erupted in the fall of 1919, it is no surprise that the nation's dailies presented them in hysterical anti-radical terms that made it virtually impossible for readers to discover the actual issues separating management and workers.

In early September, Boston's police commissioner suspended nineteen men who had tried to form a union to protest low wages and other practices they considered unfair. When the commissioner then started to recruit men to replace the suspended officers, most of the force walked off the job. The strike collapsed in less than a week, after volunteers and the state militia took over the duties of the police. Throughout the affair, dire predictions of lawlessness and anarchy were made by public officials and the press. Governor Calvin Coolidge began his national political career when he ordered in state troops proclaiming, "There is no right to strike against the public safety of anybody, anytime, anywhere." President Wilson called the strike "a crime against civilization."[21] In Los Angeles, the *Times* followed the lead of these politicians.

There were thirteen articles and editorials on the Boston police strike in the *Times;* at least eight of them must be considered mobilizing statements. The threat of anarchy was their main theme. Boston's lawlessness could easily cross the continent to Los Angeles, readers were told. In this series of stories, headline writers frequently resorted to subheaders to make their point. "MACHINE GUN FIRE FAILS TO HALT BOSTON MOB— STRIKE BRINGS ANARCHY" (September 11) read one typically overstated, essentially inaccurate headline. "BOSTON STRIKE CAUSES GRAVE WASHINGTON FEAR—SENATORS THINK EFFORT TO SOVIETIZE THE GOVERNMENT IS STARTED" (September 12) proclaimed another.

There was, in fact, considerable hooliganism in Boston during the first days of the strike; but no mob violence, no looting, and no major crime spree occurred. Nor was there any evidence of radical involvement in this strike. The policemen who tried to organize a union had called their group the Boston Social Club. They had wanted to affiliate with the American Federation of Labor so as to strengthen their effort to raise wages and redress other grievances. These facts played little role in the Los Angeles *Times'* coverage of the story. Predisposed to frame all labor disputes as part of the communist menace, and given their cue to do so by leading politicians, the editors and reports of the *Times* ended up presenting even this most non-communist of strikes as Red.

The steel and coal strikes of the fall of 1919 gave politicians and the press some scattered bits of evidence to use in their red-baiting campaign against organized labor. But in neither case did radical politics bring on the strike. The steel strike, which involved a nationwide walkout of 350,000 mostly poor production workers, had two purposes: to improve conditions and wages, and to re-establish union power in a basic industry which had broken the unions in the early 1890s. In 1918, twenty-four different craft unions formed a great organizing committee. The committee's most dynamic leader was William Z. Foster, a Wobbly and exponent of direct action before World War I, but who had most recently been the chief organizer for the conservative Brotherhood of Railway Carmen. Initially, Frank Walsh, a co-chair of the War Labor Board, assisted Foster's steel industry organizing committee.

After a year, and with more than one hundred thousand workers enrolled, the committee tried to open negotiations with the industry leader, United States Steel, but the company refused to talk. The strike began September 22nd. While as many as three hundred thousand workers joined the unions' effort, the companies called on strikebreakers, spies, deputized guards, and state and local police to break the walkout. Before it ended in a crushing defeat for the labor movement, federal troops had to be dispatched to the steel center at Gary, Indiana, to keep order. Across the country, eighteen workers died in strike-related violence.

In its early stages, the steel companies set the tone for the press' coverage of the strike by flooding the nation's newspapers with full page advertisements that identified the strike as a Red

plot carried out by revolutionaries whose final goal was the overthrow of the American system. Between September 7 and November 4, the Los Angeles *Times* carried 100 items on the strike.
During the first week, when the companies launched their propaganda offensive, there were 57 items, an average of eight per
day. All totaled, of the 100 articles and editorials on the steel
strike, only eight carried headlines that could be considered event
statements. The rest were clearly mobilizing statements which
amplified the communist menace theme of the companies' advertisements, and thus gave that industry propaganda greater
credibility.

The headlines in the *Times* had three main themes, each of
which had direct parallels in the public statements of the steel
companies. Many articles emphasized violence, especially the violence strikers allegedly directed against non-strikers. Headlines
like "[STRIKERS] THREATEN LOYAL WORKERS" [September
23), and "UNIONS RIOT AT STEEL PLANTS" (September 24) obviously presented industry propaganda as news, and helped build
public support for the companies' requests for police and military
intervention. Secondly, the *Times* news articles seemed to confirm
the companies' contentions that the strike did not reflect the true
wishes of the majority of the rank and file— e.g. "MOST STEEL
WORKERS AGAINST STRIKE" (September 19)—despite much evidence to the contrary. Finally, and most frequently, the *Times*
headlines presented the strike as part of a plot to topple American
capitalism. The fact that a great majority of the strikers were immigrants and the children of immigrants made it easy to suggest
that their actions were un-American. In many items anti-
communism and nativism were freely mixed, as they had been in
the company advertisements, which proclaimed, "There is no good
American reason to strike. . . . The strike is not between workers
and employers, but between revolutionists and America."[22]

As the confrontation began, the readers of the Los Angeles
Times saw the strike immediately framed as part of a wider alien
radical conspiracy. "STEEL STRIKE FIRST GUN IN UNION
WAR ON CAPITAL" and "SYNDICALISM IN UNION PREACHED
BY LEADER" (both September 22), the *Times* proclaimed. This
frame was amplified as the strike dragged on. Headlines like
"[FOSTER'S] AIM IS TO RUIN THE NATION" (September 30);
"SENATE TOLD OF PLOTS TO SOVIETIZE STEEL MILLS" (OC-
TOBER 5); "SOVIET GOAL OF STEEL STRIKE" (OCTOBER 21);
and "REDS ENGINEER STEEL STRIKE" (OCTOBER 25) were
the newspaper's shorthand method of linking its strike reports to
the bigger communist menace story of that year.

Like the companies themselves, the editors, reporters, and headline writers of the *Times* increasingly exploited the significance of William Z. Foster's radical past to make this linkage work. A long out-of-print pamphlet authored by Foster and E. C. Ford titled "Syndicalism" was furnished by the steel companies to public officials and newspapers, who in turn quoted it at length. Foster tried to explain that he no longer was a Wobbly, but his denials were ineffective. The pamphlet on "Syndicalism" was a convenient source of "facts," which those predisposed to seeing the communist menace in the strike turned to again and again as evidence for the truth of their story.

A Protestant Interchurch Commission of Inquiry was set up during the steel strike to investigate the charges that the companies, the press, and public officials leveled at the strikers and their leaders. This commission also tried, and failed, to mediate an end to the strike. This church group found no evidecnce of the Bolshevism, anarchism, or syndicalist violence that the press described as characteristic of the workers' actions. But what mattered most to the public, especially a public as far removed from the actual location of the strike as newspaper readers in Los Angeles, was what the press reported. Thus, the steel strike intensified the Red Scare, giving the impression of growing national support for a nationwide clampdown on all socialist and left political activities.

The bituminous coal strike scheduled to begin November 1, 1919, led directly to the infamous Palmer raids of January 1920. The United Mine Workers, headed by their new president, John L. Lewis, wanted a pay raise to make up for purchasing power lost to inflation, and a shorter work week to spread employment and keep workers from losing their jobs during the postwar slump. The mine operators refused to negotiate on the these demands, and insisted that the old contract remain in force. Federal officials indicated they would treat a coal strike as a national emergency. In the face of the operators' intransigence and apprehensive that a walkout of 400,000 miners could bring mass deportations of unnaturalized miners, Lewis declared on October 31st, "We are Americans. We cannot fight our government."[23] The miners struck anyway.

In this case, with winter already upon the country and the federal government involved from the beginning, it was easy to present the coal strike as a threat to the nation. The presence of Wobblies among the western miners also triggered anti-radical impulses. But overall the facts of the strike did not lend themselves easily to the communist menace frame. Nonetheless, this

last great strike of 1919, like the others that preceded it, was reported by the press as yet another part of the ever-more ominous
Red threat to the American way of life.

The Los Angeles *Times* published forty items on this strike,
fully three-quaters of them headed by mobilizing statements. A
few emphasized the human hardship created by the strike, e.g.,
"BLIZZARD HITS CITY WITHOUT COAL" (November 12). But
many more located the real danger of the strike in its allegedly
lawless and radical character. Headlines like "MINERS SCORN
TROOP CONTROL" (November 1), and " 'AMERICA IS FACING
ORGANIZED TREASON" and "GOVERNMENT DECLARES
STRIKE IS A COMMUNIST PLOT'" (both November 2), created
the image of anarchy in the coal fields. And, other headlines such
as "COURT ORDERS COAL MINE REVOLUTIONISTS BACK TO
WORK" (November 9) left no doubt about what the source of the
violence and disruption really was: communism. This kind of reporting was designed to lead readers to concur with calls for government intervention. In fact, federal troops and federal
mediation did bring an end to the coal strike of 1919.

Conclusion

In a very real sense, the coal strike foreshadowed and set the
stage for the final acts of the Red Scare. Having for a year framed
major international and national news stories as part of a communist conspiracy, the press helped to pave the way for federal intervention in the coal fields and the federal repression of foreign-born
radicals all across the nation which soon followed. Attorney General A. Mitchell Palmer, another ambitious politician, and young J.
Edgar Hoover, head of the Justice Department's division on alien
radicals, directed the national hunt for "subversives." On November 17, 1919, agents of the Department's Bureau of Investigation
raided the offices of the Union of Russian Workers and arrested
249 immigrants, many of whom were held for deportation. On December 21, more alien radicals, including Emma Goldman, were
seized and held for deportation to the Soviet Union. Finally, on
January 2 and January 6, 1920, nationwide raids on the Communist and Communist Workers parties were conducted.

In these final dragnet operations, as many as ten thousand
people were arrested without regard for due process. Many of
those picked up were found to have no connection with the radical
parties. Hundreds were held incommunicado, and many had to en-

dure days without food and nights without beds to sleep on. Hundreds of arrested "alien radicals" were eventually deported. The Justice Department found it difficult to prosecute radicals who were U.S. citizens because the wartime Sedition Acts were no longer enforceable. Thus, most citizen radicals were eventually released, but not before the Department had made its investigative files available to state governments and corporations. The cumulative impact of all these actions broke the back of the radical movement in the United States. That movement would never recover either the strength or tenuous legitimacy it had achieved in the early twentieth century.

The gross repression of the Red Raids would not have been possible unless the public had been prepared for it. Throughout 1919, the Los Angeles *Times* had done its best to prepare the public for the virtual elimination of the left wing of the political spectrum in the United States. And when the clampdown finally came, the *Times* acted like a cheerleader. "RADICAL RAIDS NIP RIPE PLANS FOR REVOLUTION," it announced on January 4, 1920. Three days later, on January 7, the *Times* was still rallying the public against communism, proclaiming "FIGHT REDS TO A FINISH. GREAT FUND NEEDED FOR LONG BATTLE."

Though more research along the lines presented in this essay will be required before definite conclusions can be drawn about the nation's press as a whole, it seems fair to say that this study demonstrates the viability of a media frame analysis of the Red Scare 1919–1920. This media frame analysis suggests, just like Fishman's crime wave study, that there was, and is, a very close link between the way public officials wanted the news to be interpreted and the way the press actually reported the news of the day. That the *Times* failed to even attempt objective reporting of the actual local causes and course of the major strikes of 1919 is clearly demonstrated here. This failure reflected the willingness of the newspaper's editors and reporters, and the wire service, to frame labor news in the way the government and corporate opponents of organized labor wanted it presented.

Yet, as noted above, the imposition of the communist menace frame on organized labor was not conspiratorial in its origins. Rather, the frame was initially embraced at the *Times* because the management of the *Times* itself was a corporate opponent of organized labor and predisposed to accept virtually any charges of subversion leveled at unions and striking workers by government officials and corporations. And the frame continued to be used by the *Times* because the workers of the United States provided the continuous flow of incidents which could be interpreted as part of a global communist menace.

Was the American public truly gripped by an increasingly hysterical fear of communism in 1919–1920? Certainly, government officials and the press wanted to convey this story as objective news. Uncontrollable public fears would provide a "democratic" reason for massive political repression. Quite naturally, historians who have used government documents and the daily newspapers as primary source materials have generally concluded that something like mass hysteria gripped the nation during the Red Scare. Yet these sources, including the presumably independent press, actually tell us very little about what the man and woman on the street made of the news about the communist menace. Did they really believe that Bolsheviks were at the door in their own hometown? Were they really trembling with fear over the prospect of an imminent Red takeover of the United States? All we can really say for sure, based on press accounts of the Red Scare, is that the daily newspaper readers of 1919 must have frequently been reminded about these possibilities. But whether those same newspaper readers believed the stories, and felt the emotions they were designed to evoke, we may never be able to say with certainty.

Chapter Five

Encountering Mass Culture at the Grassroots: The Experience of Chicago Workers in the 1920s

Lizabeth Cohen

In 1929, the publishers of *True Story Magazine* ran full-page advertisements in the nation's major newspapers celebrating what they called "the American Economic Evolution." Claiming to be the recipient of thousands of personal stories written by American workers for the magazine's primarily working class readership, they felt well placed to report that since World War I, shorter working hours, higher pay, and easy credit had created an "economic millennium." Now that the nation's workers enjoyed an equal opportunity to consume, "a capital-labor war which has been going on now for upwards of three hundred years" had virtually ended. *True Story* claimed that twenty years before, Jim Smith, who worked ten to twelve hours a day in a factory and then returned home "to his hovel and his woman and his brats," was likely to resort to strikes and violence when times got tough. Not so his modern-day counterpart. Today, the magazine asserted, Jim Smith drives home to the suburbs after a seven- or eight-hour day earning him three to seven times as much as before, which helps pay for the automobile, the house, and a myriad of other possessions. Now an upstanding member of the middle class, Jim has learned moderation. Mass consumption had tamed his militance.[1]

Advertising executives at the J. Walter Thompson Company shared *True Story Magazine*'s confidence in the homogenizing power of mass culture. In an issue of their own in-house newsletter devoted to "the New National Market," they too claimed that due to standardized merchandise, automobiles, motion pictures, and most recently the radio, the so-called "lines of demarcation" between social classes and between city, small town and farm had become less clear.[2]

Sixty years later, historians are still making assumptions about the impact of mass culture similar to those of *True Story Magazine*'s editors and J. Walter Thompson Company's executives.

With not much more data about consumer attitudes and behavior
in the 1920s than their predecessors had, they too assume that
mass culture succeeded in integrating American workers into a
mainstream, middle class culture. When workers bought a victrola, went to the picture show, or switched on the radio, in some
crucial way, the usual argument goes, they ceased living in an ethnic or working class world. This common version of the "embourgeoisement thesis" credits a hegemonic mass culture with blurring
class lines. When labor organizing occurred in the 1930s and
1940s, the view holds, it stemmed not from industrial workers'
class consciousness but from their efforts to satisfy middle class
appetites.[3]

How can historians break free of the unproven assumptions of
the era and reopen the question of how working class audiences
responded to the explosion of mass culture during the 1920s? Let
me first acknowledge how difficult it is to know the extent to
which workers participated in various forms of mass culture, and
particularly the meanings they ascribed to their preferences. But I
will suggest in this essay one strategy for discerning the impact of
mass culture. Shifting the focus from the national scene, where
data on audience reception is weak, to a particular locale rich in
social history sources can yield new insights into the way that
workers responded to mass culture. Chicago offers a particularly
good case since it was the best documented city in the United
States during the 1920s and 1930s. In this period, Chicago was a
laboratory for sociologists, political scientists and social workers,
and a multitude of their students. Their numerous studies of urban life, along with ethnic newspapers, oral histories, and other
local sources, can serve social historians as revealing windows into
working class experience with mass culture. Chicago's industrial
prominence, moreover, attracted a multiethnic and multiracial
work force, which gives it all the more value as a case study.

In order to investigate how workers reacted to mass culture on
the local level in Chicago, it is necessary to make concrete the ab-
straction "mass culture." This essay, therefore, will examine carefully how workers in Chicago responded to mass consumption,
that is, the growth of chain stores peddling standard-brand goods;
to motion picture shows in monumental movie palaces; and to the
little box that seemed overnight to be winning a sacred spot at the
family hearth, the radio.

While *True Story Magazine*'s Jim Smith may have bought his
way into the middle class, in reality industrial workers did not enjoy nearly the prosperity that advertisers and sales promoters as-

sumed they did. All Americans did not benefit equally from the mushrooming of national wealth taking place during the 1920s. After the wartime raises, wages advanced modestly, if at all, in big manufacturing sectors, such as steel, meat packing, and the clothing industry, particularly for the unskilled and semiskilled workers who predominated in this kind of work. And most disruptive of workers' ability to consume, unemployment remained high. Workers faced unemployment whenever the business cycle turned downward, and even more regularly, faced layoffs in slack seasons. So Chicago's average semiskilled worker did not have nearly as much money to spare for purchasing automobiles, washing machines, and victrolas as manufacturers and advertisers had hoped.[4]

But people with commodities to sell worried little about workers' limited income. Instead, they trusted that an elaborate system of installment selling would allow all Americans to take part in the consumer revolution. "Buy now, pay later," first introduced in the automobile industry around 1915, suddenly exploded in the 1920s; by 1926, it was estimated that six billion dollars' worth of retail goods were sold annually by installment, about fifteen percent of all sales. "Enjoy while you pay," invited the manufacturers of everything from vacuum cleaners to, literally, the kitchen sink.[5]

Once again, popular beliefs of the time do not hold up under closer scrutiny: industrial workers did not engage in installment buying in nearly the numbers that marketers assumed. Automobiles accounted for by far the greatest proportion of the nation's installment debt outstanding at any given time—over fifty percent. But while *True Story*'s Jim Smith may have driven home from the factory in his new automobile, industrial workers in Chicago were not likely to follow his example. One study of the standard of living of semiskilled workers in Chicago found that only three percent owned cars in 1924. Even at the end of the decade, in the less urbanized environment of nearby Joliet, only twenty-four percent of lower-income families owned an automobile, according to a *Chicago Tribune* survey. The few studies of consumer credit done at the time indicate that it was middle-income people—not workers—who made installment buying such a rage during the 1920s, particularly the salaried and well-off who anticipated larger incomes in the future. Lower-income people, instead, were saving at unprecedented rates, often to cushion themselves for the inevitable layoff.[6]

When workers did buy on credit, they were most likely to purchase small items like phonographs. The question remains, however, whether buying a washing machine, or a phonograph, changed workers cultural orientation. Those who believed in the homogenizing power of mass consumption claimed that purchasing such a standardized product drew the consumer into a world of mainstream tastes and values. Sociologist John Dollard argued at the time, for example, that the victrola revolutionized a family's pattern of amusement because "what they listen to comes essentially from the outside, its character is cosmopolitan and national, and what the family does to create it as a family is very small indeed."[7] We get the impression of immigrant, wage-earning families sharing more in American, middle class culture every time they rolled up the rug and danced to the Paul Whiteman orchestra.

But how workers themselves described what it meant to purchase a phonograph reveals a different picture. Typically, industrial workers in Chicago in the 1920s were first- or second-generation immigrants from eastern or southern Europe. In story after story they related how buying a victrola helped keep Polish or Italian culture alive by allowing people to play foreign-language records, often at ethnic social gatherings. Rather than the phonograph drawing the family away from a more indigenous cultural world, as Dollard alleged, many people like Rena Domke remembered how in Little Sicily during those years neighbors "would sit in the evening and discuss all different things about Italy," and every Saturday night they pulled out a victrola "and they'd play all these Italian records and they would dance. . . . "[8] In fact, consumers of all nationalities displayed so much interest in purchasing foreign language records that in the 1920s Chicago became the center of an enormous foreign record industry, selling re-pressed recordings from Europe and new records by American immigrant artists. Even the small Mexican community in Chicago supported a shop that made phonographic records of Mexican music and distributed them all over the United States. Some American-born workers also used phonograph recordings in preserving their ties to their original regional culture. For example, Southerners— white and black—eased the trauma of moving north to cities like Chicago by supporting a record industry of hillbilly and "race records" geared specifically toward a Northern urban market with southern roots.[9] Thus, owning a phonograph might bring a worker closer to mainstream culture, but it did not have to. A commodity could just as easily help a person reinforce an ethnic or working-class culture as lose it.

Of course, when the publishers of *True Story* spoke of a consumer revolution, they meant more than the wider distribution of luxury goods like the phonograph. They were referring to how the chain store—the A & P or Walgreen Drugs—and the nationally advertised brands that they offered—like Lux Soap and Del Monte canned goods—were standardizing even the most routine purchasing. A distributor of packaged meat claimed, "Mass selling has become almost the universal rule in this country, a discovery of this decade of hardly less importance than the discovery of such forces as steam and electricity."[10] Doomed, everyone thought, were bulk or unmarked brands, and the small, inefficient neighborhood grocery, dry goods, or drug store that sold them. Americans wherever they lived, it was assumed, increasingly were entering stores that looked exactly alike to purchase the same items from a standard stock.

Closer examination of the consumer behavior of workers in a city like Chicago, however, suggests that workers were not patronizing chain stores. Rather, the chain store that purportedly was revolutionizing consumer behavior in the 1920s was mostly reaching the middle and upper classes. Two-thirds of the more than five hundred A & P and National Tea Stores in Chicago by 1928 were located in neighborhoods of above-average economic status (Table 5.1). An analysis of the location of chain stores in Chicago's suburbs reveals the same imbalance. By 1926, chains ran fifty-three percent of the groceries in prosperous Oak Park, and thirty-six percent in equally well-off Evanston. In contrast, in working class Gary and Joliet, only one percent of the groceries were owned by chains. As late as 1929, the workers of Cicero found chain management in only five percent of this industrial town's 819 retail stores.[11] Chain store executives recognized that workers were too tied to local, often ethnic, merchants to abandon them, even for a small savings in price.[12] A West Side Chicago grocer explained: "People go to a place where they can order in their own language, be understood without repetition, and then exchange a few words of gossip or news."[13] Shopping at a particular neighborhood store was a matter of cultural loyalty. As one ethnic merchant put it, "The Polish business man is a part of your nation; he is your brother. Whether it is war, hunger, or trouble, he is always with you willing to help. . . . Therefore, buy from your people."[14]

No less important, the chain store's prices may have been cheaper, but its "cash and carry" policy was too rigid for working people's limited budgets. Most workers depended on a system of credit at the store to make it from one payday to the next. In tough times, the loyal customer knew an understanding storekeeper would wait to be paid and still sell her food. So when an A & P

TABLE 5.1
Location of Chain Grocery Stores in Chicago,
1927–1929 by Economic Status of Neighborhood.

Chain	Total stores	Total in census tracts with rental data	Percentage of stores in census tracts above median rental*
National Tea	535	530	66%
A & P	17	17	65
TOTALS	552	547	65.5%

Sources: *Chicago Telephone Directory,* alphabetical and classified, 1927;
Polk's Directory of Chicago, 1928–29; Charles S. Newcomb, *Street Address
Guide by Census Area of Chicago, 1930* (Chicago: University of Chicago
1933); "Economic Status of Families Based on Equivalent Monthly Rent-
als," Data from Table 10, *Census Data of Chicago, 1930,* box 51, folder 8,
Burgess Papers, University of Chicago Special Collections.
*using 1930 rental data, where median monthly rental was $51.30.

opened not far from Little Sicily in Chicago, people ignored it. Instead, everyone continued to do business with the local grocer, who
warned, "Go to A & P they ain't going to give you credit like I give
you credit here."[15] While middle class consumers were carrying
home more national-brand packaged goods in the 1920s, working
class people continued to buy in bulk—to fetch milk in their own
containers, purchase hunks of soap, and scoop coffee, tea, sugar,
and flour out of barrels. What standard brands working class families did buy, furthermore, they encountered through a trusted
grocer, not an anonymous clerk at the A & P.[16]

When workers did buy mass-produced goods, like ready-made
clothing, they purchased them at stores such as Chicago's Goldblatt's Department Stores, which let customers consume on their
own terms. Aware that their ethnic customers were accustomed to
central marketplaces where individual vendors sold fish from one
stall, shoes from another, the second-generation Goldblatt brothers, sons of a Jewish grocer, adapted this approach to their stores.
Under one roof they sold everything from food to jewelry, piling
merchandise high on tables so people could handle the bargains.[17]
The resulting atmosphere dismayed a University of Chicago
undergraduate sociology student, more used to the elegance of
Marshall Field's. To Betty Wright, Goldblatt's main floor was a
mad "jumble of colors, sounds, and smells." Amid the bedlam, she
observed

> many women present with old shawls tied over their
> heads and bags or market baskets on their arms. They
> stopped at every counter that caught their eye, picked

up the goods, handled it, enquired [sic] after the price,
and then walked on without making any purchase. I have
an idea that a good many of these women had no intention whatsover of buying anything. They probably found
Goldblatt's a pleasant place to spend an afternoon.

Most appalling to this student, "Customers seemed always ready
to argue with the clerk about the price of an article and to try to
'jew them down.' "[18] Betty Wright did not appreciate that behind
Goldblatt's respectable exterior facade thrived a European street
market much treasured by ethnic Chicagoans.

Ethnic workers in a city like Chicago did not join what historian Daniel Boorstin has labeled "national consumption communities" nearly as quickly as many have thought. Even when they
bought the inexpensive, mass-produced goods increasingly available during the 1920s, a new suit of clothes did not change the
man (or woman) contrary to the hopes of many contemporaries.
Rather, as market researchers would finally realize in the 1950s,
when they developed the theory of "consumer reference groups,"
consumption involved the meeting of two worlds—the buyer's and
the seller's—with purchasers bringing their own values to every
exchange.[19] Only gradually over the 1920s did workers come to
share more in the new consumer goods, but in their own stores, in
their own neighborhoods, and in their own way.

In the realm of consumption, workers could depend on the
small-scale enterprises in their communities to help them resist
the homogenizing influences of mass culture. But how did ethnic
working class culture fare against forms of mass culture—such as
motion pictures and radio—that local communities could not so
easily control? Did the motion picture spectacle and a twist of the
radio dial draw workers into mainstream mass culture more suc-
cessfully than the A & P?

Workers showed much more enthusiasm for motion pictures
than chain stores. While movies had been around since early in
the century, the number of theater seats in Chicago reached its
highest level ever by the end of the 1920s. With an average of four
performances daily at every theater, by 1929 Chicago had enough
movie theater seats for one-half the city's population to attend in
the course of a day; and workers made up their fair share—if not
more—of that audience.[20] Despite the absence of exact attendance
figures, there are consistent clues that picture shows enjoyed enormous popularity among workers throughout the twenties. As the
decade began, a Bureau of Labor Statistics survey of the cost of
living of workingmen's families found Chicago workers spending

more than half of their amusement budgets on movies.[21] Even
those fighting destitution made going to the motion pictures a priority; in 1924, more than two-thirds of the families receiving
Mothers' Aid Assistance in Chicago attended regularly.[22]

But knowing that workers went to the movies is one thing, as-
sessing how they reacted to particular pictures is another. Some
historians have taken the tack of analyzing the content of motion
pictures for evidence of their meaning to audiences; the fact that
workers made up a large part of those audiences convinces these
analysts that they took home particular messages decipherable in
the films. But investigating the variety of ways that consumers
encountered and perceived mass-produced goods suggests that
people can have very different reactions to the same experience.
Just as the meaning of mass consumption varied with the context
in which people confronted it, so too the impact of the movies depended on where, with whom, and in what kind of environment
workers went to the movies during the 1920s.[23]

Chicago's workers regularly patronized neighborhood movie
theaters near their homes in the 1920s, not "The Chicago," "The
Uptown," "The Granada" and the other monumental picture
palaces built during the period, where many historians have assumed they flocked. Neighborhood theaters had evolved from the
storefront nickelodeons prevalent in immigrant working class communities before the war. Due to stricter city regulations, neighborhood movie houses now were fewer in number, larger, cleaner,
better ventilated, and from five to twenty cents more expensive
than in nickelodeon days. But still they were much simpler than
the ornate movie palaces, which seated several thousand at a
time. For example, local theaters in a working class community
like South Chicago (U.S. Steel's enormous South Works plant)
ranged in size from "Pete's International," which sat only 250—
more when Pete made the kids double up in each seat for Sunday
matinees—to the "Gayety," holding 750, to the "New Calumet,"
with room for almost a thousand.[24] Only rarely did workers pay at
least twice as much admission, plus carfare, to see the picture pal-
ace show. Despite the fact that the palaces often claimed to be
"paradise for the common man," geographical plotting of Chicago's
picture palaces reveals that most of them were nowhere near
working class neighborhoods. A few were downtown, the rest stra-
tegically placed in new shopping areas to attract the middle
classes to the movies.[25] Going to the pictures was something workers did more easily and cheaply close to home. As a U.S. Steel employee explained, it was "a long way"—in many respects—from the

steel towns of Southeast Chicago to the South Side's fancy Tivoli Theater.[26]

For much of the decade, working class patrons found the neighborhood theater not only more affordable but more welcoming, as the spirit of the community carried over into the local movie hall. Chicago workers may have savored the exotic on the screen, but they preferred encountering it in familiar company. The theater manager, who was often the owner and usually lived in the community, tailored his film selections to local tastes, and changed them every few days to accommodate neighborhood people who attended frequently. Residents of Chicago's industrial neighborhoods rarely had to travel far to find pictures to their liking, which they viewed among the same neighbors and friends they had on the block.

When one entered a movie theater in a working class neighborhood of Chicago, the ethnic character of the community quickly became evident. The language of the yelling and jeering that routinely gave sound to silent movies provided the first clue. "The old Italians used to go to these movies," recalled Ernest Dalle-Molle, "and when the good guys were chasing the bad guys in Italian— they'd say—Getem—catch them—out loud in the theater."[27] Stage events accompanying the films told more. In Back of the Yards near the packinghouses, at Schumacher's or the Davis Square Theater, viewers often saw a Polish play along with the silent film.[28] Everywhere, amateur nights offered "local talent" a moment in the limelight. At the Butler Theater in Little Sicily, which the community had rechristened the "Garlic Opera House," Italian music shared the stage with American films.[29] In the neighborhood theater, Hollywood and ethnic Chicago coexisted.

Neighborhood theaters so respected local culture that they reflected community prejudices as well as stengths. The Commerical Theater in South Chicago typified many neighborhood theaters in requiring Mexicans and blacks to sit in the balcony, while reserving the main floor for the white ethnics who dominated the community's population.[30] One theater owner explained, "White people don't like to sit next to the colored or Mexicans. . . . We used to have trouble about the first four months, but not now. They go by themsleves to their place."[31] Sometimes blacks and Mexicans were not even allowed into neighborhood theaters. In contrast, the more cosmopolitan picture palaces, like those owned by the largest chain in Chicago, Balaban & Katz, were instructed to let in whoever could pay.[32] Thus, the neighborhood theater reinforced the values of the community as powerfully an any on the screen. This is not to deny that working class audiences were affected by the content of motion pictures, but to suggest that when people viewed movies in the familiar world of the neighborhood theater, identification with their local community was bolstered, and the subversive impact of the picture often constrained.

Thus, even if local communities did not control the production of motion pictures during the 1920s, they still managed for a good part of the decade to influence how residents received them. The independent, neighborhood theater in that way resembled the neighborhood store, harmonizing standardized products with local, particularly ethnic, culture.

Neighborhood stores and theaters buffered the potential disorientation of mass culture by allowing their patrons to consume within the intimacy of the community. Rather than disrupting the existing peer culture, that peer culture accommodated the new products. Shopping and theatergoing were easily mediated by the community because they were collective activities. Radio, on the other hand, entered the privacy of the home. At least potentially, what went out across the airwaves could transport listeners, as individuals, into a different world.

As it turned out, though, radio listening did not require workers to forsake their cultural communities any more than shopping or moviegoing did. Radio listening was far from the passive, atomized experience we are familiar with today. It was more active; many working people became interested in early radio as a hobby, and built their own crystal and vacuum tube sets. Radio retailers recognized that workers were particularly apt to build their own radios. "If the store is located in a community most of the inhabitants of which are workmen," a study of the radio industry showed, "there will be a large proportion of parts," in contrast to the more expensive, preassembled models stocked by the radio stores of fashionable districts. That radio appealed to the artisanal interests of Chicago's workers was evident in their neighborhoods in another way. As early as 1922, a Chicago radio journalist noted that "crude homemade aerials are on one roof in ten along the miles of bleak streets in the city's industrial zones."[33]

Even workers who bought increasingly affordable ready-made radios spent evenings bent over their dial boards, working to get "the utmost possible DX" (distance), and then recording their triumphs in a radio log. Beginning in the fall of 1922, in fact, Chicago stations agreed not to broadcast at all after 7 P.M. on Monday evenings to allow the city's radio audience to tune in faraway stations otherwise blocked because they broadcast on the same wave-lengths as local stations. "Silent Nights" were religiously observed in other cities as well. In addition to distance, radio enthusiasts concerned themselves with technical challenges, such as cutting down static, making "the short jumps," and operating receivers with one hand.[34]

Not only was radio listening active, but it was also far from isolating. By 1930 in Chicago, there was one radio for every two or three households in workers' neighborhoods, and people sat around in local shops or neighbors' parlors listening together (Tables 5.2 and 5.3). Surveys showed that on average, four or five people listened to one set at any particular time; in eight-five percent of homes, the entire family listened together. Communal radio listening mediated between local and mass culture much like the neighborhood store or theater.[35]

Even Chicago's working class youth, whose parents feared they were abandoning the ethnic fold for more commercialized mass culture, were listening to the radio in the company of other second-generation ethnic peers at neighborhood clubs when not at home with their families. Known as "basement clubs," "social clubs," or "athletic clubs," these associations guided the cultural experimentation of young people from their mid-teens to mid-twenties. Here, in rented quarters away form parental eyes and ears, club members socialized to the constant blaring of the radio—the "prime requisite" of every club, according to one observer. The fact that young people were encountering mass culture like the radio within ethnic neighborhood circles helped to minimize the disruption.[36]

But even more important to an investigation of the impact of the radio on workers' consciousness, early radio broadcasting had a distinctly grassroots orientation. To begin with, the technologi-cal limitations of early broadcasting ensured that small, nearby stations with low power dominated the ether waves. Furthermore, with no clear way of financing independent radio stations, it fell to existing institutions to subsidize radio operations. From the start, non-profit ethnic, religious, and labor groups put radio to their ser-vice. In 1925, twenty-eight percent of the 571 radio stations na-tionwide were owned by educational institutions and churches, less than four percent by commercial broadcasting companies.[37] In Chicago, ethnic groups saw radio as a way of keeping their coun-trymen and women in touch with native culture. By 1926, several radio stations explicitly devoted to ethnic programming broadcast

TABLE 5.2
Radio Ownership in Working and Middle Class
Chicago Neighborhoods, 1930

Class and Neighborhood	Percentage Households Owning Radios
Working Class	
Southeast Chicago (steel mills)	53.00%
East Side	69.37
South Chicago	55.90
Hegewisch	46.74
South Deering	40.00
Back of the Yards (meatpacking)	46.07
Bridgeport	48.35
New City	43.78
Old immigrant neighborhoods (small factories and garmentmaking)	37.41
West Town	41.33
Lower West Side	36.79
Near West Side	34.10
Southwest Corridor (Int'l. Harvester, West. Electr.)	55.42
North Lawndale	58.41
McKinley Park	55.03
South Lawndale	54.68
Brighton Park	53.55
Black Belt	46.44
Washington Park	61.58
Grand Blvd.	46.90
Douglas	30.85
Middle Class	
Avalon Park	83.96%
Chatham	81.26
Greater Grand Crossing	76.04
Englewood	67.61

Source: Louis Wirth and Margaret Furez, eds., *Local Community Fact Book* (Chicago: Chicago Recreation Commission 1938).

in Chicago—WGES,WSBC,WEDC, and WCRW—while other stations carried "nationality hours." Through the radio, Chicago's huge foreign-language-speaking population heard news from home, native music, and special broadcasts, like Benito Mussolini's messages to Italians living in America.[38] One of the stations which sponsored a "Polish Hour" and an "Irish Hour" is also noteworthy for bringing another aspect of local working class culture to the doors up and down blocks of the Black Belt proved the greatest business triumph of all.[47] But insurmountable economic barriers kept other Negro entrepreneurs from competing viably. Black merchants and businessmen suffered from lack of experience, lack of capital (there were only two black banks in the city to provide loans, and these had limited resources), and an inability to offer customers the credit that ethnic storekeepers gave their own countrymen or that Jewish businessmen in black areas gave black customers. The short supply of cash in black stores, moreover, kept wholesale orders small, retail prices high, and shelf stock low, all of which forced black customers to shop elsewhere.[48]

The poor showing of black business made black customers, even those deeply committed to a black economy, dependent on white businesses. But concern with black economic independence nonetheless left its mark. Within the white commercial world, blacks developed two preferences they pursued when financially able: standard brand goods and chain stores. Blacks shopping in non-black stores felt that packaged goods protected them against unscrupulous storekeepers or clerks. Not sharing the ethnic worker's confidence in his conpatriot grocer, the black consumer distrusted bulk goods. This reliance on brand names grew further when black customers who could survive without credit increasingly chose to patronize chain stores, attracted to their claims of standardized products and prices.[49]

No less important, the chain store could be pressured to hire black clerks, while the Jewish, Greek or Italian store in a black neighborhood was usually family-run. If blacks could not own successful businesses, at least they should be able to work in them. By the mid- to late 1920s, consumer boycotts to force chains to hire blacks flourished in black neighborhoods. "Don't Spend Your Money Where You Can't Work" crusades sought black economic independence through employment rather than entrepreneurship. By 1930, consumers in Chicago's enormous South Side Black Belt had pressured local branches of The South Center Department Store, Sears Roebuck, A & P, Consumers' Market, Neisner's 5 Cents to a Dollar, Woolworth's, and Walgreen's Drugs to employ blacks, some almost exclusively.[50]

With strict limitations on where blacks could live and work in Chicago, consumption—both through race businesses and more mainline chains—became a major avenue through which blacks could assert their independence. But chain stores were not the only aspect of mass culture to contribute to the making of an urban, black identity. Blacks also played a role in shaping another

TABLE 5.3
Percentage of Families Reporting Radio Ownership, 1930

A. Chicago and U.S. Community Types, by Race and Ethnicity of Families

Family Race and Ethnicity	Chicago	Urban	Rural Farm	Rural Non-Farm
Native white	74.2%	56.3%	24.0%	37.4%
Foreign-born white	54.1	46.2	32.0	35.1
Black	42.6	14.4	0.3	3.0
All families	63.2%	50.0%	20.8%	33.7%

B. Cook County and Industrial Suburbs, 1930

Suburb	Percentage
Berwyn	78.1%
Blue Island	73.7
Calument City	57.1
Chicago Heights	53.5
Cicero	65.4
Harvey	66.7
Melrose Park	57.8
Cook County overall	64.6%

Sources: United States Department of Commerce, Bureau of the Census, *Fifteenth Census of the United States: 1930, Population* (Washington, D.C.: U.S. Government Printing Office 1933); "Families in Cook County with Radios (1930)," *Daily News Almanac and Year Book for 1933* (Chicago: Daily News 1933), 801.

radio. The Chicago Federation of Labor organized WCFL, "the Voice of Labor," in its own words, to, "help awaken the slumbering giant of labor." Having suffered a variety of defeats after World War I, most notably the failure to organize Chicago's steel mills and packing plants, the Federation seized on radio in the 1920s as a new strategy for reaching the city's workers. "Labor News Flashes," "Chicago Federation of Labor Hour," and "Labor Talks with the International Ladies Garment Workers' Union" alternated with entertainment like "Earl Hoffman's Chez Pierre Orchestra" and Musical Potpourri."[39]

Radio, therefore, brought familiar distractions into the homes of workers: talk, ethnic nationality hours, labor news, church services, and vaudeville-type musical entertainment with home-town—often ethnic—performers. More innovative forms of radio programming, such as situation comedy shows, dramatic series, and soap operas, only developed later. A survey commissioned by

NBC in 1928 found that eighty percent of the radio audience regularly listened to the local, not to distant, stations.[40] Sometimes listeners even knew a singer or musician personally, since many stations' shoestring budgets forced them to rely on amateurs; whoever dropped in at the station had a chance to be heard. Well-known entertainers, moreover, shied away from radio at first, dissatisfied with the low pay but also uncomfortable performing without an audience and fearful of undercutting their box office attractiveness with free, on-air concerts. While tuning in to a radio program may have been a new experience, few surprises came "out of the ether."[41]

As a result, early radio in Chicago promoted ethnic, religious, and working class affiliations rather than undermining them, as many advocates of mass culture had predicted. No doubt radio did expose some people to new cultural experiences—to different ethnic and religious traditions or new kinds of music. But more important, workers discovered that participating in radio, as in mass consumption and the movies, did not require repudiation of established social identities. Radio at mid-decade, dominated as it was by local, non-commercial broadcasting, offered little evidence that it was fulfilling the prediction of advocates and proving itself "the greatest leveler," capable of sweeping away "the mutual distrust and enmity of laborer and executive . . . business man and artist, scientist and cleric, the tenement dweller and the estate owner, the hovel and the mansion."[42]

By letting community institutions—ethnic stores, neighborhood theaters, and local radio stations—mediate in the delivery of mass culture, workers avoided the kind of cultural reorientation that Madison Avenue had expected. Working class families could buy phonographs or ready-made clothing, go regularly to the picture show, and be avid radio fans without feeling pressure to abandon their existing social affiliations.

While this pattern captures the experience of white ethnic workers in Chicago's factories, it does not characterize their black co-workers, who came North in huge numbers during and after World War I to work in mass production plants. Blacks developed a different, and complex, relationship to mass culture. Black much more than immigrant workers satisfied those who hoped a mass market would emerge during the twenties. Unlike ethnic workers, blacks did not reject chain stores and standard brands, nor try to harness radio to traditional goals. But blacks disappointed those who assumed an integrated American culture would accompany uniformity in tastes. Ironically, by participating in mainstream

commercial life—which black Chicagoans did more than nic co-workers—blacks came to feel more independent ential as a race, not more integrated into white mi society. Mass culture—chain stores, brand name goods music—offered blacks the ingredients from which to co new, urban black culture.

Blacks' receptivity to mass culture grew out of a su source, a faith in black commercial endeavor not so very d from ethnic people's loyalty to ethnic businesses. During the a consensus developed in Northern black communities that arate "black economy" could provide the necessary glue t what was a new and fragile world together. If blacks could their producer, consumer, and investment power toward a marketplace by supporting "race businesses," the whole com nity would benefit. Less economic exploitation and more oppo nity would come blacks' way. This was not a new idea. "Bl capitalism" had been fundamental to Booker T. Washington's commodationist, self-help philosophy at the turn of the centu What changed in the 1920s was that now blacks of all politic persuasions—including the Garveyite nationalists and even th socialist-leaning "New Negro" crowd—shared a commitment to separate black economy. In the face of racial segregation and dis crimination, the black community would forge an alternative "Black Metropolis" which rejected white economic control without rejecting capitalism.[43]

At the center of the separate black economy stood "race businesses." Black consumers were told that when they patronized these enterprises, they bought black jobs, black entrepreneurship, and black independence along with goods and services, and bid farewell to white employment prejudice, insults, and overcharging. "You don't know race respect if you don't buy from Negroes," sermonized one pastor.[44] Central to the nationalist program of Marcus Garvey's United Negro Improvement Association, not surprisingly, were commercial enterprises—steamship line, hotel, printing plant, black doll factory, and chains of groceries, restaurants, and laundries.[45]

But the "black economy" strategy was only moderately successful. Those black businesses that did best were geared solely to black needs, where there was a large Negro market with little white competition. For example, undertakers, barbers, and beauticians faced few white contenders; black cosmetic companies even succeeded in selling hair products like Madame C. J. Walker's hair growth and straightening creams through nationwide chains.[46] Black-owned insurance companies whose salesmen knocked on

major feature of mass culture in the twenties—jazz. In contrast to black commercial schemes that mimicked white examples or black consumption that contented itself largely with white products, here the trend-setting went the other way. Black folk culture, black inventiveness, black talent gave the twenties its distinctive image as the "Jazz Age" and dictated the character of mainstream American popular music for many years to come.

Chicago was the jazz capital of the nation during the 1920s. Here, in the middle of the Black Belt, mixed audiences in "Black and Tan" cabarets tapped to the beat of King Oliver, Louis Armstrong, Lil Hardin, Fats Waller, Freddy Keppard, Jelly Roll Morton and others. In segregated company, blacks relished Chicago's "hot jazz" at their own more modest clubs, black movie theaters, and semi-private house parties; whites, meanwhile, danced black dances like the Charleston to black bands playing in palatial ballrooms that prohibited Negro patronage.[51]

The Chicago jazzmen's music reached far beyond the city's night clubs. Blacks—and some whites—all over the country bought millions of blues and jazz phongraph recordings, known as "race records." At record stores on Chicago's South Side, one store owner remembered, "Colored people would form a line twice around the block when the latest record of Bessie or Ma or Clara or Mamie come in."[52] With the exception of Negro-owned Black Swan Records, white recording companies like Paramount, Columbia, Okey, and Victor were the ones to produce special lines for the Negro market. But because white companies depended on the profitable sales of race recordings as the phonograph business bottomed out with the rise of radio, they had little interest in interfering with the purest black sound. As far away as the rural South, blacks kept up with musicians from Chicago and New York by purchasing records from mail-order ads in the *Chicago Defender* or from Pullman porters travelling south.[53] The radio, too, helped bring black jazz to a broad audience. Chicago stations broadcast Earl "Fatha" Hines with his band at the Grand Terrace Supper Club, and other groups performing at the Blackhawk Restaurant. Fletcher Henderson's Rainbow Orchestra played at New York's Savoy, but in time was heard in homes all over America.

Here again, then, mass culture in the form of commerical record companies and radio helped blacks develop and promote a unique, and increasingly national, black sound. And the dissemination of jazz not only contributed to black identity. It also helped shape the character of American popular music. True, white bands often reaped more financial profits from a "sweetened" and more "swinging" jazz than did its black creators in Chicago's Black Belt clubs (though black men—Duke Ellington, Fletcher Henderson and Don Redman—played an important role in turning the Chicago "hot" sound into the smoother, bigger, more tightly packaged "swing" that came out of New York.) And also true, by making a name for themselves in the music world, blacks fit right into white stereotypes of the "natural musician." Nonetheless, jazz gave black musicians and their fans recognition in the cultural mainstream, for expressing themselves in a language they knew was their own. Long before Motown, blacks were molding American popular music in their own image.

Black jazz recordings, like black employment in chain stores, became a vehicle for making a claim on mainstream society that racism had otherwise denied. When blacks patronized chain stores, they were asserting independence from local white society, not enslavement to cultural norms. No doubt their consumption of mass cultural products did give them interests in common with mainstream American society, and subjected them to the vagaries of the capitalist market. But with mass culture as raw material, blacks fashioned their own culture during the 1920s that made them feel no less black.

So it would seem that despite the expectations of mass culture promoters, chain stores, standard brands, motion pictures, and the radio did not absorb workers—white or black—into a middle class, American culture. To some extent, people resisted aspects of mass culture, as ethnic workers did chain stores. But even when they indulged in Maxwell House Coffee, Rudolph Valentino, and radio entertainment, these experiences did not uproot them, since they were encountered under local, often ethnic, sponsorship. When a politically conscious Communist worker asserted that, "I had bought a jalopy in 1924, and it didn't change me. It just made it easier for me to function," he spoke for other workers who may not have been as self-conscious, but who like him were not made culturally middle class by the new products they consumed.[54]

But beginning in the late 1920s and increasingly in the 1930s, local groups lost their ability to control the dissemination of mass culture. Sure of their hold over the middle class market, chain stores more aggressively pursued ethnic working class class markets, making it much harder for small merchants to survive. The elaboration of the Hollywood studio system and the costs of installing sound helped standardize moviegoing as well. Not only were neighborhood theaters increasingly taken over by chains, but the "talkies" themselves hushed the audience's interjections and replaced the ethnic troupes and amateur talent shows with taped shorts distributed nationally. Similarly, by the late 1920s, the local non-profit radio era also had ended. In the aftermath of the passage of the Federal Radio Act of 1927, national commerical network radio imposed order on what admittedly had been a chaotic scene, but at the expense of small local stations. When Chicago's workers switched on the radio by 1930, they were likely to hear the A & P Gypsies and the Eveready Hour on stations that had almost all affiliated with either NBC or CBS, or had negotiated—like even Chicago's WCFL, "the Voice of Labor"—to carry some network shows. The Great Depression only reinforced this national commerical trend by undermining small distributors of all kinds.

Thus, grassroots control over mass culture did diminsh during the thirties. But the extent to which this more national mass culture in the end succeeded in assimiliating workers to middle class values remains an open question. It is very likely that even though the structure of distributing mass culture did change by the 1930s, workers still did not fulfill the expectations of *True Story Magazine* editors and J. Walter Thompson Company executives. It is possible that workers maintained a distinctive sense of group identity even while participating, much the way blacks in the twenties did. Historical circumstances may have changed in such a way that workers continued to put mass culture to their own uses and remain a class apart. And increasingly over time, mass culture promoters—moviemakers, radio programmers, chain store operators and advertisers—would recognize this possibility, and gear products to particular audiences; the 1930s mark the emergence of the concept of a segmented mass market, which gradually displaced expectations of one homogenous audience so prevalent in the 1920s.

Nor should we assume—as advocates of the embourgeoisement school do—that as workers shared more in a national commercial culture, they were necessarily depoliticized. In fact, there is much evidence to suggest that a more national mass culture helped unify workers previously divided along ethnic, racial, and geographical lines, facilitating the national organizing drive of the CIO. A working population that shared a common cultural life offered new opportunities for unified political action. Sit-down strikers who charted baseball scores and danced together to popular music and union newspapers that kept their readers informed about network radio programs testified to intriguing connections between cultural and political unity. Extension of this study into the 1930s and beyond might reveal that, ironically, mass culture did more to create an integrated working class culture than a classless American one. In taking this study beyond the 1920s, it is, thus, imperative that investigators continue to pay careful attention to the context in which people encountered mass culture, in order not to let the mythical assumptions about mass culture's homogenizing powers prevail as they did in our popular images of the twenties.

Chapter Six

Affluence, Anti-Communism, and the Transformation of Industrial Unionism Among Automobile Workers, 1933–1973

Ronald Edsforth

I. Reconsidering Revisions of the Recent Past

A great many American historians have recently ventured across the great divide, World War II, which separates our half of the twentieth century from the rest of the American past, into the early Cold War. This crossing almost inevitably raises the problem of dealing with the intertwined political-cultural concepts—"the end of ideology" (the Cold War consensus) and "the affluent society" (mass consumerism)—against which the early New Left rebelled some thirty years ago. For historians of recent America, it seems all things from our youth return as a past to be reanalyzed with the advantages, and accumulated prejudices, of hindsight. Today, some three decades after the publication of the first issue of *Studies on the Left,* the problems, not of consensus history, but of the roles of political consensus and consumer-oriented affluence in the era when consensus history flourished need to be considered seriously again.

This task is especially important for American labor historians. Labor history has grown enormously in academic significance since the emergence of the New Left. In the later 1960s, it became a contested field of study, a primary battle ground in the New Left's assault on consensus history and the idea of an affluent, classless America. Labor history had been a mostly neglected field study dominated by the ideas and methods of the "Wisconsin school" and enlivened only by the persistence of Old Left scholars on its ideological fringes. After World War II, a casual observer might even have gotten the impression that labor history as history was finished. As a taught subject, it was increasingly located in specialized industrial relations programs, not history departments. Moreover, after the establishment of the great industrial unions and the New Deal order that legitimized the place of organized labor in the United States, the traditional dramatic narrative of American labor history seemed to have come to an end.

As late as the early 1960s, during the heyday of the New Frontier and progressive labor's alliance with the civil rights movement, leading labor historians like Milton Derber and Irving Bernstein strongly identified themselves with the New Deal, and their work unabashedly endorsed the accomplishments of the labor movement and of the liberals who had supported it. These postwar scholars embraced a very positive interpretation of the political character of the postwar working class. At that time, only a small group of dissenters, older members of the Old Left and a tiny vanguard of the New Left, challenged the prevailing scholarly interpretation. That interpretation described the successes of the New Deal and the industrial labor movement, and the generalized material prosperity and security they helped to create, as the principal reasons why America's organized working class had abandoned the industrial militancy and political activism seen as characterizing its turbulent years from 1933 to 1946. Today, there are still scholars who insist on the truth of this admittedly optimistic interpretation, but there are also many other more critical, pessimistic voices on the subject.

Some of these critics argue that the New Deal and the labor movement of the 1930s were failures; others even assert that these great developments were cleverly contrived bureaucratic-legal traps designed to suppress, not liberate, the working class. Moreover, among these numerous recent critics of the liberal consensus, it has become commonplace to emphasize the limits, not the extent, of postwar prosperity and security among American working people.[1] Finally, although liberal scholars had always recognized the repressive impact of the Taft-Hartley Act, and the whole domestic Cold War of which it was a part, in their interpretation of the decline of militancy and radical politics among postwar workers and their unions, none ever went as far as to suggest that these things were more important than the gains made by working people after 1932. Yet today, in some revisionist accounts of the early Cold War, it often seems as if the fate of union radicals caught in anti-communist purges is equated with the fate of the labor movement itself; so we see decline in the years 1946–1960 when by most measures the movement actually grew.[2]

Revision is, of course, a normal part of the life cycle of historical interpretation. But the character of such revision of recent American labor history warrants special attention because it seems to lead to a virtual repudiation of what are the remembered experiences of many of those people who played an active part the transformation of the labor movement after World War II. Surely, one reason for the extremely critical character of this particular revision is the relative decline of American capitalism since the prosperous 1960s. Shocked by the growing weakness of the U.S. economy and its devastating impact on older industrial cities like New York, Chicago, Detroit, Flint, and Youngstown, we have all become more skeptical about the promise of affluence and security upon which the politics of consensus still rests. Made more aware of the limitations and relative weakness of the industrial unions of today, we are apt to find it easy to emphasize those same characteristics in our study of industrial unions in past decades. Furthermore, since most labor history is now written by younger scholars like myself who cannot remember the Great Depression or World War II—who cannot, in other words, recall what it feels like to live in a world where poverty, fear, and insecurity are generalized conditions—we tend to see the great transformation of material life which began with World War II from a more distant, detached perspective. And almost inevitably that point of view leads us away from dramatic narrative and toward a more analytical history which stresses structure over experience, institutions over everyday life, and continuity over change.

Along these lines, an additional point about our present perspective needs to be made because it helps explain why recent revisions of postwar American labor history have so thoroughly rejected the positive moral authority of the New Deal and organized labor that most scholars once acknowledged. During the Reagan era, labor history clearly became an important academic refuge for individuals like myself who are frustrated veterans of the student New Left. As a result, within the field there naturally developed an identification with others who had struggled and failed to restructure the American system. We have all found ways to dignify and even romanticize the lives and hardships of distant generations of American working people.

Yet, when we have moved closer to our own times, we have not always been as generous. In fact, many of us have found it easy to blame all but the most radical members of the mid-twentieth century working class for failing to be radical enough to recognize the political limitations of their unions and New Deal government, two institutions that consistently alienated the New Left in the 1960s.[3] In other words, many younger scholars (myself included) have found in the study of modern American labor history

a way to sustain our radicalism, and simultaneously, a way to attempt an explanation the central political failure of our own
lives—the failure of the New Left to significantly transform American capitalism.

Certainly, there is nothing inherently wrong with these mo-
tives. Indeed, it does seem that careful study of the historical experience of the Old Left and the industrial labor movement with
which it was intertwined can provide, at the very least, important
questions to ask about the later historical experience of the New
Left.[4] But there are serious dangers in such an approach, especially if our present concerns lead us away from establishing em-
pathy with the majority of working people who actually joined the
industrial labor unions and/or supported the New Deal in the
1930s and 1940s, and who then in the postwar era embraced
the reformed, consumer-oriented capitalism which organized labor
and the New Deal had helped to create. Unfortunately, this is
what I believe has happened to many new labor historians.

Having rejected the Cold War liberal consensus and the materialism of the consumer-oriented affluent society in our own lives,
we find it difficult to empathize with those Americans who embraced these things as positive goods in their lives. Having always
lived in a society shaped by consumer-oriented capitalism and
New Deal liberalism, we find it hard to imagine that these things
were ever really new, that they ever could have held out the promise of a truly different and better future for American working
people. And now, having seen in recent years the erosion of
consumer-oriented prosperity and the unravelling of New Deal liberalism, and because that system's flaws are today so much in evidence, it has become even harder for us to recapture the depth of
feeling with which so many working class Americans committed
themselves to the reformed capitalism of the postwar period.

Nonetheless, two great facts of mid-twentieth-century American labor history remain, whether or not we choose to confront
them. I am referring, of course, to the fact that the New Deal order was really new, that in its day federal intervention in society
on behalf of working people and organized labor represented a fundamental break with the past. Moreover, working people (as
shown by their voting behavior in 1936 and thereafter) recognized
and appreciated this fact.[5] I am also referring to the equally important fact that the working class as a whole experienced dramatic and unprecedented improvements in material living
standards from 1941 to 1973. These facts cannot be ignored or
glossed over. Instead, we must find ways of incorporating them

into a field of study that, for the most part, has developed the themes of independence and resistance to exploitation among working people and focused on the long epochs in American history when capitalism, and the working and living conditions it produced, were very different than they generally were on the three decades after World War II.

The dominant patterns of our labor history have been derived from studying successive periods of industrial history when exploitation of workers was more direct than after World War II, when poverty was absolute and endemic, when labor unions typically had no legal rights and their suppression often turned violent, when white ethnic and racial subcultures multiplied and flourished, and when a truly nationalized popular culture did not exist. A profound transformation of American capitalism in the mid-twentieth century changed all those conditions. To interpret the impact of that transformation properly, labor historians need to develop new questions and perspectives for the postwar period. And as part of that effort it is also necessary to suspend, temporarily at least, the negative judgments made about mass consumerism during the heyday of the 1960s counterculture.

Happily, this work has begun. In the last decade , a group of historians who differ considerably in their approaches to the past have made it clear that the central problems of recent American labor history are not so much how and why workers resisted advanced (and reformed) industrial capitalism, but instead how and why advanced industrial capitalism triumphed and why the mid-twentieth-century working class embraced its culture and politics.[6] These are good questions, which quite properly suggest a rethinking of our traditional focus on working class independence and resistance. As Stanley Aronowitz has noted, in the postwar era "union workers were now of society as well as in it."[7] Describing how and explicating why this profound transformation of the organized working class' place in American society occurred now seems the primary task of historians of postwar labor.

II. Living Standards of the Postwar Working Class

There were good reasons for American workers to accept affluence as a characteristic feature of their society after World War II. Indeed, changes in the material conditions of everyday life tended to validate the public rhetoric about political consensus and the affluent society which the New Left later found so objectionable. The three decades following World War II were, in material terms, the best of all times for the American working class. By the early 1970s, in almost every measurable way—including diet, dress, health care, housing quality and home ownership, educational levels, wages, hours of work, the availability of vacations and leisure time, educational levels, life expectancy, and the possibility of retirement, insured family security, personal wealth (in savings and possessions), and access to credit—most American working people were living vastly better lives than their parents and grandparents ever did; and moreover, they knew it.[8] Relatively infrequent and short recessions, and the availability of unemployment benefits (and even company funded supplemental unemployment benefits for some unionized workers) made family incomes more certain than anyone could remember. The 1950s were actually the decade of the greatest increases in working class income and discretionary expenditures, but general improvements in material living standards continued right through 1973.

Of course, rates of improvement were not uniform. Black working class families and female-headed households in particular lagged behind the pace set by the white, male-dominated unionized industrial labor force. Nonetheless, living standards rose for the whole working class. A comparison of working class expenditures on food brings home this point. In 1918, when the grandparents of the working class of the 1960s were in the labor force, white wage earners (skilled and semi-skilled) spent an average of 40 percent of their family budgets on food, while white laborers (the unskilled laborers and hourly service workers) spent 43 percent and black workers (all job classifications) spent 48 percent of their family budgets on food.[9] These very high levels of spending on the most basic necessity in a time of nearly full employment undoubtedly reflect the very low wage levels that forced most early twentieth-century workers to struggle just to subsist.

By 1935, when the economy was going through its initial "Roosevelt recovery" from the Great Depression, white wage earners were spending only 33 percent of their family budget on food, while the white laborer spent 34 percent and the black worker 35 percent of their family budgets on food. After the Second World War, the percentage of family income going to food fell even more dramatically. These declines were coupled with basically stable spending on shelter, so that a greater and rising share of rising family incomes became available for discretionary spending. For white wage earners overall, food expenditures dropped from 30 percent to 19 percent of family budgets between 1950 and 1973. White laborers experienced a decline from 32 percent to 20 percent in the same period; for black workers food expenditures fell from 34 percent to 24 percent. However, while black family spending on shelter changed very little in the 1950s, when expenditures on food fell significantly, between 1960 and 1973 spending on housing by black families rose dramatically, from 23 percent to 39 percent of their family budgets. These last figures leave no doubt that in general material living standards of black working class families were falling behind the standards of the white working class in the 1960s when the civil rights and black power movements were able to mobilize a large part of the nation's black population.

The long-term trends of working class expenditures for the entire twentieth century clearly point to the emergence of the whole working class as true consumers in the years after World War II. By 1973, nearly two-fifths of black families, over half the families of white laborers, and nearly seven-tenths the families of white wage earners owned their own homes. Moreover, unlike most workers' dwellings of the 1930s, the vast majority of working class homes and apartments of 1973 had indoor bathtubs, flush toilets, central heating, gas or electric stoves, and electric refrigerators. By 1973, 68 percent of black workers, 89 percent of white laborers, and 95 percent of all white wage earners also owned a car. That same year, black working class families were spending 7 percent of their budget on recreation and education, while white laborers' families spent 9 percent and all white wage earners' families spent 10 percent on these things.[10]

Roland Marchand concludes his study of American advertising during the interwar period by remarking that most Americans of 1940 wished to believe in the new consumer-oriented American Dream of "You can have it all," even if after a decade of economic depression the realization of that dream seemed a long way off.[11] Yet, as the figures above illustrate, it was not really that long before material living standards did begin to rise dramatically. By 1960, it seems fair to conclude that most American workers could believe they were well on the way to actually living that new consumer-oriented dream.

III. The Affluent Automobile Workers

Automobile workers and their families were among the most privileged members of America's working class during the three decades of dramatically improving living standards that followed World War II. In material terms, the high wages and extensive benefit packages, which ultimately included pensions, health and life insurance, dental coverage, paid vacations and sick leave, and supplemental unemployment pay, placed auto workers in the vanguard of the working class. Between 1947 and 1975, the average weekly wages of automobile workers (in current dollars) rose from $56.51 to $259.53.[12] In the same period, the average weekly wages of many other industrial workers and workers in retail trade advanced, but at a considerably slower pace. For example, in 1947 the average worker in the apparel industry earned 71 percent of what the average automobile worker made each week; by 1975 the average apparel worker earned just 43 percent of the average auto worker's weekly wage.

These differences were almost certainly due to the high profitability of automobile manufacturing and sales, and to the power of the United Automobile Workers union which acted as the auto industry workers' sole bargaining agent. Even after 1975, when hard and uncertain times fell upon the automobile industry, the union (although weakened by its inability to prevent employment losses and reductions in some benefits) was still able to sustain rising incomes for its employed workers. By 1983, when the industry had just begun its recovery from the very deep Reagan recession, average weekly wages of auto workers were $524.80, nearly ten times higher (in current dollars) than they had been in 1947. By comparison, in 1983, average weekly earnings in the apparel industry had fallen to 38 percent of those in automobile manufacturing; in retail trade, average earnings were only 33 percent of the auto workers' standard.

There is much evidence to suggest that the high and usually improving material living standards of rank-and-file automobile workers were the essential underpinning of what in retrospect appears to be a long-term shift away from strikes and political activism in the automotive production centers of the postwar period. It is worth noting both the variety of this evidence, and the long time span it covers. One of the earliest pieces of evidence was uncovered by Alan Raucher just a few years ago. It is a record of a General Motors "My Job" contest held in 1947, which got nearly one hundred seventy-five thousand workers, hoping to win prizes, to voluntarily write essays on why they liked their job.[13] Of course, the circumstances of this contest make the contents of the essays suspect. Nevertheless, it does seem remarkable that Raucher discovered that for nearly all participants it was good wages, fringe benefits, and job security from the seniority system were the top reasons listed for liking their jobs.

Raucher's conclusion, that GM workers "defined their successes in large part by psychological security within the organization and by consumption and leisure pursuits off the job," is very similar to the results of Eli Chinoy's famous study of Lansing, Michigan, working people, *Automobile Workers and the American Dream,* which was published in 1955.[14] However, Chinoy, like many other radical scholars who have studied postwar working people, refused to accept the results of his own study. Chinoy found that workers staying in the industry were able to create a lifetime of aspirations for themselves out material desires and the desire for personal and family security. Yet he dismissed these aspirations as self-deluding escapism, or in other words as false consciousness.

Two remarkable scientific samplings of the attitudes of the entire UAW membership commissioned by the UAW International Executive Board in 1960 (conducted by the Lou Harris organization) and in 1967 (conducted by Oliver Quayle and Company) reveal very high levels of approval of the UAW and the gains it had helped workers make over the previous two decades.[15] Both surveys were extensive and ambitious in the range of questions asked of auto workers. In 1960 and 1967 the surveyed workers approved of the union leadership's performance by a two-to-one margin. Both surveys also reveal workers to be much more concerned about retirement and guaranteed weekly wages than they were about wage levels, hours, benefits, working conditions, job categories, or work loads and production standards. In fact, the 1967 survey of over twenty-one hundred UAW members from all regions of the country indicated that these latter issues were of markedly secondary concern.[16] Of course, these priorities do not mean that the latter issues were of no concern, but they do reveal that while most auto workers of the late 1960s were still concerned about their economic security, they were generally satisfied with the tradeoff they had made between production work and higher living standards.

This conclusion was corroborated by an employee survey conducted by the Organizational Research and Development Section of General Motor's Personnel and Administration Staff in the winter of 1972–73. This survey of a randomly selected group of nearly twenty-five hundred workers from all across the country found that the majority of auto workers felt their jobs were "good, beneficial to them, and satisfactory" while only 15 percent felt their jobs were "bad."[17] Most strikingly, nearly every worker surveyed (between 97 and 98 percent) ranked benefits and pay as either "very important" or "important" reasons for holding their jobs. This result seems particularly significant because nearly half of those surveyed indicated they thought their jobs were "boring" and that they had very little opportunity to "develop my skills" (44 percent and 45 percent respectively).[18] In other words, the tradeoff inaugurated in 1914 by Henry Ford's $5.00 day remained the principal reason for the stability of the automotive labor force.

More personal testimony on the significance of material benefits, money, and the things money could buy for the lives of auto workers and their families can be found on the many hours of interviews recorded by Kit Parker for three films he produced for the Archives of Labor and Urban Affairs.[19] These recordings were made in the late 1970s after the industry began to experience more frequent recessions. Even so, they reveal that auto workers from all parts of the industry found a great deal of their self-esteem and status in their paid-up homes, their ability to send their children to college, their vacations, and the plans they were making to travel after retirement. These interviews also revealed that younger workers wanted more things and more time off to enjoy them, and that older workers were critical of these desires.[20] Here, it seems, is evidence that two generations of auto workers had shaped their lives in accordance with the prevailing popular culture which made personal leisure and the acquisition of consumer goods viable modes of self-fulfillment. But here also is evidence that the security-consciousness of the older generation (whose memories of the Great Depression had long tempered their consumerism) was not as important among those workers who had yet to experience mass unemployment and truly prolonged unemployment.

Finally, the recently published oral history, *End of the Line: Autoworkers and the American Dream,* contains compelling testimony to the persistence of the consumer-oriented American Dream, even among those workers most disillusioned by real misery and insecurity created by the Reagan recession and the automobile industry's recent troubles. The thirty Ford workers interviewed for this excellent volume have many regrets about the life choices they have made, but they also reveal both a satisfaction with their material accomplishments and an enormous uneasiness about a future they see as having no future for working people like themselves who were able to enter the affluent society right out of high school.[21]

Although in some ways all of the evidence cited above is anecdotal, its volume, variety, and the time span it covers is impressive. Taken as a whole, this evidence has at least two important meanings. First, it seems clear that the very things the UAW emphasized in its bargaining with the Big Three automobile companies during the nearly quarter of a century when Walter Reuther was its president—long-term improvements in pay, income security, pensions, and fringe benefits—were in fact highly valued by most rank-and-file automobile workers. And secondly, it also seems clear that these same workers were not victims of false consciousness. The evidence cited above shows that auto workers most often realized the costs of the tradeoff they had made; and that those costs—in terms of boredom, frustration, lack of career goals, and lack of control over their work—were never far from their minds.

Thus, embracing the conclusion that auto workers were full participants in the mass consumer culture of the postwar era does not mean we must also embrace the idea that automobile workers passively or unconsciously accepted their own dehumanization (although this may indeed have been the case in individual instances). Instead, the available contemporary evidence of rank-and-file attitudes directs us to investigate further the character of the tradeoff, and the ways that the real discontents of auto work found outlets within the structures of the New Deal industrial order and a popular culture built on mass consumerism.

IV. Affluence and Class Conflict in the Postwar UAW

In the 1930s, the UAW-CIO earned a well-deserved public reputation as one of the most militant of the new industrial unions. At that time, the UAW also became known as the most progressive of the new unions because of the high public profile of its radical leaders, including Walter Reuther, the head of the union's General Motors department. During World War II, wildcat strikes, rank-and-file protests against the leadership's no-strike pledge, and Reuther's widely publicized ideas, first about boosting war production and later about converting the military economy to civilian uses in peacetime, maintained the UAW's standing as the political vanguard of America's industrial working class. But then, in the aftermath of the long General Motors' strike of 1945–46, when Reuther became UAW president, the union appeared to reject this role, purging radicals and shopfloor militants, while at the same time embracing the Cold War and the watered-down progressivism of Truman's Fair Deal. By the 1960s, in fact, when Walter Reuther was frequently consulted by Presidents Kennedy and Johnson, the UAW seemed to most observers to be very much part of the political establishment.

How is this apparent about-face to be explained? Here it is not necessary to retell in detail the history of the United Automobile Workers union; much of that history is already familiar to students of modern American labor. Yet recent scholarship has called into question longstanding interpretations that stress either the pressure put on the union by government and the big corporations and/or Reuther's alleged treachery as fundamental causes of the transformation of the UAW. This scholarship has, in fact, made it possible to offer a more positive interpretation that highlights (1) the ability of working people to continue the class struggle against corporate management within the new postwar industrial relations order, and (2) their simultaneous willingness to embrace mass consumer affluence and anti-communism as the ideological foundations of the postwar political culture.

The struggle to establish an industrial union in the automobile industry had been a long and difficult one. The deeply entrenched anti-unionism of the automobile companies, local political establishments, and press, as well as the antipathy and confusion among a great many working people, all had to be overcome before the UAW was securely organized as a powerful force in the nation's most important manufacturing industry. Between 1933 and 1946, as part of that struggle, automobile workers in Detroit, Flint, Toledo, Cleveland, and other Midwestern production centers frequently turned to militant tactics—including work slowdowns, unannounced departmental shutdowns, mass strikes, rallies, flying squadrons of pickets, and of course, the famous sitdown strikes—to achieve their goals. The General Motors sit-down strike of 1936–37, the Ford strike of 1941, wartime wildcat strikes, the 113-day GM strike of 1945–46, and a massive job action/rally at Detroit's Cadillac Square in April 1947 are only the most memorable of what were in fact a long series of militant auto worker actions. On other less well-remembered occasions during those years, auto workers demonstrated their class-conscious solidarity by sending caravans of pickets and truckloads of food to assist strikers in other cities—and other industries.

The militant class consciousness of many automobile workers was, of course, a result of the insecurity and work speedups brought on by the Great Depression. However, the particular shape and duration of the auto workers' militancy resulted from a bottom-up restructuring of shop floor life, which has been fully delineated only in recent years. In the mid-1930s, significant numbers of auto wokers, often led by tiny cadres of political radicals, created shop steward networks in some of the industry's biggest plants. The rank-and-file shop steward movement survived political turmoil within the union between 1937 and 1942, and was revived and strengthened during the war years. In 1944–45, it provided both the inspiration and the organization behind a wave of unauthorized wildcat strikes that challenged the UAW's national leadership and its no-strike pledge. Thus, for nearly a decade (and in some localities like Flint even longer), these shop steward networks sustained rank-and-file activists and the militant class consciousness of midwestern auto workers.

As World War II came to an end in 1945, many auto plants seethed with discontent over real wages. UAW members also feared reconversion plans that included a two-pronged management drive to reassert full control over the workplace, and simultaneously, with the help of the new federal labor bureaucracy, force union leaders to act "responsibly" by limiting the scope of collective bargaining and disciplining their militant members. At General Motors, workers' discontent was effectively channeled by UAW vice-president Walter Reuther into the bitter 113-day walkout that began in November 1945 after the rank and file by a six-to-one vote authorized a strike.

The strike won Reuther the loyalty of many union members who had previously been against him or had taken no part in union politics. It also enhanced his reputation as a progressive working class leader with ideas, energy, and a commitment to carrying forward the legacy of the CIO, the New Deal, and Franklin Roosevelt. However, the strike did not, as Reuther and his supporters had hoped, expand the union's bargaining power. In the end, workers anxious to once again receive paychecks were forced to accept only improvements in seniority protection and a wage increase pegged to a percentage already agreed to by the other big car makers and CIO unions in other industries. It was a bitter conclusion to a protracted struggle, one that left many GM workers skeptical about the efficacy of militant, confrontational tactics.[22] The failure of this strike to achieve its stated aims was followed in the spring of 1947 by the failure of mass auto worker protest to stop, or even amend, the Taft-Hartley Act, and by Ford's successful breaking of the Foremen's Association of America in a 47-day lockout. Taken together, these three events mark the end of a remarkable era of sustained auto worker militancy.[23]

After 1947, strike activity in the automobile industry declined over the long run, but neither steadily nor uniformly. In part, this decline may be seen as the result of the purge of communist and radical rank-and-file leaders that Walter Reuther carried out during his first few years as overall union president. Yet the conditions in the automobile factories that produced militancy, especially disputes over job classifications, work loads, and production standards continued to prompt workers to resist management authority.

The period of declining auto worker strike activity that began in 1948 was in fact never free from strikes and other evidence of auto workers' resistance to the dehumanization of their work. Old ways of handling grievances changed slowly at first. In fact, what William Serrin later dubbed "the civilized relationship" between organized labor and management in the automobile industry never really emerged at the shop floor and local plant level. For example, as Steve Jefferies has recently shown, all through the 1950s, workers at Chrysler, and particularly at its big plants in Detroit, fought management's attempts to alter shop floor bargains through the use of the wildcat strike weapon. Chrysler workers revived the use of this tactic in the later 1960s and early 1970s, years when younger workers at Lordstown and other General Motors plants also frequently struck over local issues.[24]

Other forms of class-conscious militancy also punctuated the early postwar period. In 1950, Chrysler workers stayed off the job for 104 days to secure a contractual pension plan comparable to that implemented at Ford the previous year. Then, three years later, when inflation created by the Korean War sapped workers' purchasing power despite Cost of Living Adjustment (COLA) provisions in their current contracts, widespread wildcat strikes at Ford and General Motors forced the companies as well as reluctant union leaders to open up those contracts and negotiate a new wage and benefits package.

This led to a major change in UAW policy. Previously, as part of its bargain with companies, it had tried to centralize all contractual bargaining. However, steadily rising local demands based on widespread grievances over local conditions, work rules, supervision, and production standards forced Reuther and the union's executive board to permit local unions to bargain locally with management even after contractual agreement at the national level had been achieved. Thus while the industry had infrequent national strikes after 1950, there were numerous local strikes (both authorized and unauthorized) in the late 1950s, and then again in the later 1960s and early 1970s.[25]

Management's ability to exert its authority over workers at the point of production varied considerably from company to company, and from plant to plant within each of the Big Three. On the whole, General Motors and Ford both seem to have done a better job of establishing what Henry Katz has recently called "disciplined regularity" in their plants during the 1950s.[26] Nelson Lichtenstein's careful studies of Ford's massive River Rouge complex reveal the movement towards disciplined regularity began in the workplace itself.[27] The end of the Second World War brought an end to the circumstances—including cost-plus contracts, small-batch production, individual and team pacing, and the dilution of the authority of foremen and supervisors—that had enabled workers on the auto shop floor to revive shop steward networks and exercise considerable control over working conditions and production standards. As all the automobile companies reconverted to civilian production, they also insisted on re-establishing what they claimed was their right to manage. To do this, they removed foremen and supervisors from the shop floors and, by putting them in white collars and offices, enhanced their authority as managers. The companies also reinstated and further rationalized assembly-line methods, disrupting the solidarity of work groups and shop steward networks formed during wartime. The return of tens of thousands of veterans to their jobs in the industry added to this disruption of rank-and-file work groups.

Even more important, the cooperative relationship between the big industrial corporations and the federal government that had emerged during the war years helped management efforts to curtail union power and rank-and-file militancy. Backed by a federal government generally more concerned with national security than extending the New Deal, and by a conservatively reformed National Labor Relations Board in particular, auto company managers began to insist that the UAW make its members live up to a strict interpretation of contracts prohibiting strikes for their duration.

Ford and General Motors had more immediate success than Chrysler. After 1950, the year General Motors and the UAW signed their much-heralded five-year contract that included wage improvements, a pension plan, upward revision of the original (1948) COLA formula, and new hospital and medical benefits, patterns of routinized bureaucratic labor relations and a general

absence of rank-and-file strike activity began to emerge. Yet, as
Craig Zabala has recently demonstrated in great detail, GM workers' grievances rose almost continually in the whole postwar period, and especially quickly in the years 1952–1957 and 1961–
1969. Zabala's work makes a forceful case for the thesis that
workers learned how to use the grievance bargaining process, and
particularly its initial more informal steps, as a way of exerting
considerable control over their work.[28]

In short, "disciplined regularity" did not reflect worker passivity or absence of conflict. Instead, in the 1950s and 1960s auto
workers learned how to use the political and legalistic structure of
the postwar workplace to their own advantage. This means that
hundreds of thousands of auto workers in fact actively resisted dehumanization on the job, even as they embraced the relative affluence the job made possible. What changed most between 1945 and
1960 were the location and the form of resistance. Increasingly
workers fought for control and dignity locally through the contractual procedures created by the union and the companies as part of
the New Deal restructuring of industrial relations.

Disciplined regularity started to break down and strikes to increase in the mid-1960s, about the time the first members of the
postwar generation entered the work force. In 1964, local
production-related grievances provoked a national strike against
General Motors, and kept members of twenty-eight local unions off
the job even after a new contract was signed and ratified. In subsequent years, rank-and-file auto workers became increasingly
restive in the workplace. Absenteeism and tardiness rose, more
grievances were filed, local unions made more demands at contract time, and hours lost to work stoppages increased. As both
Serrin and Emma Rothschild pointed out in their widely read
studies of the early 1970s, the national contract strikes against
Ford in 1967 and General Motors in 1970 were called in part to
allow young militants to "blow off steam" and thus make contract ratification easier. In those strikes, the UAW under Walter
Reuther and then Leonard Woodcock clearly acted, to use C.
Wright Mills' perceptive phrase, as a "manager of discontent." But
union leaders were also being responsive to older workers' grievances, especially the declining purchasing power of wages that resulted from the Vietnam War–driven inflation, and a demand for
a "thirty years and out" early retirement program.[29]

By the early 1970s, a generation gap had clearly developed
within the UAW. Older auto workers had actually lived through
the struggle to establish the union power that helped to usher in

two and a half decades of rising living standards; they were alienated from a younger generation of auto workers which included historically high numbers of blacks and women, and seemed very much influenced by the Black Power movement and the so-called counterculture. At the time, this generation gap appeared to be a decisive factor in UAW politics. The older (mostly white male) workers, who had always in Doug Fraser's words, "accepted the auto shop as a fact of life"; and were "reasonably happy" in their private everyday lives, now wanted early retirement.[30] Of course, this demand was at least partly grounded in the high levels of material security already obtained by that older generation. It also indicated a breakdown of the basic social-cultural consensus that had prevailed among workers in the auto industry for several decades. Where older workers had long been able to find satisfaction in the social interactions of their various work groups within the automobile factories, they now found themselves confronted by the same kind of racial, gender, and cultural tensions that were dividing America as a whole at the time.

These tensions, and the significance of the generation gap, exploded upon the national scene in the now famous Lordstown "troubles" of 1972. The very high percentage of young workers who took part in the unauthorized sabotaging of production, and the authorized strike at the General Motors' Lordstown, Ohio, Chevrolet Vega assembly plant that year quite naturally led management, politicians, and the national news media to hold the counterculture and its anti-work ethic responsible for the upheaval.[31] Yet, with a clarity that only hindsight brings, we can now see that the socio-cultural explanation for the reappearance of rank-and-file militancy in the automobile industry was, and is, insufficient. Lordstown's troubles were actually rooted in a dramatic speedup that GM tried to force upon workers as part of a quick-fix strategy designed to meet the rising threat of small car imports. As Gary Bryner, the twenty-six year old Local 1112 (Lordstown) president, said at the union's convention in 1972,

> It may be just a little different than as portrayed by the press. . . . Our fight was against speedups and for working conditions, decent working conditions, and for dignity in the work place, which was a constant fight for us all.[32]

Speedups, arbitrary discipline, and intolerable working conditions were primary causes of the wildcat strikes which erupted in the older Chrysler Corporation Detroit plants in the late 1960s and early 1970s. But in Detroit, race, and especially the organization of the Dodge Revolutionary Union Movement (DRUM) among younger black militants, created divisions within the militant work force that enabled the union hierarchy to work with management to suppress the local insurgency, first by actually using its UAW staff to break a strike, and then by refusing to fight the company over the dismissal of the DRUM leaders. Nonetheless, what ended the militancy at Chrysler in 1973 should not be confused with what had caused it in the first place. As Jefferies has written, "more detailed study suggests the strike issues were very similar to those which aroused protests ten, twenty, and even thirty-five years before."[33]

As we now know, a serious decline in the fortunes of the American automobile industry and American automobile workers had already begun by the early 1970s. It was, finally, not the counterculture or racial and gender tensions, that shocked union leaders out of the "civilized relationship" with management. The ever-increasing threat of new speedups, contract givebacks, prolonged layoffs, and ultimately plant closings—real events that combined with double-digit inflation to threaten the hard-won security and material affluence of workers' lives—were the most fundamental causes of the latest, and still ongoing, transformation of labor relations in the automobile industry.[34]

V. The Importance of Walter
Reuther's Leadership

With this admittedly selective overview of the history of the postwar automobile industry in mind, we can now reverse perspectives and take a "top-down" look at Walter Reuther's contribution to the political culture of the postwar UAW. Today, we are distant enough in time to consider Reuther's policies more dispassionately than was possible while he was alive and his cohorts still controlled the union. Reuther was an ambitious union leader who very much wanted to lead the UAW and, in doing so, a political/ social transformation of postwar America. But after the unsuccessful General Motors strike of 1945–46 and the passage of the Taft-Hartley Act, Reuther realized his dreams of a corporate state and government economic planning could not be realized. Instead, he increasingly pursued the best he could achieve for his union, what

Lichtenstein has described as "a sort of privatized welfare state."[35]

To achieve this end, UAW leaders seemed to concede management's so-called "right to manage," promising in contractual agreements to act "responsibly" by enforcing work rules among their members. Anxious to secure gains they had already made, absorbed by the effort to consolidate power within the union, and chastened by the failure of the General Motors strike and by the victory of Republicans and conservative Democrats at the polls in November 1946, the union under the direction of its newly elected international president, Walter Reuther, moved decisively in the direction of "responsible behavior." Disciplinary actions against militant members were upheld, and officers of the local unions were made accountable for disruptions of production and other contract violations.

Rank-and-file workers were told in no uncertain terms to channel their demands and discontents into the official grievance procedure. Between 1946 and 1950, Reuther systematically replaced political opponents and dissidents who held appointive positions within the UAW. He also campaigned vigorously against opponents in local union elections. These actions, combined with changes in management policy and the new dues checkoff system, to undermine and very soon destroy the unofficial shop steward networks that had sustained the rank and file's class-conscious militancy for a decade or more.

These observations raise many questions, among them. How was the Ruether faction able to establish political dominance as well as a policy of "responsible behavior" in the UAW? And why did the political factionalism and entrenched radicalism, which had shaped the inner life of the union for so long, disappear so quickly in the later 1940s?

When these questions are raised, almost immediately the words "Cold War" and "anti-communism," and maybe even "red-baiting" and "purge" leap to mind. Of course, these things did play an important role in rapidly changing labor relations in the automobile industry and the political life of the UAW after 1945. The Cold War created a wider political climate in which the radicals of the UAW's left-center leadership faction, led by R. J. Thomas and George Addes, and the radicals who so often led rank-and-file militants at the local level, became impossible to defend. The Taft-Hartley Act made labor anti-radicalism the law of the land, but even before Taft-Hartley became law, Walter Reuther and his supporters had made anti-communism and red-baiting an integral part of their drive to establish unified political control over the UAW, and to destroy the shop steward networks that were the primary source of the militancy endangering the union's "responsible" image. As George Addes recalled in 1982, "It was unbelievable that you could go out and wave the red flag, call names and convert membership."[36] Unbelievable for Addes and other members of the left-center coalition perhaps, but not so unbelievable if the depth and character of the ideological reservoir upon which Reuther was drawing is understood, as Reuther himself so well understood it.

Undoubtedly, then, it is true that Walter Ruether's faction took control of the UAW between 1946 and 1948 in large part because they were Cold Warriors who red-baited opponents and, when given the chance, removed the opposition from union offices. However, it is also true that Reuther's faction triumphed because their opponents, in biographer John Barnard's words, "demonstrated the left's difficulty in perceiving the true character of the ordinary beliefs."[37]

If we stopped our analysis at this point, as Reuther's critics have always done, the answers to our questions about the political defeat of the union's Left leaders and the swift demise of the wartime shop steward networks would seem to fit very nicely into one of the traditional interpretive frameworks of American labor history. Repression and red-baiting did in the Left. However, if we stop here, our interpretation will remain incomplete and seriously flawed. We need to ask more questions, especially about "the true character of the ordinary worker's beliefs," and we need to ask them in the light of those two great facts of postwar labor history—the newness of the New Deal and the dramatic improvements in living standards and personal security which set mid-twentieth-century working people apart from previous generations, and very possibly the generation that followed them. For instance, is it really fair to say that repression and the Cold War alone explain both the decline of strike activity and the emergence of the "disciplined regularity" that followed that decline? Should both, or indeed either, of these developments be pictured as essentially forced upon rank-and-file workers by organizations and events out of their control? If we answer yes to this question, must we also assert that Walter Reuther's landslide victories in the UAW presidential balloting in 1947 and afterwards, and auto workers' overwhelming preference for Truman over Henry Wallace in 1948, were coerced? Doesn't it make more sense to insist that the great majority of the automotive working class accepted

Reuther, Truman, and the whole reformed postwar American system, at least in part, willingly? Surely, if we assent to this approach, we are still left with the problem of explaining working people's willingness to embrace what so many radical critics condemned as an inhumane and undemocratic system; but at least we will be building on the two great facts of postwar labor history, instead of having to search for ways to deny or ignore them.

Melvyn Dubofsky's important essay, "Not So Turbulent Years," makes it clear that in most cases of labor militancy during the 1930s, a minority of what he calls "sparkplug unionists" sustained class-conscious activity while the majority of workers participated only infrequently or not at all. Usually the militant unionists were themselves led by an even smaller number of political radicals—Communists, Socialists, and Trotskyites—who no matter how effective they were as union organizers, could never convince more than a tiny portion of the working class to join their political parties. Most of the workers of the 1930s were not only non-militant, Dubofsky asserts, they were profoundly anti-radical.[38] Popular anti-radicalism certainly checked the political ambitions of the radicals who organized rank-and-file auto workers in the 1930s and early 1940s. In fact, most radical organizers urged workers to vote for FDR and other Democratic candidates during those years. More positively, in the tolerant climate fostered by the New Deal and the CIO, radicals who were valued for their organizing skills and energy often won the respect of large numbers of anti-radical working people because establishing a union was the paramount goal they shared.[39]

All this changed with the onset of the Cold War. When the companies, government agencies, politicians, and union leaders all began to speak the anti-radical rhetoric of the Cold War consensus, they did not have to work very hard to convince the automotive working class to reject communism and other left politics; most working people were already convinced. Especially after the disappointing results of the long General Motors strike, they were anxious to get on with the task of making America into the consumer-oriented land of plenty that business and political leaders, the mass media, and their own UAW president said it should and could be. In addition, among the many Eastern European first- and second-generation immigrant workers and their friends in the industry, overt anti-communism spread quickly as the Soviet Union established political control over Poland and the other Eastern European and Balkan nations so recently liberated from the Nazis.

Throughout the postwar era, Walter Reuther spoke out in fa-
vor of making the system work by making sure that workers and
their families could be consumers. Beginning with an article he
aptly titled "Our Fear of Abundance," which first appeared in the
New York Times Magazine in September 1945, Reuther made it
clear that he understood, perhaps better than any of his contemporaries in the labor movement, the dynamics of a second industrial revolution that could make consumers out of workers. His
long campaign for full employment and a guaranteed annual wage
reflected not just his knowledge of how changes in production, the
industrial labor movement, and the New Deal had transformed
American capitalism; it also reflected his empathic understanding
of the beliefs of most auto workers.[40]

As we have seen above, a great variety of evidence indicates
that postwar auto workers endorsed and incorporated into their
lives the new consumer-oriented American Dream. Those workers
believed Ruether in 1946 when he quoted the Federal Reserve's
first *Postwar Economic Study* to insist,

> A rise of 40 or 50 percent above pre-war levels in con-
> sumption goods will be possible and necessary. This
> would mean that people would buy more cars than they
> did in the 1930s, many more ice-boxes, and several
> times the amount of some other goods and services.[41]

After 1946, those same auto workers gave Reuther increasingly
uncritical support when, as president of the UAW, he negotiated
contracts with the Big Three employers that consistently put them
among the most secure and best-paid of America's mass-
production work force. As his recent biographer, John Barnard,
has written, "Reuther secured those material means to a better
life that the union's members wanted."[42]

And, of course, Reuther did more. As the leading anti-
communist social reformer in the American labor movement,
Reuther became a symbol of the way that the materialism inherent in the new consumer-oriented American Dream (and the modern business unionism that sought to secure that Dream for
workers) could be fused with more idealistic goals. Thus, it was
Reuther's genius as a true working class leader to articulate and
champion an ideology that was both a product of the labor struggles of the 1930s and 1940s and a blueprint for what Stanley
Aronowitz has recently called the "social contract unionism" of the
postwar era. "How can we stop Communism?" Reuther asked in
Collier's in 1948,

There is no formula. There is only the never-ending task of making democracy work, keeping it alive and fighting injustice; expanding and enriching it by tangible achievement. Stopping Communism is only a negative aspect of that positive, infinitely more important work.[43]

VI. Consumer-Oriented Americanism

In a beautifully compressed way, the words of Walter Reuther quoted above fuse Cold War anti-communism with post–New Deal labor liberalism and the popular culture of mass-consumer affluence. Indeed, as Reuther's linking them together reveals, these three things lie at the core of the political ideology of the mid-twentieth-century organized working class. This ideology—which might be termed "consumer-oriented Americanism"—was rooted in the transformation of the United States from a producer-oriented to a consumer-oriented society, a transformation that had begun to reshape the everyday lives of the most advanced sectors of the working class as early as the 1920s. From its origins in the often crude initial efforts to nationalize the political and popular cultures of that decade—the Red Scare, Americanization, and the new saturation marketing campaigns—this ideology has penetrated white ethnic and, to a lesser extent, racial subcultures. And after 1945, as an ideology which permeated both politics and popular cultures, it made the United States a progressively more homogeneous society.

Certainly, since the 1950s, rising populations of Hispanic and Asian-Americans and the emergence of the Black Power and women's movements have prevented anything like complete cultural homogenization from occurring. Yet, it is still impossible to look at the content of everyday life today and not recognize the extent to which consumer-oriented Americanism has been embraced by, at the very least, the dominant population of whites of European origin.

This widespread faith in consumer-oriented Americanism explains many of the difficulties in our interpretation of the transformation of politics within the postwar UAW, especially why the majority of the organized automotive working class rejected their own radical rank-and-file union leaders, and accepted a post–New Deal order that put the Cold War ahead of the extension of social justice and of social welfare programs. Consumer-oriented Americanism succeeded first and foremost because it was grounded in

something auto workers felt in their everyday lives, very real improvements in living standards and personal security, which continued through the postwar era. But this ideology also succeeded
precisely because of its ability, through its continual renewal in
politics and popular culture, to simultaneously invoke the terrors
of Communism and the new American Dream of an ever-widening
circle of those who enjoy the pleasures of high-tech consumption
and new leisure time pursuits.

In the ideology of consumer-oriented Americanism, anti-
communism was always linked to the promise of an ever-richer
material existence, as Reuther's postwar speeches and articles reveal. It was not, in other words, a mere political device to be used
or not used as it suited the purposes of political or union leaders.
Anti-communism was the necessary Manichean complement to
the politics and popular culture of affluence. It completed the ideology of consumer-oriented Americanism by turning defense of democracy into acceptance of bi-partisanship, and very important,
by transforming individual materialism (the key dynamic value of
mass-consumer society, though a potential sin in the Christian
tradition) into a positive good. Or to put it more bluntly, anti-
communism made accumulation into a moral crusade.

It was precisely this last point that the radicals among
the UAW's "sparkplug unionists" and early postwar leadership
could never understand. And it was this lack of understanding
that made them vulnerable to what their survivors still call "Reuther's purge." Certainly, Reuther was not himself committed to
a simplified (what we might call today Reaganite) version of
consumer-oriented Americanism. As part of, not just a leader of,
the mid-twentieth-century working class that had formed itself
in the struggle to create industrial unions and implement the New
Deal, Reuther did not want to roll the clock back to 1929. In the
postwar era, Reuther became, through his own efforts and the efforts of others like Eleanor Roosevelt, a symbol of the determination to preserve and extend the legacy of the New Deal, Franklin
Roosevelt, and the progressive CIO of the 1930s. He thus became
a leading spokesman for the liberal variant of the politics of
consumer-oriented Americanism within the UAW and the nation
as a whole.

The transformation of rank-and-file militancy and the rise of
Walter Reuther in the postwar UAW were intimately linked. Unless we see that both were inspired by the same dramatic changes
in everyday life and the same basic ideological commitments, we
will be forced to present these events in paradoxical ways. How-

ever, once we understand the power of consumer-oriented Americanism as an ideological matrix that linked and gave meaning to the separated realms of modern everyday life—to the workplace, family, and citizenship—the paradoxes fade. For the postwar auto workers who generally supported Walter Reuther and consumer-oriented Americanism, the rejection of the radicals who had been instrumental in building up the UAW and sustaining its militant tradition through the unofficial shop steward networks was both repressive and democratic, intolerant and popular. Anticommunism and anti-radicalism were not forced down the throats of most of the postwar automotive working class; they were embraced as intrinsic components of an ideology that made sense of their place in a complex society. Moreover, as we have seen above, the anti-communism of postwar workers did not mean workers necessarily abandoned class consciousness or workplace struggles to better their lives.

After World War II, the workers of the UAW were in the vanguard of their class in both material and political terms; but they were not alone. By the mid-1960s, the majority of America's organized working class who were not victims of the second Red Scare embraced, or at least tolerated, anti-communism because it was an integral part of the New American Dream to which they had committed their lives. Theirs was not an unobtainable dream; nor were their lives empty because of it. Indeed, for at least a quarter of century, the material promises of consumer-oriented Americanism were fulfilled in improvements in everyday life that made them the most affluent working class in American history.

Chapter Seven

"If a Body Catch a Body": The *Catcher in the Rye* Censorship Debate as Expression of Nuclear Culture

Pamela Steinle

In 1951, the American public was introduced to 16-year-old Holden Caulfield, the narrator and central character of J. D. Salinger's first and only novel, *The Catcher in the Rye.* Described in early reviews as "an unusually sensitive and intelligent boy" and as "unbalanced as a rooster on a tightrope,"[1] Holden was and has remained a figure of varied interpretation and much controversy. As recently as 1981, *Catcher* had the dubious distinction of being at once the most frequently censored book across the nation and the second-most frequently taught novel in public high schools.[2] Except for a brief respite in the early 1970s, *Catcher* has been the focal point of literary censorship for the past 35 years— a focus exhibited not only in its premier status on book-banning lists but through repeated references in popular literature and television.[3]

From its initial reception to the present, *The Catcher in the Rye* has been identified as a favorite and formative novel by adolescent and college-level readers alike.[4] In 1961, *Catcher* made its second appearance on the paperback bestseller list of the *New York Times Book Review,* causing *Times* critic Robert Gutwillig to comment that while use in college classes explained some of its high sales figures, "the appeal of *The Catcher in the Rye* extends also to the younger brothers and sisters of the college crowd."[5] At the same time, Edward Corbett reviewed *Catcher* for *America,* and noted that "I have never witnessed on our campus [a Midwestern Jesuit college] as much eager discussion about a book as there was about *The Catcher in the Rye.*"[6] Twenty-five years later, critic Sanford Pinsker argued for *Catcher's* formative value and described himself as "one who fell in love with *The Catcher in the Rye* early, and who has been trying to figure out what that has meant ever since."[7] Richard Stayton took the same approach in a 1985 review, concluding that "Salinger's spiritual odyssey had reached out beyond two decades to teach me a new perspective on myself."[8] Finally, in a bizarre demonstration of *Catcher's* uneasy grip upon the imagination, assassin Mark David Chapman offered *The Catcher in the Rye* as intended justification for the murder of ex-Beatle John Lennon in 1980. Chapman read silently from the novel as he was arrested and, at his sentencing, read aloud the passage which gives *Catcher* its title:

> Anyway, I keep picturing these little kids playing some game in this big field of rye and all. Thousands of little kids, and nobody's around—nobody big, I mean—except me. And I'm standing on the edge of some crazy cliff. What I have to do, I have to catch everybody if they start to go over the cliff—I mean if they're running and they don't look where they're going I have to come out from somewhere and catch them. That's all I'd do all day. I'd just be the catcher in the rye and all.[9]

Simply told, *The Catcher in the Rye* is the tale of 16-year-old Holden Caulfield, who is flunking out of his third prep school and suffers a breakdown of sorts when he leaves school to spend three days on his own in New York City. Holden is the idealistic narrator of the story, which he tells in retrospect from a sanitarium in California. With meticulous adherence to contemporary teenage vernacular, the text is peppered with mild obscenities as Holden condemns much of the postwar adult world. Salinger depicts American society as largely "phony"—a term Holden applies to various definitions of contemporary success: corporate achievement, paradigmatic marriage, physical attractiveness, movies, athletics, and "belonging" via conformity. The "craziness" of Holden's perspective is suggested by the fact that he is well on the way to such success himself if only he would accept it. The novel ends as it begins: with Holden in the sanitarium, expecting to return to "normal life" in the near future, yet with little indication as to how he will do so.

On the surface, then, *Catcher in the Rye* is a rather mundane novel—it is not immediately clear why it has gained the lasting affection and engendered the vehement hostility of so many participants in lengthy and heated public controversies across America. Beyond the opening arguments over whether the novel is "American" or "un-American," the debate over *Catcher's* value and appropriate readership is a Geertzian "note in a bottle." Laden with value judgments and assumptions, the debate is essentially a discourse on the constitution and possibility of moral values and

ethical conduct in mid-twentieth-century America. That this discourse is at least in part an expression of the impact of America's
development and first use of the atomic bomb upon the American
cultural imagination is the thesis of this chapter.

To decipher the dialogue of the *Catcher* debate, I examined the
national discourse on *Catcher* from 1953 to 1983, as it appeared in
newspaper and magazine accounts, editorials, letters to the editor,
and school board minutes. I reviewed the *English Journal, PTA
Magazine,* the American Library Association's *Newsletter on Intellectual Freedom,* and numerous religious publications throughout
this period to understand the role definitions and views of censorship that participants brought to the debate. Finally, I conducted open-ended interviews with past and present participants
in the debate in suburban Alabama, California, New Mexico, and
Virginia.[10]

The *Catcher* censorship debate reflects common experiences
and expression across the thirty-five years of localized controversy—a commonality often explicitly recognized by participants.
One such common element was the complaint about offensive language—by one parent's count, 237 "goddams," 58 "bastards," 32
"chrissakes," and one "fart"[11]—which frequently initiated local
controversies. This is curious since Holden himself repeatedly tries
to erase obscenities written by others. In fact, the initial focus on
language was not the actual center of the debate; rather, language
use was a relatively easy issue for controversy participants to address. Instead, the crux of the *Catcher* debate was whether or not
adolescents should read a novel that effectively portrays postwar
America as a society characterized by social pretense, injustice, in-
equality, and—above all—alienation. Even as the vast majority of
participants, including those against *Catcher,* explicitly agreed
with Salinger's depiction, the question of whether it was appropriate reading for adolescents dominated the dialogue as the controversies reached full steam at school board meetings and in
exchanges of letters to the editor in local newspapers.

Yet locating the center of the debate does not explain its longevity or the peculiar angst which characterized both the dialogue
and the participant interviews and recollections. Many participants were aware of *Catcher's* controversial history, yet teachers
continued to assign it as "necessary" reading, and people who had
never before been involved in censorship actions sought to ban it—
and, on both sides, often at considerable personal cost to their local reputation, marriage and family relationships, and physical
and emotional health.[12] While local controversies were frequently

resolved by *Catcher's* retention as reading on reserve, requiring parental approval, the most valuable outcome for many was a renewal of belief in the democratic process as a consequence of first-hand confrontation with the meaning of tolerance and responsibility in the pursuit of individual freedom.

Consider the interview statement of a postman and school board member in the Alabama controversy:

> Personally, if it was my decision and it was going to be a final decision, I'd have a bonfire. But, you know, I know, I don't have a final decision and I've got to use some reason too, and a parent wants their children to read things I consider vulgary or trash, that's the parent that'll have to answer, that'll have to watch that child.
>
> The Constitution gives certain rights and you can't just sweep those things under the mat. That's why I said, you know, if I had to be objective I'd get rid of 'em: if I had the final say, they wouldn't be here. But I know that's not the final say and I don't say it, that's not the way it's going to be. So, the only solution I know is what we did. It's, ah, they're still available. The parent wants to do it, go read 'em.[13]

Such democratic resolution of the local controversies often led to a good deal of back-patting and good-spirited handshaking among participants, and indeed might be further applauded by Robert Bellah (et al.) who, in *Habits of the Heart*,[14] decried as well as documented the lack of sincere, local, democratic participation in postwar American society. However, the value of the form of resolution directs attention away from the unresolved question of exactly what it is that is at stake in an adolescent's reading of *The Catcher in the Rye*. In the course of the debate what is claimed to be at stake is the "character" of American adolescents. On one side, the reading of novels critical of American experience is deemed necessary to prepare adolescents for responsible adulthood. A parent in one of the 1960 controversies lauded the efforts of other pro-*Catcher* participants "who wish their children to be free, and they take the position that the freedom to read, training to read, training of critical thinking is invaluable."[15] An educator writing for *PTA Magazine* in 1963 linked this position with his interpretation of *Catcher:*

> We should judge books not so much on the basis of the world they portray as by the judgments they make on

that world. What kind of life are they asking for? *The Catcher in the Rye* . . . is calling for a good world in which people can connect. . . . [16]

In opposition, protesting participants believe that reading *Catcher* will "weaken the moral fiber of the students," by serving as "a teenage primer to debauchery."[17] In the same 1960 controversy, another parent compared adolescents' reading of *Catcher* to the training of dogs by "rubbing their noses in filth,"

> destroying their desire and will to be good citizens or their faith in principles and the good character of others. . . . To shock a young person who is passing through the most sensitive and idealistic years of his or her life into insensitiveness only defeats constructive ends.[18]

The division, then, is over whether to prepare adolescents for or to protect them from adult disillusionment, and it is a split I believe indicates a contemporary crisis in the process of middle class enculturation. In modern middle class American parenting, as in expressive forms of culture such as the novel, adolescence has served as a complex symbol of cultural innocence and hope for the future. While the sheer pace of social change and the factor of individual mobility have long made it difficult to prepare an American child for an adulthood of uncertain circumstances, it has been assumed that whatever that adulthood might encompass, it would take place in an ever-brighter future. In the postwar period, however, recognition of the increasing dissonance between American ideals and the realities of social experience has become unavoidable, and it is precisely this cultural dissonance that is highlighted by Salinger's novel.

The widely shared critical interpretation of the title passage is that Holden sees his own late adolescence as a precipitous jump or fall from the cherished ideals and innocence of childhood to the inauthentic and cynical social reality of adulthood.[19] As "the catcher in the rye," Holden, like those who seek to censor the novel, seeks to "catch" children before they can fall over the "crazy cliff." Furthermore, a crucial fact about *Catcher*—as opposed to interpretive readings of it—is that Holden does not reject the historically central values of individualism, family, democracy, and equality: He criticizes their faulty enactment in American society and lambasts the tautological replacement of morality with normality, and its corollary value of conformity. In this sense, *Catcher* is indeed a very American novel, as Salinger's carefully drawn characterization of Holden is the very embodiment of the American Adam, and his eloquent critique of contemporary society is recognizable as part of the long-standing "determining debate" given coherent definition by R. W. B. Lewis.[20]

However, Holden is situated in a context in which hopefulness and belief in the endless availability of new beginnings—so characteristic of the American Adam—are no longer credible. When Huck Finn as the prototypical adolescent Adam "lights out for the territories," he is not only moving forward in time and space but in the hopeful pursuit of ideals that have been strengthened from being tested by the challenge of experience. In marked contrast, when Holden confronts his own morality, any perception of hope for individual distinctiveness is dashed by his recognition of contemporary chaos and anonymity:

> That's the whole trouble. You can't ever find a place that's nice and peaceful, because there isn't any. You may *think* there is, but once you get there, when you're not looking, somebody'll sneak up and write "Fuck you" right under your nose. Try it sometime. I think even, if I ever die, and they stick me in a cemetery, and I have a tombstone and all, it'll say "Holden Caulfield" on it, and then what year I was born and what year I died, and then right under that it'll say "Fuck you." I'm positive, in fact.[21]

Even more jarring is the replacement of the image of Huck on a raft with the image of Holden astride a nuclear warhead. Where Huck's escape route portends the sense of adventure inherent in a new beginning, Holden's fantasied "escape" is consciously suicidal and prescient of *Dr. Strangelove:*

> Anyway, I'm sort of glad they've got the atomic bomb invented. If there's ever another war, I'm going to sit right the hell on top of it. I'll volunteer for it, I swear to God I will.[22]

Hence, where *Catcher* emphasizes the increasing difficulty adolescents face attempting to bridge the chasm between the worlds of childhood and adult experience, the very sense of the future itself is here called into question. Indeed, the metaphorical "ghost at the banquet"—or in this case at the debate—whose presence explains the angst and extraordinary personal investment of participants in local controversies, is the specter of nuclear annihilation. Just as Holden, wishing to refuse the "killing adjustments" required by his impending participation in adult society, finds he cannot return to the innocence of childhood, America, with the development and use of the Bomb—however necessary or justifiable—reached a state of maturity that rendered the ideology of American innocence finally untenable. *Catcher in the Rye* appeals to contemporary readers through their familiarity with its Adamic narrator; the lack of resolution in the novel speaks not only to the futility of contemporary experience but to the frightening absence of a future of any certainty.

In fact, debate participants shared a vague yet pervasive fearfulness of a present and future over which they have little, if any, control. Fearfulness was the common denominator and often the dominant characteristic of every interview I conducted. When asked what he thought was at the root of a 1960–61 California controversy, a local high school principal repeated the response of many participants: "I think it just stems from fear."[23] Also typical was his inability to expand upon or articulate the actual nature or source of this fear: Instead, he fell into a meditative silence for a few minutes and then abruptly began to speak of how the specific issue of *Catcher's* status was resolved—"controlled"—by the school board.

While statements by many participants suggested they were more comfortable speaking of ways they managed their uneasiness about the fate of American society rather than the source of that uneasiness, a few participants either directly specified or alluded to the threat of nuclear annihilation—often in seemingly incongruous contexts. A pro-*Catcher* parent in Alabama stated that there are "so many other areas of concern, that censorship is just a small part of it, because there is the nuclear, the school prayer [long pause], all that goes together."[24] Another pro-*Catcher* parent argued:

> In these perilous times, it is not just a case of war and peace but a question of the survival of mankind and our ideals. We have to educate our children to become responsible citizens.[25]

A 1981 essay, suggestively titled "The Censorship War: Librarians at the Battlefront," was more specific about the peril. Encouraging the fight against censorship of novels such as *Catcher,* librarian Charles Park wrote:

> The freedom to learn, to have access to information, is being threatened today. The stakes are higher, higher

than ever before, for we are all very much in the shadow of a mushroom cloud.[26]

Critic Marcus Klein included *Catcher* among significant mid-century American fiction and emphasized the nuclear context in which to understand it. Here, Klein's interpretation is typical of references to nuclearism in the works of many literary critics and historians:

> The terror beyond evil is the murder that occurred in the Second World War together with the prospect become familiar of entire and utter annihilation. We are all half-dead of it already. . . . [27]

Adolescent readers also placed *Catcher* in this context. A sixteen-year-old female high school student who wrote "I accept *The Catcher in the Rye* as part of myself," argued that "Holden's perambulating thoughts and abusive language help paint the picture of bitter confusion which surrounds this boy as he gropes about for stable bearings, wondering if there are any." "The bitterness," she further explained,

> is derived in part from the uncertainty of the future. It is the fear that you are looking forward to something that won't exist that makes you acrid and spiteful. Maybe the future will consist of rehashed memories; you are only closer to dying each day as you wallow in your rut remembering how you and the gang played kick-the-can when you were twelve.[28]

That the "uncertainty of the future" is an allusion to the threat of nuclear annihilation is clarified not only by her fear that the future "won't exist" but by the congruence of her statement with those of adolescents writing on nuclearism. In a 1978–1980 study, Cambridge psychiatrist John Mack asked 10th to 12th grade students, "Have nuclear advances affected your way of thinking about the future, your view of the world, and time?" Typical student responses were:

(A) I think that, unless we do something about nuclear weapons the world and the human race may not have much time left (corny, huh?).

(B) It gives me a pretty dim view of the world and mankind but it hasn't really influenced me.

(C) Everything has to be looked at on two levels: the world with the threat of ending soon, and life with future, etc. The former has to be blocked out for everyday functioning because very few people can find justification for living otherwise. But [it] is always there—on a much larger scale than possibilities of individual deaths, car accidents, etc.—even though the result to me personally would be the same.[29]

Adolescent reliance on denial as a method of psychic survival is at least in part a learned response. As Mack concluded:

The experience of powerlessness of children and adolescents, the sense that they have that matters are out of control, is not different from the way most adults feel in relation to the nuclear arms race. Little can be done to help our young people unless adults address the apathy and helplessness that we experience in relation to the arms race and the threat of nuclear war.[30]

Indeed, even as Americans "profess not to be troubled," a 1983 Harris poll found that "two-thirds of America expected a nuclear war sometime in the next twenty years."[31] The increasing frequency and lowering age of clinical depression as well as escalating adolescent suicide[32] further suggest that America is failing to provide its youth with a sense of a viable future.

Correspondingly, in 1987 Phyllis La Farge documented responses of alternating fearful awareness and concerted denial in the drawings and written work of children from kindergarten to high school. One response pointed out the apparent irrelevance of education in light of the nuclear threat:

I'm angry because I feel I won't have a future like most people and I ask myself, why do I take classes I hate, such as science and math when maybe I won't live to use my knowledge from those classes in college. I feel helpless. I keep trying to kid myself and forget about any possibilities of a nuclear war.[33]

Furthermore, children recognize the paralysis and helplessness of adults in the face of the nuclear threat. For example, a grammar school student wrote:

Dear President Reagan,
    I am sure that my parents don't like knowing that I may never reach 21 or even 12 since I'm only 11. You may not be causing it but you can control it in the U.S.[34]

This child recognizes parental powerlessness but believes that the power to insure the future lies within Presidential authority. As children mature, recognition of adult powerlessness becomes less manageable, and adolescent suspicions that it is not powerlessness as much as complicity evoke their anger. One high school student, sounding very much like Holden Caulfield, wrote:

> It [nuclear advances] has shown me how stupid some adults can be. If they know it could easily kill them I have no idea why they support it. Once in a while it makes me start to think that the end of my life might not be as far off as I would like it to be.[35]

It is this fear of nuclear holocaust, not the fear of four-letter words, that I believe is at the heart of the *Catcher* debate. The lack of faith in the American character expressed in the *Catcher* controversies is rooted not in doubts about the strength of adolescent Americans' character but in recognition of the powerlessness of American adults—as parents, professionals and community leaders—to provide a genuine sense of the future for the adolescents in their charge. *The Catcher in the Rye* is an indictment of adult apathy and complicity in the construction of a social reality in which the American character cannot develop in any meaningful sense beyond adolescence.

And it is an indictment that, however accurate, many adults wish their children to avoid as long as possible. Phyllis La Farge concluded from her work that, "never losing hope is what all parents fervently want for their children," which leads them to "try to encourage hopefulness by keeping silent about the nuclear weapons, the arms race, and other issues."[36] *The Catcher in the Rye* confronts adults with not only the impossibilities of this wishful protection but with its dysfunctional consequences: In its "very American" embrace of the pursuit of life, liberty, and happiness, and in the embodiment of the American Adam in the radical idealism of Holden Caulfield, it is mature American society that is "un-American" in its apathy, denial, and pursuit of superficial comforts in the shadow of nuclear annihilation.

Chapter Eight

The Domestication of Rock and Roll: From Insurrection to Myth

Larry Bennett

For the audience attending the Monterey Pop Festival in June 1967, two of the most astonishing acts were The Who and The Jimi Hendrix Experience. Both bands hailed from England, though Hendrix was a native of Seattle, Washington, and their approaches to stage performance were nearly unknown in the United States. Pete Townshend's guitar playing was The Who's visual center. Townshend manipulated the instrument violently, playing "power chords" with wide windmill sweeps of his right arm. As he played guitar, Townshend also roamed across the stage, punctuating his horizontal movement with acrobatic leaps. Townshend regularly brought The Who's sets to a close by smashing his guitar on the stage. As Townshend hacked the group's Monterey performance to an end, Keith Moon reciprocated the downstage violence by kicking over his drum kit. Townshend, vocalist Roger Daltrey, and bass player John Entwistle walked off the stage at about the moment the last drum bounced to the floor.

Guitarist Jimi Hendrix had observed The Who in London, and during his band's appearance at Monterey he was determined to top Townshend's stage gyrations. Hendrix was a master of guitar distortion, at times seeming to lose track of melody and rhythm altogether, but invariably reining in his instrument and storming through signature tunes such as "Purple Haze" and "Foxey Lady." At Monterey Hendrix joined his sonic assault to wild stage antics. He trumped Townshend's leaps and power chords by seeming to play the guitar with his teeth, and to close his performance Hendrix poured lighter fluid on his guitar and ignited it.

In just a few years popular music had experienced a remarkable transformation. At the beginning of the 1960s record producers controlled the song selection and performance styles of singers such as Lesley Gore, Bobby Rydell, and Bobby Vee. When these singers appeared before live audiences they were expected to deliver controlled replicas of their recorded songs. The performer was subordinate to the song and its arrangement. The performers who succeeded during this era were careful professionals, or they were directed by careful professionals.

The stage performances of The Who and The Jimi Hendrix Experience were not intended to reproduce recordings. Nor were Pete Townshend and Jimi Hendrix engaging in the "soloing" or extensions of recorded performances favored by jazz musicians. Rather, these musicians were staging ritualistic performances in which they seemed to give up their rational, musicianly selves to the power of the music. In this respect Townshend and Hendrix recalled nineteenth-century Romantic musicians such as Paganini and Liszt, whose theatrical performances also combined technical virtuosity and visionary soulfulness.

Also like their Romantic predecessors, members of The Who and The Jimi Hendrix Experience lived wild personal lives, the visionary performer's source of the exhilaration and pain that may be recycled as art. Yet in the years that followed the Monterey Pop Festival the careers and lives of The Who and of Jimi Hendrix took different courses. Like a true nineteenth-century Romantic, Hendrix mixed private and musical conflagrations, succumbing to a drug overdose in 1970. The Who carried on through the 1970s, although the band lost much of its fire following the death of Keith Moon. Ironically, by the late 1980s Pete Townshend, the demonic model for Hendrix's stage exploits, had given up regular performing and was working as an editor for a London publishing house.

Jimi Hendrix's life and death conform to one of the principal paradigms of the rock and roll subculture: the impassioned performer who flames briefly, brightly, and imaginatively before self-destructing. Through sound recordings, films, and videotapes Hendrix continues to live for young followers of rock and roll. In the view of many of these fans, Hendrix undoubtedly gave his life for his music. For informed parents and antagonists of rock and roll, Hendrix's story communicates a related message. They note Hendrix's freakish appearance, eccentric performances, and desperate reputation, and link these to rock and roll's unsavory milieu of lavish spending, sex, and drugs. In their view, the music kills indiscriminately.

Pete Townshend's less conventional story, which includes elements that are for most people quite conventional, such as maturing and finding employment in an orthodox profession, also sheds light on the life of rock and roll performers. Townshend must have found the legacy of The Who very difficult to bear as he approached his forties, and rather than continue to go through the motions of recreating past musical deeds, he gave up performance with his old band.[1]

The contrasting stories of Hendrix and Townshend underline the central paradoxes of rock and roll as a component of popular culture in the United States. On the one hand, millions of young fans find in rock and roll an emotionally liberating sonic experience, and some portion of these listeners absorb important political cues from particular performers. Although adversaries of rock and roll are usually loath to notice these messages, possibly because of their forceful precision as social commentary, performers such as The Beatles, Frank Zappa, Steely Dan, Bruce Springsteen, The Clash, and U2 have attacked militarism and racism while advocating economic justice and individual self-reflection. Rock and roll is not simply music for idiots; however, it has also not produced a revolution.

On the other hand, critics of rock and roll have accused it of inducing moral decay, undermining literacy, and subverting basic social values. Just how these degradations are accomplished is not often specified, and only rarely do commentators outside the subculture recognize the economic underpinnings of rock and roll in the "entertainment industry." One of the exceptions is Allan Bloom, who after devoting considerable energy to identifying rock and roll's contribution to the "closing of the American mind," adds that the rock and roll industry is "perfect capitalism."[2] Bloom, however, does not explore the nature of this connection. A professional economist might challenge Bloom's assertion; but it is of particular interest because of its acknowledgment that rock and roll is not so much an aberrant or deviant feature of popular culture in the United States as an artistic form linked to economic structures well within the social mainstream.

In the pages to follow I explore these paradoxes. In the first place, we will look at characterizations of rock and roll by both friendly observers and critics, noting a set of fairly consistent, distinctive interpretive threads. What links each of these interpretive threads is a tendency to misconstrue the role and the place of rock and roll within popular culture in the United States. From this account of how rock and roll is interpreted we will turn to the construction of a paradigmatic rock and roll "career," noting the usual meanings attached to phases of the rock and roll life and also observing the mythic character of this paradigm. In essence, by tracing the relationship between what often happens to rock and roll performers and the widely shared understanding of how rock and roll sweeps performers through their lives, we can begin to explain both the continuing appeal of the music to its practitioners and listeners as well as its domestication as a popular culture form.

Various Roads to Hell

Commentators on rock and roll have devoted a substantial amount of energy to defining the meaning of the term, but in practice it remains a very slippery notion. This slipperiness is due, in part, to rock and roll's diverse sources and the variety of genres it encompasses. For instance, sociologist Simon Frith finds sources of rock and roll in black music, country music, folk music, and pop music, while Charlie Gillett, in his encyclopedic history, *The Sound of the City,* identifies five distinguishable rock and roll genres as early as the mid-1950s.[3] Contemporary rock and roll is no less diverse, and indeed, is so cross-pollinated that defining the boundaries of its performance is probably futile. Consider this juxtaposition: In the mid-1980s former folk singer Paul Simon released well-received recordings supported by pop instrumentalists from South Africa; coincidentally multi-instrumentalist and singer Prince fashioned a musical synthesis incorporating sources as diverse as James Brown and The Beatles. Yet many rock and roll listeners appreciated both performers.

Even if we could precisely define the parameters of rock and roll performance we would not have a satisfactory definition of the term, as attention to singing and instrumental styles only begins to deal with the pervasiveness of its cultural effects. Rock and roll also incorporates millions of fans whose ambitions, behavioral norms, and consumption patterns are shaped by their musical preferences. These consumers of rock and roll, in turn, are served by an extensive economic network of large entertainment corporations and struggling "indie" recording labels, the manufacturers and marketers of auxiliary products such as clothing and posters, and the regional and local promoters, clubs, and auditoriums booking performers for on-stage performances.

Given these complexities, the following discussion treats rock and roll as a subculture.[4] There are several advantages to this approach. It is inclusive, permitting the discussion of performers representing a wide array of genres. Furthermore, my intention is to explore how meaning is attached to rock and roll by performers, fans, and critics alike. Thus, rock and roll's status can be emphasized as a cultural medium not wholly outside the mainstream, but also not clearly within the mainstream. Viewing rock and roll as a subculture also underlines how rock and roll performers and fans have developed a self-conscious sense of their own history, which includes heroes, villains, and widely held attitudes on a variety of topics. In the pages to follow, the characterization of rock and roll incorporates these elements: a wide-ranging set of overlapping musical genres, a large, loyal, and self-conscious cadre of fans, and a substantial segment of the entertainment industry itself.

Since the emergence of rock and roll in the 1950s, three main lines of interpretation have sought to define its social meaning. The first of these may be termed the "high culture" position, which emphasizes rock and roll's deficiency as a medium of artistic expression. A second critical perspective is "moralistic," pointing to the immoral content of rock and roll lyrics and lifestyles, and ultimately the immoral effect of rock and roll on listeners. Partisans of rock and roll accept some of the claims of the preceding views, but recast their implications to define rock and roll as a socially critical, populist musical form. In the words of historian George Lipsitz:

> Like the mass demonstration and wildcat strike, the good time in rock-and-roll songs elevates the world of play over the world of work, and carves away a limited sphere of autonomy in an increasingly regimented environment.[5]

The high culture perspective actually preceded the invention of rock and roll. Since the emergence of mass culture media early in the twentieth century, critics had attacked the standardization and commodification of mass art forms such as movies and popular songs, as well as their psychically manipulative effects on their consumers. Thus, Theodor Adorno, in disparaging even the comparatively refined media of Broadway show tunes and central European operetta, could speak of songs in which "everything can be replaced by something else." As for the effect of popular songs, he added that "they reckon with the immature, with those who cannot express their emotions and experiences, who either never had the power of expression or were crippled by cultural taboos."[6]

Compared to Broadway musicals and operetta, rock and roll pioneers such as Elvis Presley, Bill Haley, and Little Richard were the objects of outright hostility. Television critic John Crosby described Presley as an "unspeakably untalented and vulgar young entertainer," while in the aftermath of rioting at a Hartford, Connecticut, rock and roll concert in 1956, a local psychiatrist termed rock and roll a "communicable disease."[7]

At this point the moralistic critique of rock and roll emerged and to some degree intermingled with the high culture perspective. Rock and roll was characterized as a primitive means of expression, a point underlined by the low-budget recording techniques used by independent producers such as Sam Phillips and the fevered live performances of Presley, Little Richard, and others. Critics of rock and roll typically were disturbed by the sexual suggestiveness of these performers, which no doubt played a large part in their popularity among teenagers. The producers of Ed Sullivan's television show, one of popular entertainment's principal gatekeepers in the 1950s and 1960s, struck just the right bargain between marketing and morality. Presley was invited to perform before a national television audience, but the cameramen were instructed not to record his already legendary pelvic undulations.

The threat to public morals embodied by Presley and his comrades was linked to another cultural taboo in the South, where many of the early rock and roll performers were based. In late March 1956, the *New York Times* reported that the Executive Secretary of the North Alabama White Citizens Council had claimed that "the National Association for the Advancement of Colored People had 'infiltrated' southern white teenagers with 'rock and roll' music."[8] In seeking the removal of "immoral" records from jukeboxes, Asa Carter of the White Citizens Council was voicing a widespread concern that rock and roll contributed to racial mixing.

One of the crucial characteristics of rock and roll's development is its periodic retrenchment, which at times is the result of younger performers seeking to rejuvenate their art through the incorporation of older styles, but at other times grows out of pressure exercised by recording company executives and producers. In the late 1950s, rock and roll's threat to teenage morals and racial separation was met head-on by the recording industry. The new music's leading performer, Elvis Presley, was signed to a contract by a major recording company, RCA-Victor, and thereafter produced less intense recordings, retired from public performances, and devoted considerable energy to a movie career.[9] Other incendiary performers such as Chuck Berry, Jerry Lee Lewis, and Little Richard had brushes with the law, moved to more orthodox musical styles, or failed to sustain their early popularity. By the early

1960s, the spark of rock and roll was contained. Major record companies recruited film and television personalities such as Tab Hunter and Rick Nelson to make sanitized recordings for the teenage audience, and there was little chance that wilder performances could cross over from "race" or "rhythm and blues" markets to the larger white teenage audience. As soon as race records became hits in regional markets or among black teenagers, more controlled "cover" versions would be released by white performers. For instance, two of Pat Boone's early hits, "Ain't That a Shame" and "Tutti Frutti," had been recorded first by Fats Domino and Little Richard, respectively.[10]

This period of quiescence was temporary. In the early 1960s new performers sprang up across the country and invaded America from across the Atlantic. The British Invasion, led by The Beatles and The Rolling Stones, reintroduced volume, rhythmic dexterity, and social commentary to rock and roll. Ironically, many of the English invaders anchored their early performance repertoires with cover versions of songs by the likes of Chuck Berry and Little Richard. But in the mid-1960s black performers recording for independent labels such as Motown (The Four Tops, The Supremes, The Temptations) and Atlantic (Aretha Franklin and Otis Redding) also reached large and appreciative white audiences. Across the United States "garage bands" recorded in a variety of styles. For every garage band like The Young Rascals (later, simply The Rascals), which developed a durable "white soul" style, there were dozens of groups like The Count Five, The Knickerbockers, and The Thirteenth Floor Elevators that recorded one hit song and disappeared. As in the mid-1950s, much of rock and roll was being produced and consumed with only limited intermediation by corporate decision makers; and indeed, the audience was expanding so rapidly that even the best-known performers, with contracts to record for major recording companies, were given substantial leeway in preparing their recorded performances.

These were heady times, and by the end of the 1960s rock and roll's principal themes of teenage adventure and sexual exploration were transformed to a more self-conscious critique of mainstream culture. Tom Smucker, in a recollection of his weekend at the Woodstock Festival in the summer of 1969, wrote: "Rock, and its constellation of associations—Dope, Hippie Ideals and Styles—gave a form for our middle-class avant garde rebellion against tedium and repressions that wasn't associated with the irrelevant and abhorrent situations of the past."[11] Smucker's use of "rock" as an alternative for "rock and roll" suggests the seriousness with which this critique was offered. The music had grown up, and, in communicating values such as cooperation, personal introspection, and emotional honesty, rock and roll performers and proponents of their music were distancing themselves from the generation of Bill Haley, Elvis Presley, and Little Richard.

Gillett recalls that publications such as *Rolling Stone* magazine acclaimed "the new musicians as visionaries with a spiritual purity that could permanently alter art, politics, and society."[12] In many instances these very rock and roll performers were surprised by the expansiveness of their fans' expectations. Stanley Booth, traveling with The Rolling Stones on tour in the United States in 1969, recounts the band's indifference to their American audience's demand for political statements. Songs such as "Streetfighting Man" and "Sympathy for the Devil," which members of the band viewed as vehicles for rollicking exhaltation, were construed by their fans as calls to direct political action.[13]

In the late 1960s there were also shifts in the characterization of rock and roll by commentators outside the subculture. A variety of intellectuals, often academics or artists, offered approving commentary on rock and roll, at times noting the growing artistic facility of performers, in other instances praising the emotional directness of rock and rollers. Yet as the rock and roll subculture expanded, seemed to become more autonomous, and appeared to permeate every corner of daily life, troublesome new concerns were voiced by observers on the outside. In 1968, Benjamin De-Mott, an English professor at Amherst College, wrote something like a novice's guide to rock and roll for the *New York Times Magazine*. DeMott's analysis was generally favorable, but one of his comments suggests an emerging variant of the moralistic critique of rock and roll: "Rock seems at moments only a footnote to the pot or drug experience, not an independent meditative engagement in its own right."[14]

Hostile critics developed this line of analysis much more strenuously, as evidenced by the following reaction to The Rolling Stones' "Sticky Fingers" album: "Is the milieu that nurtured the Stones—a young, despairing world of violence, ugliness, drugs and an unmistakable impulse toward self-destruction—still out there waiting for the anti-heros of old? Will the tribes still gather to enjoy the Stones' personal exhortation to reduce civilization to pot-smoking ruins?"[15] Rock and roll decadence had been added to the arsenal of the moralistic commentators.

During the 1970s a variety of trends within the subculture gave force to this critique. Big stars were amassing remarkable fortunes and often spending their wealth quite foolishly. Performers developing a new genre, heavy metal, produced music at truly deafening levels and composed lyrics with routine references to violence and satanism. By the mid-1970s another new genre, disco, won the opprobrium of "hard rockers" with its highly produced, lyrical recordings, but at the same time introduced a club scene in which gays played a very visible role.

These developments signaled the fragmentation of what a few years before had seemed to be a nearly monolithic rock and roll audience, and by the mid-1970s both fans and friendly critics complained of "sell-out" releases by the likes of Paul McCartney, the enfeeblement of John Lennon and The Rolling Stones, and the soporific professionalism of other popular performers such as Fleetwood Mac. In the wake of this malaise, younger musicians in England and the United States began to fashion the punk movement. Punks reduced their instrumental attack to guitar, bass, and drums; on stage, they produced harsh, loud music, at strikingly fast tempos. In the case of some of the leading punk bands, notably The Clash, an unprecedented social critique—emphasizing the realities of the class system and the pervasiveness of racism—was embedded in the lyrics of songs such as "Career Opportunities," "London's Burning," and "White Riot." On the street, punks introduced provocative styles of dress, coiffure, and make-up suggesting fascinations with sexual perversion and death.[16] However, as Simon Frith noted in 1977, punk's principal target was not bourgeois society, but the record industry itself:

> The reason why teenage music must be remade is because all of the original rock 'n' rollers have become boring old farts, imprisoned by the routines of showbiz, by the distant calculations of profit-making, by delusions of rock as art and bourgeois commodity. From this perspective the return to rock 'n' roll roots is, in itself, a radical rejection of record company habits and punk's musical simplicity is a political statement. The ideology of the garage band is an attack on the star system.[17]

Frith's analysis is singular in two respects. First, he notes a new twist in the rock and roll subculture's sense of itself because the punks not only were aware of the legacy of previous performers such as The Rolling Stones, Led Zeppelin, The Jefferson Airplane, and The Grateful Dead, but they were seeking to undo part of that legacy. Their movement was a retrenchment to rock and roll roots in which performers eschewed the trappings of fame and fortune, fancy instruments, and pseudo-artistry. In addition, Frith presages the ultimate decline of the punk movement. Teenage punk performers recording for tiny record labels could attack aging performers and their major companies, but in the long run the more ambitious and successful among them would probably come to terms with CBS, Warner-Elektra-Atlantic, or A&M. Performers needed the industry in order to survive, and relatively few punk fans were inclined to sustain a cause whose goal was the fracturing of the recording business.

The rock and roll industry rode out the punk insurgency. Some of the most talented new performers, such as Elvis Costello and Talking Heads, began to reach listeners well beyond the original punk audience. Others, like the Sex Pistols, disintegrated very quickly. Rock and roll commentators often characterized the 1980s as a period of excessive genre fragmentation, in which relatively insulated clusters of fans appreciated specific forms of rock and roll without extending their attention to any of a wide array of alternative styles. Probably the most significant consequence of this genre segmentation was the separation of white and black listening audiences.[18]

In the era of Ronald Reagan the drumbeat of the moralistic attack on rock and roll continued, leading to such events as the Senate Commerce, Science, and Transportation Committee's hearings on rock and roll lyrics, which were instigated by the Parents Music Resource Center (PMRC). The essential aimlessness of the hearings is suggested by the *New York Times'* account of Dee Snider's (vocalist with the heavy metal band, Twisted Sister) testimony: "Mr. Snider defended his song 'Under the Blade,' saying it had nothing to do with bondage, rape and sado-masochism, as Mrs. Gore [of PMRC] had charged, but rather dealt with the apprehension one faces before undergoing surgery."[19] Nonetheless, reacting to pressure from the PMRC and other right-wing groups, recording companies and retailers began to place warning labels on "offensive" releases, typically awarding this designation to rap and heavy metal performers.[20]

Although Tipper Gore of the PMRC is unlikely to agree, rock and roll is here to stay; but for reasons that neither rock and roll adversaries—the high culture critics and moralists—nor the rock and roll partisans have satisfactorily explained. The moralists cannot come to grips with rock and roll's contribution to the social assimilation, or more simply, the growing up of teenagers and young adults. On the one hand, rock and roll instructs fans in very orthodox ways of consumption; on the other, the subculture's assumptions regarding how performers age and lose their integrity demonstrate the futility of willful, independent action by individuals. The high culture critics cannot account for the ongoing vitality of rock and roll, whether measured by the appearance of new and newer performers, often inventing their own styles, or by more conventional standards such as attendance at on-stage performances and purchase of recordings.

But by looking at the paradigmatic rock and roll career we can identify the sliver of freedom promised to performers and fans even as the subculture presumes the ultimate flaming out of the rock and roll fire. Rock and roll partisans rarely can account for the subculture's particular form of social marginality, which is defined by rock and roll's inability either to enter the pantheon of esteemed arts or spark a revolution in youth attitudes, social practice, or political commitments.[21] Again, by looking at what often happens to rock and roll performers and the meanings typically attached to these passages we can explore some of the roots of this marginal status.

Stations of the Crossover

The identities, lives, and artistic objectives of rock and roll performers are of great importance to their fans. Observers of the music industry note that recording companies market performers as much as performances; so from this perspective interest in the performers' lives is a useful ingredient in selling recordings. Furthermore, as a particular market within the music industry, rock and roll's publicity machinery has been unusually active. Since the 1950s dozens of magazines, newspapers, and newsletters have reported on the lives, artistic turmoils, and business dealings of rock and roll performers. In the 1950s and early 1960s these publications were typically "fanzines," which in Simon Frith's words, focused on performers' "human interest details" by pitching them weighty questions such as "What is your favorite color?"[22] Contemporary publications, such as *Rolling Stone* and *Spin,* devote more attention to artistic questions, but these are still presented in the context of the lives and personal minutiae of performers.

However, to characterize the interest in performers' lives in this fashion does not do full justice to the sources of this interest. Since the early 1950s, when David Riesman discussed a "minority

group" of popular music listeners who appreciated the music of
"unadvertised small bands," insisted on "rigorous standards of
judgment," and often expressed "dissident" political values, commentators on popular music have noted the existence of a fraction
of listeners who have demanded more of this music than pleasing
background sounds and sentimental lyrical expression.[23] In the
1960s, listeners' interest in the lives of performers was grounded
in the concern for authentic performance, an outgrowth of rock
and roll's incorporation of black and folk music conventions, both
genres emphasizing direct emotional expression by performers,
which was coupled with the rock and rollers' self-conscious exploration of political themes in their own performances.[24]

Yet the fascination of rock and roll listeners with rock and roll
lives has an even more fundamental source, which is suggested by
Gillett's contention that rock and roll emerged at the point when
youthful performers began to make music for a youth audience.[25]
From this perspective, what made Elvis Presley more exciting
than Frank Sinatra (as well as long-in-the-tooth rock and rollers
such as Bill Haley) was that he was a teenager who had more or
less stumbled into a recording career. Not only was his obscure
background a source of inspiration, but how he coped with wealth
and fame offered a continuing story. Twenty years later this con-
flation of performer and audience gave power to the punk movement, through its effort "to abolish the distance, and then the
difference, between performer and audience."[26] On the one hand,
bands such as The Ramones demonstrated that exciting music
could be made by untutored musicians. On the other hand, fans
played a major role in defining the image of the movement. For
example, Dave Laing reports that a particular punk fan, Sid Vicious, was credited with developing punk's first dance, the pogo.
Vicious later achieved greater notoriety when he was recruited to
play bass in the Sex Pistols.[27]

In short, listener interest in the lives of rock and roll performers is not simply an outgrowth of record company marketing.
Many rock and roll fans seek to understand the artistic objectives
of performers, and beyond musical aesthetics, look to performers
as sources for their personal styles of dress and behavior. However,
the careers of rock and roll performers and the reporting of these
careers in newspapers, magazines, and electronic media tend to
follow a narrowly confined course. There is a characteristic rise
and fall in the careers of rock and roll performers, and within this
overall framework are several well-defined crossroads. In describing this overall pattern and some of its principal variations we can

identify a fundamental source of rock and roll's partial cultural incorporation as well as the political quiescence of its fans.

Cult, Crossover, Transcendence, and Sell-Out

The prototypical rock and roll career begins in a specific locale, which is usually a large city but may be an atypical smaller community such as a college town. An individual performer or band begins to build a following through live performances, and given sufficient degrees of success and ambition, at some point makes recordings. At this stage of such a prototypical career, the recordings will be made by a small or independent company rather than one of the major entertainment corporations such as Warner-Elektra-Atlantic. With continued success on stage or through these first recordings, the performers will move on to perform outside the home community and possibly sign a recording contract with a major company.

The performer or band who moves through these early stages of a career will have developed a small, loyal core of "cult" fans, who have attended many performances and may even know members of the group personally. Indeed, some performers continue to have a cult following even after signing and recording with a major label. Through listener word of mouth, sympathetic attention from radio station programmers and disk jockeys, and live appearances in smaller clubs or as an opening act for major performers, an intense though geographically dispersed cult following can be achieved.

As the number of rock and roll acts is legion, one can reasonably ask how the cult following originates. Why don't listeners simply attend themselves to the readily accessible recordings and performances of established performers? The most obvious reason for the ongoing initiation of these loyal audiences is the excitement provoked by new performers, quite often through live performance. More fundamentally, though, one must also note how listeners use performers' songs and personal styles to give themselves a sense of identity, cues for dress, and the prospect of a community of fellow listeners. For the followers of "uncommercialized, unadvertised small bands" this process of identification is an important means of differentiating themselves in society. Established performers can also give identity and meaning to listeners, but they do not allow fans to differentiate themselves in the same way. George Melly captures this use of performers and their music perfectly in this comment on "swinging London" in the mid-1960s:

Pop had become a moment, the moment when a sound, a group or an artist was poised between the appreciation of a coterie and wide acceptance; the equivalent of the moment in the City when it becomes known that a private company is going public.[28]

The cult phase in rock and roll careers is hardly universal. In the first place, there are the examples of contrived groups, such as The Monkees in the 1960s, or more recently, New Kids on the Block, which are wholly the creation of record industry insiders.[29] These performers do not work their way up through a local club circuit, and their initial, major label recordings are heavily promoted. The history of rock and roll is likewise filled with the formation of supergroups—Cream; Crosby, Stills, Nash, and Young; Emerson, Lake, and Palmer; Asia; The Firm; The Traveling Wilburys—whose members were already well-known performers. Again, these combines do not pass through a cult stage.

As a means of interpreting the careers of rock and rollers, the cult phase is important because of its overtones of symbiosis between performers and listeners. Performers compose songs and offer stage performances that are rooted in a local milieu and the experience of direct interaction with audiences. Fans can assume a strong identification with performers, whose stage personas they know well and whose recordings, due to their limited circulation, are "their own." In a sense, the career of every rock and roll performer represents a fall from the cult phase—even though many performers, in fact, have not had such followings.

The most common break with cult status is through "crossing over," which may be signaled by signing a contract with a major recording company and a subsequent adjustment of performance style.[30] In the 1980s, association with a major label usually resulted in marketing performances through videos, which can have a profound impact on a performer's visual presentation. Performers that cross over seek a larger audience, and thus, tend to remold themselves in a more mainstream image.

Of course, a performer's cult following may object to this reshaping of image and sound, especially if the transformation threatens the performer's aura of uniqueness. In the early 1980s this was the case when high speed punk bands from the West Coast such as X and The Blasters moved from independent to major labels. A few years later, fans and critics examined very closely new releases by The Replacements and Husker Du, Midwest "thrash" bands that left their indie labels to sign with subsidiaries of Warner-Elektra-Atlantic. Specifically, old fans wondered whether their major-label recordings would still capture the cacophonous sound of their early recordings and if, in turn, their live performances would lose their wild edge.

The history of rock and roll is littered with the stories of crossover performers. Surely the most famous crossover was Elvis Presley, who emerged in the 1950s as a sexually charged rock and roller, but by the early 1960s was a crooning movie star. Several extremely popular performers in the 1970s, such as Fleetwood Mac and Peter Frampton, began their careers in the 1960s as less orthodox rock and rollers. In the early 1980s, Human League, an English dance band, achieved worldwide success with lilting synthesizer arrangements of romantically titled songs such as "Don't You Want Me." Only a few years before, at the height of the punk craze the band had formed as a collection of nonmusicians, initially releasing a pair of songs called "Being Boiled" and "Circus of Death."[31] This is the classic crossover path: from material and performances based on the eccentric conceptions of band members to a group persona evoking marketable values such as glamour and romance.

Some performers manage to achieve larger audiences, and even win the acclaim of journalists, critics, and listeners outside the rock and roll audience, without seeming to cross over. This was the experience of The Beatles in the 1960s, Bruce Springsteen in the 1970s, and to varying degrees Michael Jackson, U2, and John Cougar Mellencamp in the 1980s. In the case of The Beatles, their gradual "transcendence" of rock and roll crested with the release of the "Sgt. Pepper's Lonely Hearts Club" Band album in April 1967. The reaction to "Sgt. Pepper" was described a few months later in *Newsweek:*

> The sounds The Beatles made, the words they sang, reached such levels of irony, allusiveness, wit, poetry and put-on that the mighty Liverpudlians could be said to have come through with the first modern work that blended all heights of brow and levels of culture. The album sold by the millions and was analyzed ecstatically by critics who had previously concentrated on the subtleties of Henry James and John Donne.[32]

This is the essence of transcendence. An entry in the mass circulation—not the rock and roll—press proclaims an artistic achievement that places the performer outside the parameters of rock and roll. Interestingly, some of the outward signs of transcendence correspond to crossing over: greater sales of recordings, performances before larger audiences and employing different media, new contracts with major record companies. Transcendence may also be signaled by the performer's stepping outside the world of rock and roll to make comments on political issues or by participating in philanthropic exercises. In recent years U2 has participated in the "Live Aid" benefit concert to fight world hunger and performed as part of Artists United Against Apartheid. John Cougar Mellencamp has helped organize and has performed at a number of "Farm Aid" benefits to raise funds for farmers in economically distressed portions of the midwestern United States.

Nevertheless, transcendence can, like crossing over, alienate a performer or band from their original audience. For example, by the time The Beatles released "Sgt. Pepper's Lonely Hearts Club Band" the group no longer gave live performances. Michael Jackson, whose transcendence has been marked by the rare feat of huge sales to black and white fans alike, has become a Hollywood recluse, recording and giving public performances only infrequently.

Thus, for the original fans of particular performers, and as widely observed career transitions, crossing over and transcendence may be characterized in another fashion, as "selling out." This is the label applied to performers who lose sight of their original artistic intentions and withdraw from the symbiotic connection with a community of listeners. Performers themselves will acknowledge this loss, as did John Lennon following the break-up of The Beatles:

> As soon as we made it, we made it, but the edges were knocked off. Brian [Epstein] put us in suits and all that and we made it very, very big. But we sold out you know. The music was dead before we even went on the theatre tour of Britain. . . . We always missed the club dates because that's when we were playing music. And then later on we became technically efficient recording artists, which was another thing. We were competent people, you know and whatever media you put us in we can produce something worthwhile.[33]

In Lennon's view The Beatles' music was "dead" years before the group released the succession of recordings that made them the world's most acclaimed musicians. Lennon's recollection includes all of the elements usually associated with selling out: manipulation by management, loss of contact with live audiences in intimate performance settings, proficiency in dealing with media outside the strict confines of rock and roll. In this understanding of the rock and roll performer's career, great success and acclaim yield failure.

Fratricide

Rock and roll, like jazz, is a musical idiom in which groups of musicians—bands—are the typical vehicles of performance. Many rock and roll bands provide instrumental support for a featured vocalist, but some of the most prominent bands have adopted a collective identity: The Beach Boys, The Beatles, The Rolling Stones, The Jefferson Airplane, The Grateful Dead, Fleetwood Mac, The Sex Pistols, The Clash, Talking Heads, U2, REM. By contrast, the more common jazz practice is to identify bands with a leader—Miles Davis, John Coltrane, Thelonius Monk, McCoy Tyner, Wynton Marsalis, and so on. Some of the most successful rock and roll bands have also been quite long-lived, of the foregoing groups the Rolling Stones and Grateful Dead have performed for more than twenty years. Among small jazz bands only the Modern Jazz Quartet and The Art Ensemble of Chicago, with their uncharacteristic collective identities, have achieved a similar longevity.

In spite of this temporal staying power, the members of a rock and roll group are often at odds with one another, and these internal wranglings are an ongoing subject of rock and roll reportage and discussions among fans. This phase in the rock and roll career is "fratricide," squabbling with intrafamilial overtones, usually among the overrepresented rock and roll gender, males. On occasion, this term has literal application, as in the much-publicized stage battling of The Kinks' Ray and Dave Davies, but rock and roll bands have also been the arena for marital disharmony. Fleetwood Mac may have achieved the most complicated web of matrimonial/sexual squabbling, as recorded in this summary:

> [Lindsay] Buckingham and [Stevie] Nicks drifted apart during the summer of 1976, and Christine McVie celebrated her divorce from husband John [McVie] by getting herself sterilized. . . . She then embarked on a two-year affair with Dennis Wilson of the Beach Boys while further complications arose when Currie Grant, the band's long-serving lighting engineer, revealed his involvements with both Christine and Stevie in the pages of *Rolling Stone*.[34]

The significance of fratricide rests in its everyday undercutting of the communal assumptions of rock and roll music making and listening. Record companies have long marketed "families," "brothers," and "sisters," who have not been, in fact, related. In addition, the visual presentation of rock and roll groups has often sought to underline communal values, with the early Beatles in their matching, lapelless suits and "mop tops" as the exemplar of this strategy. In the 1960s, this marketing ploy was redefined as bands assimilated the hippie ethos and its emphasis on emotional directness and material sharing. Song-writing credits for particular compositions were assigned to the entire group (e.g., "Light My Fire" by The Doors), and San Francisco–based groups such as The Jefferson Airplane used their earnings to make collective investments.[35]

"Better music through good vibes" is the outgrowth of this faith in musical communalism, although few proponents of this notion in the 1960s acknowledged its sources in rock and roll marketing. In practice, fratricide was the rule. The disintegration of The Beatles, documented in the film "Let It Be," is the characteristic case. For the individual Beatles the collective identity of the group became stifling, with the result that their later recordings were essentially individual performances released under The Beatles rubric. When John Lennon's romantic attachment to avant-garde artist Yoko Ono resulted in Ono's joining the band in the recording studio, The Beatles' collective identity was effectively terminated.[36]

Artistic disagreements are another provocation to fratricide. In the early 1980s The Clash, the most influential English punk group, as well as the punk band whose ideological orientation most closely paralleled the stance of politically engaged rock and rollers in the 1960s, fell into discord. Vocalist Joe Strummer and bass player Paul Simonon took offense at guitarist Mick Jones' inclination to play more commercial music, asking him to leave because he had "drifted apart from the original idea of the Clash."[37]

For musicians and listeners alike, the communal myth is an important component of rock and roll culture. While more technically skilled jazz musicians do not argue—they simply break up and recombine their bands—rock and rollers seeks to overcome technical deficiencies through spiritual camaraderie ("feel") and improve their sound collectively by sticking together. Romantic disputes, quarrels over money, or accusations that some members of the band want to sell out give lie to the communal myth. One of the principal tableaus of the rock and roll career is the ruinous squabbling that accompanies a group's musical decline.

Slumming

Another mark of rock and roll decline is "slumming," performers' acknowledgment of their diminished status and attendant efforts to carry on in the afterglow of previous triumphs. Rock and roll slummers agree to appear in clubs or arenas that they once would have scorned. In performance, they rely on tried and true older material rather than risk listener indifference to new songs. In presenting themselves to their audience they adopt personas that evoke past successes rather than ongoing musical creativity.

Two descriptions of Johnny Rotten, leader of the punk standard-bearing Sex Pistols, underline some of the main elements of slumming. The first, by critic Greil Marcus, characterized Rotten in the Sex Pistols:

> There was a black hole at the heart of the Sex Pistols' music, a willful lust for the destruction of all values that absolutely no one could be comfortable with—and that was why, at his greatest, Johnny Rotten was perhaps the only truly terrifying singer rock and roll has ever known. Certainly, no one has yet seen all the way into the nihilistic madness of "Holidays in the Sun," the Pistol's last single.[38]

The second description, of Rotten fronting another band, Public Image Ltd. (PIL), was written eight years later:

> In earlier editions of PIL, Rotten demanded to be billed as John Lydon, his real name, but he's recently come to accept the marketing value of the more infamous moniker. Rotten's music has followed a similar course, from the punk anarchy of the Pistols to the pop nihilism of early PIL to the canny careerism that received a strong response from the Pavilion crowd. . . . Still, it was a little strange to hear the man who once threatened to shatter all rock conventionalism now working the hall like any other arena-rock hack, goading the crowd for more applause and reviving the Pistols' "Holidays in the Sun" from a decade ago.[39]

In ten years "Holidays in the Sun," a violent song that alludes to the horrors of Nazi concentration camps, had become a "greatest hit" to be used as a live performance show-stopper.

John Lydon's readoption of Johnny Rotten is also notable:

Following the break-up of the Sex Pistols Lydon had returned to his original name in an effort to distance himself from his punk persona. In the face of declining public notoriety, he apparently revised the need for such distancing. In practice, the readoption of Johnny Rotten was strictly a ticket-selling device. On stage, Lydon was employing a far more congenial pose than he had as Johnny Rotten, the Sex Pistol. Finally, it is worth noting that the 1988 description of Lydon/Rotten is taken from an account of a concert in which PIL was opening for a better-known rock and roll band, INXS, whose fame was just then on the rise. Lydon was coping with downward mobility.

Elvis Presley was the classic slummer. Following a decade of appearances in teen-oriented movies and withdrawal from live rock and roll performance, Presley agreed to his manager's plan to return to the stage in a Las Vegas hotel/casino. Presley modeled his Las Vegas persona on the image of a lesser singer, Tom Jones, who nonetheless was a popular Las Vegas act. In Las Vegas, Presley regained some of his self-confidence as a performer, made huge sums of money (mainly for manager Tom Parker), but accepted musical arrangements and material that took him even farther afield from his roots in rock and roll.[40]

Slumming is formalized in "rock and roll revival" shows, events that typically feature a number of performers from some golden era of the past: 1950s rock and roll, the British Invasion, surf music, Woodstock, and so on. Performers may bridle at this kind of packaging, especially those, like Chuck Berry, who do not envision themselves as has-beens:

> Beginning around 1973, nearly every year Richard Nader booked me at Madison Square Garden in New York City for the Revival of the Fifties show. I thought the title was dumb because rock 'n' roll never had heart trouble and thus did not need to be revived.[41]

Nevertheless, the rock and roll revivals do turn performers into the living dead. Middle-aged men and women churn out songs that they composed and performed as teenagers. What had once been performances of scintillating immediacy become lumbering run-throughs. There is a clear subtext to this form of slumming. Rock and roll is teenager's music, and once rock and rollers grow up they can no longer create new music.

An unusual variant of slumming is represented by the career of David Johansen, who led a hard-rock band, The New York Dolls, in the early 1970s. The Dolls were known as much for cross-dressing as their music, and as Johansen recalls "I got to be, like, 28 years old, and I said: 'Hey, let's face it, pal: You're a grownup now.' "[42] After performing solo for a few years, Johansen adopted the performing persona of Buster Poindexter, a vocalizing lounge lizard whose repertoire includes Broadway show tunes and other pop songs. Johansen literally slums as Poindexter, appearing in small clubs in New York and a few other cities; and indeed, he often assumes the new persona so thoroughly that he will not acknowledge his earlier career. Some portion of Buster Poindexter's audience probably does not even realize that David Johansen was a member of The New York Dolls. Johansen has confronted slumming in an unorthodox and creative way by embracing it and, in effect, transforming himself.[43]

The End

As with other occupations and callings, rock and roll careers come to an end, but it is characteristic of rock and roll endings to trivialize the social salience of performers and the meaning of their music. For many performers, the career phase that we have just discussed, slumming, is "the end." Years of occasional rock and roll revival shows assure performers a safe, marginal place in the shadows of show business. Other rock and rollers sustain more visible and lucrative careers, but they do not make continuing musical contributions. For example, drummer Ringo Starr of The Beatles has become an unobtrusive supporting actor in Hollywood film productions.

Two other ends provide insights on the place of rock and roll in American culture. The first of these is "grueling death," notably the variety of drug and alcohol abuse-related deaths that have struck rock and roll performers, but also including the occasional suicide. Among the very prominent performers who have succumbed to drugs or alcohol are Elvis Presley, Janis Joplin, and Jimi Hendrix. Musicians in the punk generation have more frequently committed suicide, including Sid Vicious of The Sex Pistols and Ian Curtis of Joy Division. For parents and other critics outside the rock and roll subculture, "grueling death" communicates two social meanings. First, the rock and roll life is a deviant path that offers to outsiders no lessons worth learning. Second, rock and roll is a terminal, nihilistic music. Even its practitioners come to this realization, and as a consequence, they cut their own lives short.

For many performers and listeners, grueling death is also the logical extension of rock and roll's sonic and lyrical excesses. But

within the subculture some performers who succumb to grueling
death metaphorically return to life. This other, related end is
"death and transfiguration." Drug casualty Jimi Hendrix continues to influence rock and roll musicians, and since his death
record companies have scoured their tape vaults to continue the
release of his recordings. The Doors, a band that broke up following the death of vocalist Jim Morrison in 1971, inspired a new generation of fans in the late 1970s and early 1980s. Sales of their
recordings were brisk, and Morrison's grave in Paris' Père-
Lachaise Cemetery became a shrine for young musical pilgrims.
Death and transfiguration has been the particular fate of John
Lennon, who was murdered by a mentally disturbed fan, Mark
David Chapman, in 1980. Although Lennon had recorded infrequently during the 1970s, the memory of The Beatles remained a
powerful force in the rock and roll subculture. Since Lennon's
death, The Beatles nostalgia industry has flourished through
books, films, television documentaries, and record repackagings.

Death and transfiguration, whose beneficiaries also include
founding rock and rollers Buddy Holly and Richie Valens, as well
as Elvis Presley; accidental fatalities such as guitarist Duane Al-
lman (killed in a motorcycle accident); and young, prematurely
lost musicians like Ian Curtis, give rock and roll a hierarchy of
deities and an insular sense of its own history. For some rock and
roll listeners contemporary musicians cannot have the impact of
these lost heroes. Rock and roll is a treacherous romantic quest
fated to repeat its dance of death as new heroes join the pantheon
of the dead. It is not a living commentary on the conditions of
young people, life in a society torn by political and technological
change, or prospects for the future from the vantage point of those
who will live through it.

Rock and Roll and Political Quiescence

The preceding pages have offered, in part, a descriptive account of rock and roll careers. The particular cases that we examined are representative of the sequence of stages and alternative
courses characteristic of the professional rock and roll life, and to
these examples we could add dozens more. But in addition, the
overarching pattern that we have outlined is a widely employed
paradigm, which, as indicated by the sources of the examples we
have reviewed, is used by many performers, rock and roll journalists, and listeners. Its overall shape, with individual elements cor-
responding to "rise," "tension," "decline," and "fall," is elegantly

tragic. It imposes order on the evolution of particular performers, the rise of new subgenres, and the seemingly inexorable reconfiguring of rock and roll; but more important, it helps define the nature of the rock and roll's cultural marginality.

Not every performer passes through the whole sequence of career phases that we have described, and some of the career categories can overlap, but enough careers conform to the main outlines of the paradigm to give it force. Its essence can be stated simply. Performers speak in meaningful terms to their audience for a limited time; once they have mastered the business of recording and promotion, their ability to communicate with their audience is already impaired. There is little that is truly unique in the performances or vision of individual rock and rollers. Ultimately, all performers burn out or fall into the habit of recycling past performances. As bearers of the rock and roll torch they are replaced by younger successors, who themselves will soon enough be superseded.

The rise and fall of rock and roll performers is not wholly unique. For example, an examination of the careers of film stars and the commentary on their careers might produce a similar pattern. Nonetheless, there remains an important difference between the ways in which rock and roll and film performers present themselves to their audiences. In spite of the elaborate production and marketing machinery that supports the work of rock and rollers, the latter usually give the impression of controlling their own performance. Individual performers and bands normally claim credit for their own compositions, play the musical instruments, and appear more or less alone on the performing stage. The elaborate apparatus of filmmaking is much more visible—from the opening credits of movies. Consequently, for film stars the decline or at least routinization of their magic can be understood as a condition growing out of their place in an industry. Yes, there is also a constraining industry of rock and roll, but the decline of performers is typically attributed to declining creative powers, loss of intensity, or simple aging. In the last instance, rock and rollers—excepting the occasional David Johansen/Buster Poindexter—clearly do not have the option available to maturing matinee idols, which is to become a skillful character actor or actress.

This paradigm thus makes sense of the fundamental contradiction of rock and roll: a genre defined by its marketers, performers, and listeners as "youth music," performed by individuals who cannot escape time. The intellectual and emotional force of individual performers is typically related to their empathic quality. Given this presumption, evaluation of performers is grounded in the consideration of how well they speak of and to the concerns of their audience. In this understanding of rock and roll, compositional genius, lyrical acuity, and instrumental virtuosity are secondary factors. What is primary is absorbing and then reflecting the concerns of a demographically defined audience.

For performers, who are just as aware of the paradigm as journalists and listeners, the bind presented by this formulation is not merely metaphorical. Some of rock and roll's most highly charged performers simply burn out in well-publicized deaths. This has been the fate of Elvis Presley, Brian Jones of The Rolling Stones, Jimi Hendrix, Janis Joplin, Jim Morrison, and Sid Vicious. Pete Townshend's withdrawal to the publishing industry represents an illuminating minority solution. As Townshend and the other members of The Who approached middle age, the band's ability to shift to new subject matter and performance styles became impossible. Regardless of what Townshend, Daltrey, and Entwistle wanted to become, their audience demanded The Who of pop art tee-shirts and Woodstock. Townshend finally left rock and roll altogether. In walking away from the music Townshend at least avoided the fate of Chuck Berry, a talented lyricist and guitarist condemned to repeat the performances of his 20s and 30s through his 40s and 50s.

The paradigmatic rock and roll career with its rise, tension, decline, and fall gives a good account of how performers and their music have been situated in American culture since the mid-1950s. While the well-publicized consumption preferences of rock and rollers—exotic clothing, alcohol and drugs, ornate mansions, and so on—have given their fans some aspirational objectives that are basically consistent with broader social preferences, the insistent spontaneity and the youth-based social commentary of even the most talented and ambitious performers have been neutralized. Try as they may, rock and roll performers have been neither convincing nor tenacious outlaws.

Simon Frith has observed that rock and roll's reputation as "socially subversive" is the object of a redefinition by a new breed of performers who "start by accepting, celebrating even, music's commodity status, by defining revolt as style, politics as gesture. . . ." [44] These English performers described by Frith refuse to present themselves as autonomous commentators on an unjust society, and instead lace their "disposable pop" with unsettling juxtapositions and other avant-garde devices that implicate their listeners as consumers. One consequence of this strategy would appear to be the submergence of the performer, which prevents the listener from identifying with and then rejecting the "sell-out."

As an antidote to the performers' trap described in this chapter, Frith's new-style pop music is certainly a more knowing performer's pose. Nevertheless, the immersion of such performers in stylized pop music may signal a further marginalization of critical rock and roll, as the oblique strategies of the most gifted rock and rollers produce music, which like avant-garde jazz, is appreciated by an isolated coterie of fans. For the larger audience there will remain devotees of the rock and roll myth, young musicians weaned on the legendary flare-ups and burn-outs of Elvis Presley, Jimi Hendrix, and Sid Vicious, who recreate the styles and lives of their predecessors with hardly a nod toward the world outside the arena concert circuit and the teenager's music room.

Chapter Nine

Closing Thoughts: Popular Culture and National Anxiety

Larry Bennett

In the conservative America of the 1980s and early 1990s, just as the terrain of public policy debate has shifted to the right, so have the politics of culture. One sign of this shift was the appearance, near the end of the Reagan years, of a cluster of books urging reconstitution of the United States' education system. Notable among these were volumes by Secretary of Education William Bennett and academicians Allan Bloom and E. D. Hirsch, Jr. Although their particular emphases varied, in the view of each of them America's schools fail to meet the needs of current and future generations. Bennett, who subsequently became the Bush administration's "drug czar," is a disciplinarian who would reduce the breadth of contemporary curriculums by eliminating "faddish" social studies and "pop culture" offerings. Bloom focuses his attention on a minority of students, whom he would educate in the classics as a means of guaranteeing a self-conscious and refined cadre of national leaders. Hirsch is more populistic, proposing a curriculum of "cultural literacy" essential for any competent adult. Hirsch's objective is also more directly pragmatic than Bloom's: an educated workforce buttressing an America that is more internationally competitive.[1]

Just behind this fearsome threesome's attack on contemporary education is an auxiliary fusillade directed at popular culture. Part of their argument claims that educators have been too attentive to popular culture, admitting topics and techniques to the classroom that undercut traditional educational values. More significantly, these critics attack the content of popular culture, noting its anti-intellectualism, fetishization of sex and leisure, and withdrawal from the "real world." Of course, Bennett, Bloom, and Hirsch express views that, in varying degrees, are shared by a considerable portion of the United States' political elites, as evidenced by contemporary controversies over the offensiveness of rap music, whether or not the U.S. flag deserves constitutional protection, and government financial support for "obscene" art.

At the heart of the antagonism toward television, rock and roll, and popular cinema shared by Bennett, Bloom, Hirsch, and others is an anxiety over the United States' declining world stature. Considering the West's 1989–1990 "victory" in the Cold War, this anxiety at first appears surprising. However, we should bear in mind that since the middle 1980s business leaders, policy experts, and journalists have routinely identified the principal nemesis of the United States as its trade rival Japan. Moreover, the collapse of the Warsaw Pact prefigured the reunification of Germany, another country whose economic might concerns many Americans.

If we imagine the United States as an obsolete Detroit gas-guzzler lumbering toward the twenty-first century, we can underline the nature of this anxiety about popular culture. Bennett, Bloom, and Hirsch look in the rearview mirror and observe the Vietnam debacle. Racing ahead of them in the economic fast lane are disciplined, culturally homogeneous nations like Japan and Germany. On the highway's shoulder, Bennett, Bloom, and Hirsch observe the smoking hulk of the Soviet Union, wrecked not only by a command economy but also by a mob of unassimilated ethnic populations. Glancing about their own vehicle they are menaced by an unruly underclass and a feckless younger generation. For Bennett, Bloom, and Hirsch, the dilemma of the United States is not that the barbarians are approaching, but rather that the barbarians are multiplying rapidly in their very midst.[2]

The contemporary right-flank assault on popular culture shares many themes with an older group of leftist commentators, who observed the United States at the peak of the "American Century." In the 1950s Dwight MacDonald's essay, "A Theory of Mass Culture," attacked the homogenization of American culture and linked it to the formation of a quiescent, uninquisitive public.[3] Nor was MacDonald's critique the original formulation of this position. Since the 1930s, members of the Frankfort School of social criticism, notably Theodor Adorno, Max Horkheimer, and Leo Lowenthal, had offered similar commentary on popular entertainment media.[4] Critical commentary on popular culture, in fact, persists among leftist scholars, though its themes of wasteful personal expenditures, environmental degradation, and debased public discourse generally differentiate it from the work of conservative observers.[5]

Despite the different emphases and clearly different intentions of writers such as Bloom and Dolores Hayden, their criticisms of the content of contemporary popular culture deserve serious attention. The decline of literacy in the United States, which in some fashion has to be related to our national penchant for television viewing, as well as such popular youth pastimes as MTV and video games, is a worrisome trend. An economic development that worries many economists is the American reluctance to commit earnings to personal savings; in turn this bears some relation to the personal consumption ethos permeating the substance and presentation of the popular arts in this country.[6] More troubling still is the sense of alienation felt by many Americans, which exists side by side with various seemingly quixotic movements for individual and social transformation.[7] Again, one cannot help but think that a popular culture in which norms of individual competition and acquisitiveness are so deeply embedded has a hand in each of these conditions.

These trends are indeed cause for concern, and yet a careful reading of the essays presented in this volume suggests that much of the commentary on popular culture oversimplifies the causal connection between the content of popular cultural products and media and the values internalized by individuals. In addition, the character of particular media, which we often discuss as if determined by forces wholly internal to their organization of production and technology, in fact, is usually shaped in equal measure by political conflict and adjustment directed at accommodating new media to prevalent social values. In other words, media reflect as well as shape social values. Finally, there is what might be called a "shadow life" within popular culture that results from the interaction of the media and prevailing social values, the syntheses resulting from these interactions, and the more or less random impacts of these syntheses over time. In short, the content of popular culture is less predictable than many commentators would have us believe. Contrary to the conservative critique, films, rock and roll, and fashion are not simply agents of social destabilization; nor, as the less nuanced leftist critics sometimes propose, is popular culture merely a means of mass political indoctrination.

The Elusiveness of Popular Culture

Like critics of the fine arts, observers of popular culture typically base their interpretations on readings of the substantive content and stylistic conventions found in particular books, films, videos, and musical recordings. Viewed simply as artistic objects, examples of these media are often stimulating and interesting, and the critic's role is usually thought to center on evaluation of artistic intent and execution. To the extent that critics seek to examine the impact of these products, the usual procedure is to infer impact from their content. This is a sensible enough strategy, but it begs the question of whether or not recordings, films, and books "mean" for their audiences what critics suppose their producers intended.

In essence, what we think we know about popular culture is largely comprised of impressions of what culture producers seek to communicate. This circumstance, however, represents a constraint rather than an insuperable barrier. As several chapters in this volume demonstrate, by locating popular culture products and media in a broader social context, the analyst can begin the process of relating product to consumer, inferring the consumer's sensibility, and gauging how these interactions then reshape social reality. Lizabeth Cohen's essay confronts this challenge directly through her examination of a local context in which mass culture products were received. Her research quite convincingly uncovers a variety of neighborhood conventions, patterns of ethnic loyalty and distrust, and personal adaptations of mass culture products that undercut the "embourgeoisement" thesis of mass culture/working class interaction—and more generally the approach to popular culture that equates product meaning and cultural effect.

Pamela Steinle's look at local controversies generated by J. D. Salinger's *The Catcher in the Rye* captures the discontinuity between the popular culture artifact and the consumer from another angle, in this instance the ambiguous relation of author and audience. Steinle's book-banners and -defenders express antithetical reactions to Salinger's novel, yet the two views of *Catcher in the Rye* grow from analogous emotional responses to the American condition. But could even the most prescient critic of the book have predicted its striking the latent chord of nuclear anxiety that Steinle's account so frequently finds? One doubts it. Holden Caulfield's weekend spree in Manhattan cannot, by ordinary means, be connected to post-World War II concerns over nuclear war and the obliteration of the planet. Nevertheless, this appears to be an important part of *Catcher in the Rye*'s cultural resonance.

In some cases, the characteristic relation between popular culture producers and consumers is clearly symbiotic, as my essay on the formalization of rock and roll careers as rock and roll myth suggests. In rock and roll, the social distance between culture producers and consumers is relatively narrow. And while record company executives and producers have indeed sought to mold performers and their performances to particular markets, new performers routinely appear and redefine expectations of performance. The formation of the rock and roll myth is itself a response to the four-way contradictions among corporate marketing considerations, the generally accepted notion of rock and roll as youth music, individual expression, and the maturing of performers. The myth distorts reality by casting the performer as creative hero in a race with time, when in fact, the race is with market categories. Nevertheless, rock and roll's corporate apparatus is never quite able to control and deliver the safe product with which most recording company executives would feel most comfortable. The music continuously reshapes itself, and one source of its constant motion is the power of the rock and roll myth.

In practice, some of the best accounts of the characteristic features of popular culture in the United States, such as Frances Fitzgerald's *Cities on a Hill*, dispense altogether with the direct reading of media and products. Fitzgerald's study of four transformative communities provides such compelling portraits of their members' personal odysseys, collective behavior, and group norms that she can then convincingly work back to inferences regarding how these communities respond to and use the media. A noteworthy example of this process is her explanation of the Religious Right's seemingly intuitive manipulation of television. Fitzgerald's informants time and again recalled the anxiety brought into their homes by television coverage of civil rights actions, urban crime, and gay and lesbian mobilization. But by the same token, television broadcasts by the likes of Jerry Falwell reassured them and, indeed, regenerated their sense of membership in a righteous, politically empowered community.[8]

In addition to extrapolating the meaning of popular culture from the apparent content of popular culture media and objects, commentators also often identify the substantive character of particular media with their technological character.[9] Nancy Rosenbloom's description of the short-lived and uneasy alliance between New York Progressives and the film industry provides a useful corrective to this assumption. Technologies do not simply spring on us, and we typically structure the application of technologies in light of prevailing social norms, often following a period of political controversy and debate.

The principal theme that emerges from considering the essays in this volume, as well as the work of a variety of other observers of popular culture, is, rather than the determinacy of popular culture, its elusiveness. In contrast to the views of both the contemporary right-wing critics of popular culture and the leftist tradition, the content of popular culture in the United States is varied and fluid. One signal of this fluidity is the discontinuity between content and impact of the popular cultural product. The close observer of popular culture also notes the imperfect control over products exercised by dominant economic institutions. This is an obvious lesson of Lizabeth Cohen's study, whose mass product manufacturers and media programmers would surely have liked to consolidate simple, more or less undifferentiated markets across Chicago's diverse communities of the 1920s. Instead, the products of mass culture were subject to varied and unpredictable applications.

Nor, as Pamela Steinle's essay demonstrates, is mass passivity the sure consequence of the general circulation of popular culture media and mass culture products. Intellectuals may well abhor the kinds of political mobilization that follow the publication of books like *The Catcher in the Rye*, but the fear of some of the early mass culture critics—that radio, television, mass circulation literature narcotize the population—clearly misread the situation. At this time the salient questions for the observer of popular culture concern what kinds of popular media products fire political controversy, how these reactions are likely to be manipulated, and what these controversies reveal about the population's deeper temperament.

Analyses such as Michael Burkun's, as well as Howard Abramowitz's and Cohen's essays, do bring to light some persistently unsavory themes in American popular culture such as nativism, racism, and anti-Semitism. Moreover, popular media such as television and newspapers often play important parts in sustaining and disseminating these themes. Nevertheless, these strains of American culture were observable long before the maturation of contemporary popular media; and even today, they are probably passed along in their most extreme forms by these traditional media: word of mouth and personal example.

If the patterns of popular culture production and consumption do not fall into the relatively simplified categories used by much past commentary, can we make any generalizations at all about the overall shape of popular culture in the United States? Ronald Edsforth's discussion of Walter Reuther and automobile workers in the postwar period offers one such overall characterization, by his linking the ethos of personal consumption to the grand fight against communism. In this view of postwar America, the shift to consumer-oriented production, the rise to affluence of the union-ized working class, and the casting aside of previous taboos against self-gratifying commodity consumption were rationalized by corporate executives, union leaders, and the rank-and-file workers alike as the necessary postscript to World War II. In or-der to overawe the Soviet threat, the principal domestic responsi-bility of the United States was to build a consumer economy that would be the world's envy. Was this simply manipulation? To a degree it surely was, but its force as an ideology must also be at-tributed to its plausibility for a large part of the American work-ing class.

Yet to argue that the implications of popular culture and con-sumption patterns in the United States must be understood against the backdrop of a broader historical and social context is not to suggest that they play no independent role in giving shape to American life. Quite evidently, the media provide something akin to a network of launching pads, which, when one or another fad, phobia, or controversy bubbles up in some particular locale, rockets it across regions and time, dislocating it from any specific, directly experienced context. Howard Abramowitz's analysis of the post-World War I Red Scare and its amplification by daily newspa-per coverage is a rendering of just this process.

Barkun's discussion of Coxey's Army makes another important point about the evolution of popular culture and its relation to the politics of the United States. Not only is the general dissemination of conventional as well as some highly eccentric political ideas a consequence of the prevailing means we use to gather and monitor "news," the maturation of the press and electronic media have also redefined the nature of political action. There were surely exam-ples of "sacramental" political action long before the march of Cox-ey's Army, but with the arrival of the mass circulation press such efforts to join "the sacred and the mundane" assumed a new character.[10] Politics, which in the United States had been played through the processes of identifying interest and mobilizing influ-ence in well-defined political forums, could now be recast as the expression of collective need and personal magnetism. Under the spell of Carl Browne and a legion of successors the popular press and television have provided the means for transmitting a whole array of new political tactics. Indeed, it is evident that these me-dia are much more effective communicators of political tactics than of conventional political discourse.

Barkun's observations may thus be linked to the position of a contemporary media critic such as Neil Postman, who argues that television has turned politics from a forum for competition and resolution of competing interests to a stage adapted to individual performances.[11] When one considers the presidency of Ronald Reagan, who seemingly managed to calm and uplift the spirit of a public that usually disagreed with his policies, Postman's argument appears wholly convincing. Nonetheless, it lacks the historical rooting provided by research such as Barkun's. From the start, it appears that Carl Browne realized that a new style of politicking was in order if the daily press were to be put to its most effective use in publicizing Coxey's Army.

Fearing the Popular

Ultimately, popular culture in the United States cannot be reduced to the formulas employed by many critics on both the political left and right. Although most popular culture products are mass-produced and intended to meet predetermined consumer preferences, and the intellectual requisites for enjoying these products are none too impressive, this is not all there is to popular culture. Individuals working in many popular culture media attempt to communicate highly personal messages to attentive audiences, and an ongoing stream of popular culture items provokes our attention in unforeseeable ways. Moreover, the consumers of popular culture products regularly impose their own meanings and derive their own pleasures from them.

Yet what is most interesting about the "unlikely consensus among certain voices from the right and the left about the intrinsic evils of new technologies and the monstrous mass cultures to which they give birth" is the way the two ideological strands intertwine and seep into the mainstream of popular culture analysis by journalists, politically unattached intellectuals, and others.[12] The right-wing camp's contribution to most such "value-free" interpretation is concern over the effects of open-ended structures of socialization such as cinema and recordings, as opposed to those old reliables, the church and family. The latter, it is usually assumed, will send the right signals, especially to younger people: study hard, work hard, be satisfied with reasonable material success. No such assumptions govern the interchange between television, records, films, and kids. The left's concerns, which again can be observed in the work of many popular culture commentators, is clearly related: maybe people, especially younger people, really do want the popular culture trash that envelops them.

Like the jeremiads of Bennett, Bloom, and Hirsch, this fear of

the popular is another sign of our national anxiety, and as it filters into day-to-day interpretation of popular culture, renders serious investigation almost impossible. Indeed, it most paralyzes
the response to those popular culture items that, in fact, break the
mold of "safe product." An extremely telling example of this situation is the reaction to director Spike Lee's 1989 film, "Do the
Right Thing." Lee's film is a fictional account of race relations in a
small section of Bedford-Stuyvesant, in New York City's borough of
Brooklyn. "Do the Right Thing" includes all the elements that
bring discomfort to most observers of American popular culture.
Its soundtrack is an intensely noisy assemblage of rap music and
angry, vernacular dialogue. At the same time, some of its scenes
are palpably erotic. Its plot pits blacks against whites in sometimes violent confrontation. Just as one would expect, much of the
published reaction to "Do the Right Thing" was hostile, accusing
Lee of racism, pitching his film above the heads of his audience,
even distorting the upcoming mayoral election in New York City.[13]

At the heart of "Do the Right Thing" is a remarkably sophisticated interpretation of how popular culture fits within the U.S.
patterns of demographics, economic life, and social class. By considering the film's exploration of the ways in which such presumed
ephemera as hairstyles, pop music, and fan allegiance to performers interact with the social structure, one can identify a considerably more clear-headed understanding of the significance of
popular culture than that proposed by the likes of William Bennett, Allan Bloom, and E. D. Hirsch. In addition, one can specify
the deeper, unspoken sources of hostility to the film.

"Do the Right Thing" is, in the first place, an extremely knowing presentation of popular culture artifacts—coiffure, dress, music—among young blacks in the late 1980s. In the case of one
character, Radio Raheem, Lee portrays an incessantly pacing
ghetto kid, who, without his huge boom box and its blaring tape of
Public Enemy's "Fight the Power," would be utterly lost. As it
turns out, Radio Raheem loses his life in the wake of a chain of
events that includes his provoking the local pizzeria owner, Sal,
with his blasting music.

In analogous ways, popular culture preferences are used to define other characters and relationships. Politically radical Buggin'
Out sports the film's most outlandish "high top fade" haircut,
while racial mistrust is underlined by blacks and whites disagree-
ing over matters such as the relative merits of baseball pitchers
Dwight Gooden (black) and Roger Clemens (white).

Yet Lee's portrait of this single block in Bedford-Stuyvesant does not stop with the presentation of street life and styles. Structuring the film's events is a series of overlapping racial and ethnic cleavages. The most obvious divide separates Sal and his two sons, who run the last Italian business in the community, Sal's Famous Pizzeria, from the local black majority. At the edge of the main story is the apparently prospering Korean grocery across from Sal's, which in the course of the movie is several times the object of disparagement by neighborhood blacks, and in the closing conflagration is nearly engulfed by the spreading violence. Though Lee does not develop the relationship at length, pizza carrier Mookie's tempestuous scenes with his girlfriend, Tina, also suggest that all is not well between blacks and Puerto Ricans in this small corner of Bedford-Stuyvesant.

Yet "Do the Right Thing"'s locale is not merely the battleground for hostile racial and ethnic groups. It is also a neighborhood in which the small entrepreneur is on the run. One of Sal's sons, Pino, despises the neighborhood and its inhabitants and urges his father to move their business. Sal, who apparently remains in the community for reasons beyond expediency, nonetheless responds to Pino by arguing that there would be too much competition if they relocated to their own neighborhood. In effect, like most of the black characters in "Do the Right Thing," Sal and his two sons are trapped in Bedford-Stuyvesant.

Lee's portrayal of neighborhood outsiders, notably the police, is similarly nuanced. In the prelude to "Do the Right Thing"'s closing riot, Radio Raheem, who has forced his way into the pizzeria and fought with Sal, is restrained by the police. One of the white police officers employs a choke hold to lift Raheem off the ground, in so doing strangling him. Radio Raheem's killing seems to signal that the police, and by extension, city government, are principal oppressors of the neighborhood's people. Yet even the police are not monolithic, for as the murderous policeman increases his hold on Raheem, one of his white colleagues pleads with him that he is using too much force. Moreover, as one watches the police squad cars arrive at the corner too late to prevent the initial fighting, and then dash off into the darkness before the full-scale rioting begins, it is evident that no more than the local residents do the police control Bedford-Stuyvesant.

The fight inside Sal's Famous Pizzeria, the killing of Radio Raheem, and the torching of the pizzeria that follows are precipitated by a dispute that places in sharp relief the relationship between popular culture and the social cleavages in the neighborhood. Buggin' Out, who is the most politically conscious of the younger blacks in the film, argues with Sal over the pizzeria's

"Wall of Fame." The Wall of Fame is one of those assemblages of celebrity photographs one observes in pizza parlors, neighborhood restaurants, and taverns across the country. Not surprisingly, Sal's preference for celebrities begins and ends with sports and entertainment figures of Italian descent, and Buggin' Out claims to find this offensive. After all, this is Bedford-Stuyvesant.

Sal is unimpressed by Buggin' Out's logic, who in turn attempts to organize a boycott of the pizzeria. The film's climax occurs when Buggin' Out, Radio Raheem, and a third friend, Smiley, enter Sal's to once more confront him over the Wall of Fame. At first glance, Spike Lee seems to be setting in motion a tragic train of events with the flimsiest of means, an argument over which overrated media figures should grace the walls of a pizza joint. A number of reviewers emphasized this point, commenting that "trivial matters" elicit the film's closing riot.[14] The corollary of this perception, which was also adopted by a number of reviewers, suggests that Lee views racial conflict as inevitable, ready to erupt upon the slightest of provocation.[15]

I would propose an alternative interpretation, which is, I think, more consistent with the film's overall presentation of the neighborhood and its residents. In "Do the Right Thing" the flotsam and jetsam of popular culture—hairstyles, clothing, music, celebrities—are consumed by local people as a means of expressing their own individuality. In this light, Buggin' Out's weird haircut, just like Radio Raheem's boom box and, crucially, Sal's Italian-American heroes—serve to give a measure of meaning and individuality to otherwise constricted lives.

One element is common to all of the principal characters in "Do the Right Thing": They know that they are not going anywhere. For Mookie, Sal, Radio Raheem, and the rest, popular culture artifacts provide relief from the monotony and sense of hopelessness pervading their lives, yet through their contrasting uses of popular culture they also exacerbate the community's cleavages. Sal and his sons express themselves as well as their solidarity with Italian-American culture by reserving the Wall of Fame for Frank Sinatra, Al Pacino, and the like. Buggin' Out has his own heroes, such as Michael Jordan, and he insists that his piece of the popular culture collage share in the Wall of Fame's recognition. Through this seemingly trivial disagreement Spike Lee is, in effect, specifying the point at which individuals' adoption of popular culture products exacerbates more fundamental social divides. Contrasting patterns of immigration to New York, disruptions of the urban economy, and the legacy of past discrimination may be the root sources of black–Italian confrontations, but what many contemporary blacks and Italians observe, across the racial divide, are "others" who dress differently, like different sports, and have different heroes. And these differences are enough in themselves to aggravate intergroup hostilities.

At this point, Mr. Bennett and Professors Bloom and Hirsch might join the discussion to note that Spike Lee's characterization of popular culture as an ingredient in stirring interracial hostility is wholly consistent with their attacks on Hollywood films, rock and roll, and video games. Yet, in fact, do their respective advocacies of discipline, philosophy, and the basics offer a realistic alternative to Mookie's baseball, Sal's Italian-American entertainers, and Radio Raheem's rap? Given the realities of the United States' two-tiered economy, the lingering disabilities confronting racial minorities, and the decrepitude of public services, including education, in inner-city neighborhoods, the solutions proposed by Bennett, Bloom, and Hirsch, can benefit at best only a handful of Lee's characters. For the rest, cutting ugly reality with popular culture remains a bearable, if not satisfactory, solution.

Through both his exuberant presentation of life on the street in Bedford-Stuyvesant and his plotting of "Do the Right Thing," Spike Lee characterizes the uses and ambiguities of popular culture in a fashion paralleling the work of cultural analyst Dick Hebdige. In his study of English punks, *Subculture: The Meaning of Style*, Hebdige writes that members of the punk subculture, through their preferences in music, clothing, and hairstyles: "were engaged in that distinctive quest for a measure of autonomy which characterizes all youth sub- (and counter) cultures."[16] The principal characters in "Do the Right Thing" employ popular culture items in an analogous way: For them, clothes, music, and admired entertainment figures provide a means to define satisfying, expressive personas, which are otherwise unavailable through their work, experience at school, or their families. But there is more to the use of popular culture than this, because these individual adaptations also tend to produce collective identities. Hebdige in *Subculture* devotes considerable attention to the separate identities of punk precursors such as Mods, Teddy Boys, and Skinheads, while Lee turns his plot on the nagging disparities between black and Italian-American estimations of musicians, sports figures, and actors.

Hebdige does not claim that the formation of subcultures represents any sort of conventionally efficacious political action. Although they seized a "measure of autonomy," punks made no headway at controlling their work situations or the politicians who governed them, but they did manage to take control of their thoughts, appearance, and immediate environments. Again, Mookie, Buggin' Out, Radio Raheem, and Sal strive for much the same in "Do the Right Thing," but the tragedy of the film is that when two relatively powerless groups strive for cultural autonomy in the same benighted neighborhood, chaos ensues, and neither of the local groups gains from it.[17]

In the end, popular culture gives meaning to individuals and groups in "Do the Right Thing," and at the same time underlying cleavages brought to the surface by contrasting preferences in dress, music, and entertainers tear apart the neighborhood. This is a complex and insightful message; but just as several commentators have only noticed the "trivial" sources of the film's final conflagration, some observers refuse to accept the nuances of Spike Lee's presentation. Or, noting the film's ambiguity, they refuse to accept the possibility that the film's audience can understand its complexity. In the words of one reviewer:

> All these subtleties are likely to leave white (especially white liberal) audiences debating the meaning of Spike Lee's message. Black teenagers won't find it so hard, though. For them, the message is clear from the opening credits, which roll to the tune of "Fight the Power." . . . The police are your enemy. White people are your enemy.[18]

It is rare when the fear of the popular is more succinctly expressed.

It is not "Do the Right Thing" 's aggressive music, harsh plot, or stream of profanities that provoked its hostile critics. The film's true crime is Spike Lee's deliriously exciting presentation of a neighborhood in which poverty, individual pessimism, and blocked social mobility are the ground rules of everyday life. Such is the stuff of earnest documentaries for discerning audiences, not popular entertainments. A single powerful movie does not salvage the bulk of popular culture in the United States, and this is not the point of looking so closely at "Do the Right Thing." However, by examining how Spike Lee has constructed his story we have observed a critical elaboration of some of the main features of contemporary American culture that quite escapes the likes of William Bennett, Allan Bloom, and E. D. Hirsch, Jr.; and moreover, we have identified just what makes so many people uneasy with popular culture in general: not its predictability; rather, its indeterminacy.

NOTES

Chapter One. Popular Culture and Politics in Modern America.

1. For a sampling of this recent literature see the essays in Paul Buhle, ed., *Popular Culture in America* (St. Paul MN 1987); Lary May, ed., *Recasting America: Culture and Politics in the Age of the Cold War* (Chicago 1989); Ian Angus and Sut Jhally, eds., *Cultural Politics in Contemporary America* (New York 1989); Arthur Asa Berger, ed., *Political Culture and Public Opinion* (New Brunswick N.J. 1989).

2. Their seminal essays from the 1960s and 1970s are collected in Herbert Gutman, *Work, Culture, and Society in Industrializing America* (New York 1977) and in Warren Susman, *Culture as History: The Transformation of American Society in the Twentieth Century* (New York 1984).

3. "History as Myth and Ideology," in *Culture as History*, 5.

4. For a representative debate on "mass culture," see Norman Jacobs, ed., *Culture for the Millions? Mass Media in Modern Society* (Boston 1964), the proceedings of a symposia held in June 1959.

5. The essay is in Adorno and Horkheimer, *Dialectic of Enlightenment* (London 1979); see especially 154–156. On the Frankfort school, see Martin Jay, *The Dialectical Imagination: A History of the Frankfurt School and the Institute of Social Research, 1923–1950* (Boston 1973), ch. 6; and Christopher Brookeman, *American Culture and Society Since the 1930s* (New York 1984), ch. 8.

6. "Mass Society and Its Culture," in Jacobs, 22.

7. *One-Dimensional Man* (Boston 1968 ed.), 12, 14.

8. These events prompted the London publisher, Routledge & Keegan Paul, to reissue *Understanding Media* in 1969. The original was published in New York in 1964 by McGraw-Hill.

9. These essays are collected in the volume *Against Interpretation* (New York 1981).

10. *Steppin' Out* (Chicago 1981), 258.

11. See Robert Westbrook, "Politics as Consumption: Managing the Modern American Election," in Richard Wightman Fox and T. J. Jackson Lears, eds., *The Culture of Consumption: Critical Essays in American History, 1880–1980* (New York 1983) for a most perceptive account of the emergence of this trend.

12. "Bicentennial Blues," *It's Your World* (Arista Records, 1976).

13. *CULTURE, Inc.: The Corporate Takeover of Public Expression* (New York 1989), 156.

14. *Amusing Ourselves to Death: Public Discourse in the Age of Show Business* (New York 1985), 155–156.

15. Stuart Ewen, *Captains of Consciousness: Advertising and the Social Roots of Consumer Culture* (New York 1976) and *All-Consuming Images: The Politics of Style in Contemporary Culture* (New York 1988); Todd Gitlin, *The Whole World is Watching: Mass Media in the Making and Unmaking of the New Left* (Berkeley and Los Angeles 1980) and *Inside Prime Time* (New York 1983).

16. "Power, Hegemony, and Communication Theory," in Angus and Jhally, 62.

Chapter Two. Coxey's Army as a Millennial Movement.

1. Lester V. Berrey and Melvin van den Bark, *The American Thesaurus of Slang* (New York 1952, 2nd ed.), 343, 494, 786. Eric Partridge, *A Dictionary of Slang and Unconventional English* (New York 1970, 7th ed.), 186, 684, and *Slang Today and Yesterday* (London 1970, 4th ed.), 430.

2. The fullest account of the Western "armies" appears in Carlos A. Schwantes, *Coxey's Army: An American Odyssey* (Lincoln, Neb. 1985). See also Donald L. McMurry, *Coxey's Army: A Study of the Industrial Army Movement of 1894* (Boston 1929; reprinted New York 1970), 241–242.

3. Richard Hofstadter, *The Age of Reform: From Bryan to F. D. R.* (New York 1959), 165.

4. McMurry, 47, 60, 115. Henry Vincent, *The Story of the Commonweal* (Chicago 1894; reprinted New York 1969), 120. Embrey Bernard Howson, *Jacob Sechler Coxey: A Biography of a Monetary Reformer, 1854–1951* (Ph.D. dissertation, Ohio State University, 1973), 140.

5. W. T. Stead, " 'Coxeyism': A Character Sketch," *The Review of Reviews* 10 (1894), 47–59.

6. The text of the proposed legislation appears in Howson, 422–424, 432–435.

7. Ray Stannard Baker, *American Chronicle* (New York 1945), 7.

8. Carl Browne, *When Coxey's "Army" Marcht* [sic] *on Washington 1894* (San Francisco 1944), 4.

9. Baker, 8. Osman C. Hooper, "The Coxey Movement in Ohio," *Ohio Archaeological and Historical Publications* 9 (1900–1901), 155–176.

10. *Bulletin No. 3* (Massillon, Ohio: J. S. Coxey Good Roads Association of the U.S., 1894), in Ohio Historical Society's microfilm of Jacob Sechler Coxey, Sr., papers at the Massillon Museum (hereafter "Coxey Papers").

11. Browne, 6.

12. Jacob S. Coxey, *Coxey: His Own Story of the Commonweal* (Massillon, Ohio 1914), 94 (Coxey Papers).

13. Browne, 5; McMurry, 33.

14. Schwantes, 33.

15. McMurry, 38.

16. Shirley Plumer Austin, "Coxey's Commonweal Army," *The Chautauquan* 18 (1894), 332–336.

17. Vincent, 15.

18. Baker, 9.

19. *Bulletin No. 3.*

20. *Bulletin No. 3.*

21. *Coxey's Sound Money* (Massillon, Ohio) Dec. 5, 1896, 7 (emphasis in original).

22. Browne also told Ray Stannard Baker that he had part of the soul of the Greek orator Callisthenes. Baker, 8.

23. *Bulletin No. 3.*

24. Hooper.

25. *Bulletin No. 3.*

26. Baker, 9.

27. Browne, 2.

28. Untitled album of Coxey's March photographs, Massillon (Ohio) Public Library (emphasis in original). The final four lines do not appear in Browne's line drawing of the banner in *Bulletin No. 3.*

29. *Bulletin No. 3.*

30. *Bulletin No. 3.*

31. Browne, 6 (emphasis in original).

32. Christopher Hill, *Antichrist in Seventeenth-Century England* (London 1971), 118.

33. Quoted in Christopher Hill, *The World Turned Upside Down: Radical Ideas During the English Revolution* (New York 1972), 112.

34. Hill, *The World Turned Upside Down*, 119.

35. Reports of Browne's sermonizing appear in, among others: Stead, Vincent, 69; McMurry, 66–70. A photograph in the Massillon Public Library shows Browne speaking in Hagerstown Md., with the Commonweal banner next to him.

36. *Coxey's Sound Money*, Oct. 8, 1896, 4–5.

37. Hofstadter, 75–76.

38. *Coxey's Sound Money*, Oct. 8, 1896, 4–5.

39. *Bulletin No. 3* (emphasis in original).

40. *Carl's Camp Courier of the Commonweal of Christ* (Camp Liberty Md.) July 4, 1894, 1 (Coxey Papers) (emphasis in original).

41. Stead.

42. Carl Browne, broadside (1894) (Coxey Papers).

43. Undated broadside (c. 1894) (Coxey Papers).

44. Malcolm O. Sillars, "The Rhetoric of the Petition in Boots," *Speech Monographs* 39 (1972), 92–104.

45. Undated broadside (c. 1894) (Coxey Papers).

46. Eric Partridge (ed. Paul Beale), *A Dictionary of Slang and*

Unconventional English (New York 1984, 8th ed.), 1046. *Oxford English Dictionary* (1970) 9, 661. Harold Wentworth and Stuart Berg, *Dictionary of American Slang* (New York 1960, 2nd ed.), 464.

47. *Coxey Good Roads and Non-Interest Bond Library, No. 2*, 30; *Sound Money* 1, no. 1, June 6, 1895, suppl. n.p. (Coxey Papers).

48. Vincent, 109.

49. *Carl's Cactus* (Washington D.C., Aug. 16, 1895, n.p. (Coxey Papers).

50. A crucifixion cartoon by Browne appeared in *Coxey's Sound Money*, October 22, 1896; Heston's cartoon appeared at least three times in one month: October 1, 1896; October 8, 1896; and October 29, 1896.

51. Hofstadter, 78.

52. No dispute exists concerning the presence of anti-Semitic themes in Populist rhetoric, although considerable controversy surrounds Hofstadter's contention that anti-Semitism was a significant element. See, for example, Norman Pollack, "Fear of Man: Populism, Authoritarianism, and the Historian" and Irwin Unger, "Critique of Norman Pollack's 'Fear of Man,'" *Agricultural History* 39 (1965), 59–67 and 75–80, respectively.

53. Arthur H. Nethercot, *The First Five Lives of Annie Besant* (Chicago 1960), 248, 284–285.

54. Bruce F. Campbell, *Ancient Wisdom Revived: A History of the Theosophical Movement* (Berkeley and Los Angeles 1980), 69. Emmett A. Greenwalt, *California Utopia: Point Loma: 1897–1942* (San Diego 1978, 2nd ed.), 6–7.

55. Campbell, 27.

56. Vincent, 109–110.

57. Greenwalt, 10–11.

58. Stead.

59. Vincent, 112.

60. Nethercot, 392–393.

61. Account from the *Philadelphia Inquirer*, reprinted in *Sound Money*, June 20, 1895, 5.

62. Account from the St. Louis *Chronicle*, reprinted in Coxey's *Sound Money*, July 30, 1896, 12.

63. *Coxey's Sound Money*, September 17, 1896, 4, and November 5, 1896, 16.

64. *Coxey Good Roads and Non-Interest Bond Library, No. 2*, 25–26.

65. Howson, 139.

66. Baker, 11.

67. Daniel Boorstin, *The Image, or What Happened to the American Dream* (New York 1962), 10–12.

68. James H. Moorhead, "Between Progress and Apocalypse: A Reassessment of Millennialism in American Religious Thought, 1800–1880," *Journal of American History* 71 (1984), 524–542; Ernest R. Sandeen, *The Roots of Fundamentalism: British and American Fundamentalism, 1800–1930* (Chicago 1970), 172–173; Frederic Cople Jaher, *Doubters and Dissenters: Cataclysmic Thought in America, 1885–1918* (New York 1964); Ruth Alden Doan, *The Miller Heresy, Millennialism, and American Culture* (Philadelphia 1987), 13–14.

69. Richard Hofstadter, *The Paranoid Style in American Politics and Other Essays* (New York 1965), 3–4. See also Michael Barkun, *Disaster and the Millennium* (Syracuse 1986), 145–146.

70. Michael Barkun, "The Language of Apocalypse: Premillennialists and Nuclear War," in Marshall W. Fiskwick and Ray B. Browne, eds., *The Godpumpers: Religion in the Electronic Age* (Bowling Green, Ohio 1987), 159–173.

71. Leonard Zeskind, *The "Christian Identity" Movement: A Theological Justification for Racist and Anti-Semitic Violence* (Atlanta: Center for Democratic Renewal, 1986); Alan D. Sapp, "Basic Ideologies of Right-Wing Extremist Groups in America" (Warrensburg Mo.: Center for Criminal Justice, Central Missouri State University, 1985).

72. John Wilson, "British Israelism: The Ideological Restraints on Sect Organization," in Bryan Wilson, ed., *Patterns of Sectarianism: Organization and Ideology in Social and Religious Movements* (London 1967); John Wilson, "The Relation Between Ideology and Organization in a Small Religious Group: The British Israelites," *Review of Religious Research* 10 (1968), 51–60.

73. Herbert W. Armstrong, *The United States and Britain in Prophecy* (Pasadena, Cal.: 1980).

74. Zeskind.

75. Mrs. Sarah E. V. Emery, *Seven Financial Conspiracies Which Have Enslaved the American People* (Lansing Mich. 1894, rev. ed.; reprinted Westport, Conn. 1975).

Chapter Three. Progressive Reform Censorship, and the Motion Picture Industry, 1909–1917.

1. John Collier, "The Problem of Motion Pictures," reprinted from the Proceedings of the Child Welfare Conference, Clark University, Worcester, Mass. June 1910.

2. Robert J. Fisher, "Film Censorship and Progressive Reform: The National Board of Censorship of Motion Pictures, 1909–1922," *Journal of Popular Film* 4 (1975), 143–156; Kathleen D. McCarthy, "Nickel Vice and Virtue: Movie Censorship in Chicago, 1907–1915," *Journal of Popular Film* 1 (1976), 37–55.

3. See especially Robert Sklar, *Movie-Made America* (New York 1975); Garth Jowett, *Film: The Democratic Art* (Boston 1976); Lary May, *Screening Out the Past: The Birth of Mass Culture and the Motion Picture Industry* (New York 1980). For a preliminary treatment of the relationship between Progressivism, censorship, and the motion picture industry, see Nancy J. Rosenbloom, "Between Reform and Regulation: The Struggle over Censorship in Progressive America, 1909–1922," *Film History* 1 (1987), 307–325.

4. See especially Daniel T. Rodgers, "In Search of Progressivism," *Reviews in American History* 10 (1982), 113–132, for a historiography of the last fifteen years. For a recent analysis, see Richard McCormick, *The Party Period and Public Policy: American Politics from the Age of Jackson to the Progressive Era* (New York 1986), 263–355. See also Richard McCormick and Arthur Link, *Progressivism* (Arlington Heights Ill. 1983).

5. See especially Robert J. Fisher, "The People's Institute of New York City, 1897–1934: Culture, Progressive Democracy, and the People" (Ph.D. diss., New York University, 1974), and Moses Rischin, *The Promised City* (Cambridge, Mass. 1962), 212–218; Edgar A. Russell, "Work of the People's Institute as Originated and Carried on by Charles Sprague Smith," *Craftsmen* 10 (May 1906), 182–189; Charles Sprague Smith, "Ethical Work of the People's Institute, A People's Church," *Outlook* 79 (April 22, 1905), 1001–1003; and "The People's Institute of New York and Its Work

for the Development of Citizenship Along Democratic Lines," *The Arena* 38, July 1907, 49–52.

6. See John Collier, "The People's Institute," *The World Today* 16 (February 1909), 170–175 and Charles Sprague Smith, "The People's Institute of New York."

7. John Collier, "Cheap Amusements," *Charities and the Commons* 20, April 11, 1908, 73–76.

8. For an explanation of the relationship between the People's Institute and the National Board of Censorship of Motion Pictures see Fisher, "The People's Institute," 208–252. See also Charles Matthew Feldman, *The National Board of Censorship (Review) of Motion Pictures. 1909–1922* (New York 1977).

9. Especially Thomas R. Gunning, "D. W. Griffith and the Narrator–System: Narrative Structure and Industry Organization in Biograph Films, 1908–1909" (Ph.D. diss., New York University, 1986), 433–457. Gunning explains that the MPPC was incorporated on September 9, 1908, and that the licenses with the manufacturers and the importers were signed on December 18. See also Robert Anderson, "The Motion Picture Patents Company: a Reevaluation" in Tino Balio ed., *The American Film Industry* (Madison 1985 revised ed.), 133–152; and Jowett, *Film*, 33–34.

10. Richard Abel, *French Cinema: The First Wave, 1915–1929* (Princeton 1984), 9–39.

11. Announcement to Exhibitors from Motion Picture Patents Company, February 1, 1909. Motion Pictures Patents Company Administrative Files (hereafter MPPCAF) Edison Archives, Edison National Historic Site, National Park Service, United States Department of the Interior.

12. John Collier, Direct Examination, "United States vs. Motion Picture Patents Company and Others, Case No. 889, Eastern District Pennsylvania, September 1912–April 1914" (Washington, D.C.: U.S. Government Printing Office) 5, 2896.

13. Announcement to Exhibitors, February, 1, 1909, MPPCAF.

14. See especially Gunning, 469–479.

15. See Russell, 185.

16. See especially Charles Sprague Smith, *Working with the People* (New York 1908).

17. Charles Sprague Smith to Hon. William A. Armstrong, May 21, 1908, People's Institute manuscript Collection, box 9, Manuscripts and Archives Division, New York Public Library (hereafter NYPL).

18. Collier, "Cheap Amusements," 75.

19. See Robert C. Allen, "Motion Picture Exhibition in Manhattan 1907–1912," in John C. Fell, ed., *Film Before Griffith* (Berkeley and Los Angeles 1983), 162–175, and Russell Merritt, "Nickelodeon Theaters, 1905–1914: Building an Audience for the Movies," in Tino Balio ed., *The American Film Industry* (Madison 1976), 83–102.

20. Collier, "Cheap Amusements," 76.

21. John Collier, "The People's Institute," *The Independent* 72 (May 30, 1912), 1148.

22. See Rosalind Rosenberg, *Beyond Separate Spheres: Intellectual Roots of Modern Feminism* (New Haven 1982).

23. John Collier to Sonya Levien, n.d., Levien Manuscript Collection, Huntington Library, San Marino, California, box 20.

24. John Collier to Manufacturers of Motion Pictures, March 15, 1909, Edison Document File. See also *Report of the National Board of Censorship of Motion Pictures* (New York: National Board of Censorship, 1911), 5–7.

25. Executive Committee Precedents, March 8, 1909–June 23, 1915, National Board of Review of Motion Pictures Collection, box 170, NYPL.

26. Executive Committee Precedents, August 6, 1909.

27. Executive Committee Precedents, July 15, 1909.

28. General Committee Precedents, March 12, 1909–June 11, 1915, National Board of Review of Motion Pictures Collection, box 120; see especially April 15, 1909. See also National Board of Censorship of Motion Pictures, Pamphlet no. 2, August 14, 1909, George Kleine Collection, box 38, Manuscript Division, Library of Congress.

29. Collier to Manufacturers of Motion Pictures, March 15, 1909, Edison Document File.

30. John Collier to Dwight MacDonald, March 26, 1909, George Kleine Collection, box 6.

31. Collier to MacDonald.

32. National Board of Censorship of Motion Pictures, "Suggestions for a Model Ordinance for Regulating Motion Picture Theaters" (New York n.d.). See also Sonya Levien, "New York's Motion Picture Law," *The American City* 9 (October 1913), 319–320.

33. John Collier, "The Learned Judges and the Films," *The Survey* 34 (September 4, 1915), 514.

34. Mayor William J. Gaynor, "Mayor Gaynor's Veto," *The Moving Picture World*, 15, January 11, 1913, 135–136.

35. Howe, quoted in W. P. Lawson, "Standards of Censorship," *Harper's Weekly*, 60, January 16, 1915, 63.

36. Howe in Lawson.

37. Howe in Lawson.

38. Josephine Redding to William McGuire, n.d. [after June 11, 1915], and McGuire to Redding, July 22, 1915; W. Frank Persons to Edward Sanderson, Director of the People's Institute, February 10, 1917; and W. G. McGuire to Sherwood, February 2, 1917; all in National Board of Review Collection, boxes 42, 43, 8, respectively. See also "Special Bulletin on Motion Picture Comedies" [April 1915], Edison Document File; *The Standards and Policy of the National Board of Review of Motion Pictures* (New York 1917); *The Standards of the National Board of Review of Motion Pictures* (New York 1917).

39. See Barrett's Report, August 1914, National Board of Review Collection, box 118.

40. For examples of the standards set by the National Board under Collier and Howe, see "National Board of Censorship of Motion Pictures," August 1909, George Kleine Collection; *Annual Report of the National Board of Censorship of Motion Pictures* (New York 1913), 9–12; *The Policy and Standards of the National Board of Censorship of Motion Pictures, Revised May 1914* (New York 1914).

41. See John Collier, *From Every Zenith* (Denver 1963).

Chapter Four. The Press and the Red Scare, 1919–1921.

1. Frank Luther Mott, *American Journalism* (New York 1962), 609.

2. Peter M. Sandman, David M. Rubin, and David B. Sachsman, *Media Casebook: an introductory reader in American mass communications* (Englewood Cliffs N.J. 1972), 48–49; and Mott, 547.

3. Edward Herman and Noam Chomsky, *Manufacturing Consent* (New York 1989), 4; Sandman et al., 45–46.

4. Quoted in Sidney Kobre, *The Development of American Journalism* (Dubuque, Iowa 1969), 509.

5. *The Brass Check* (Pasadena 1936), esp. chs. 25–28.

6. Robert E. Park, *The Immigrant Press and Its Control* (New York 1922), 303; see also Kobre, 518; Sandman et al., 46; Mott, 593.

7. Park, 365.

8. Herman and Chomsky, 16.

9. Herman and Chomsky, 2.

10. *The Press and Foreign Policy* (Princeton 1967), 10. Also see Maxwell McCombs and Donald Shaw, "Newspapers versus Television: Mass Communication Effects across Time," in McCombs and Shaw eds., *The Emergence of American Political Issues: The Agenda-Setting Function of the Press* (New York 1977), 5; Doris Graeber, *Mass Media and American Politics* (Washington, D.C. 1989), 287; W. Phillips Davidson et al., *Mass Media* (New York 1976), 181.

11. *Only Yesterday* (New York 1959 Bantam ed.), 32.

12. Todd Gitlin, *The Whole World Is Watching: Mass Media in the Making and Unmaking of the New Left* (Berkeley, Calif. 1980), 6–7. Also see Erving Goffman, *Frame Analysis* (New York 1974).

13. *Manufacturing the News* (Austin, Texas 1980), 10.

14. Mark Fishman, "Crime Waves as Ideology," *Social Problems* 25 (1978), 542.

15. Quoted in Lynn Bowman, *Los Angeles: Epic of a City* (Berkeley and Los Angeles, 1974), 277.

16. John Walton Caughey, *California* (Englewood Cliffs, N.J. 1953), 475.

17. Quoted in James R. Green, *The World of the Worker* (New York 1980), 95.

18. Quoted in Robert L. Friedheim, *The Seattle General Strike* (Seattle 1964), 86–87.

19. Quoted in Friedheim, 101.

20. Friedman, 169.

21. Both men are quoted in Foster Rhea Dulles and Melvyn Dubofsky, *Labor in America: A History* (Arlington Heights 1984, 4th ed.), 224.

22. Quoted in Samuel Yellen, *American Labor Struggles, 1877–1934* (New York 1974 ed.), 272.

23. Quoted in Dulles and Dobofsky, 228.

Chapter Five. Encountering Mass Culture at the Grassroots.

1. True Story Magazine, *The American Economic Evolution* 1 (New York 1930), 32–34, 67.

2. Walter Thompson Company, *Newsletter*, no. 139, (July 1, 1926), 157–159, RG 11, J. Walter Thompson Advertising Company Archives (hereafter JWT).

3. Stuart Ewen, *Captains of Consciousness: Advertising and the Social Roots of the Consumer Culture* (New York 1976); Stuart and Elizabeth Ewen, *Channels of Desire: Mass Images and the Shaping of American Consciousness* (New York 1982); Richard Wightman Fox and T. J. Jackson Lears, eds., *The Culture of Consumption* (New York 1983). While this is also the general thrust of Roy Rosenzweig's argument, he does suggest that in bringing diverse groups of workers together, the movies unintentionally may have helped them mount a more unified political challenge in the 1930s. But they did not organize out of a working class consciousness. Having shared in middle class culture in the 1920s, they fought to sustain and expand their access to it, which was being endangered by the depression. Roy Rosenzweig, *"Eight Hours for What We Will": Workers and Leisure in Worcester, Massachusetts, 1870–1930* (New York 1984).

Sociologists have also shared the assumptions of contemporary observers who were confident of the homogenizing power of mass culture. See Daniel Bell, *The End of Ideology* (New York 1962);

John Goldthorpe and David Lockwood, *The Affluent Worker in the Class Structure* (Cambridge, Mass. 1969). For criticism of the embourgeoisement thesis, see John Clarke, Chas Critcher, and Richard Johnson, *Working Class Culture: Studies in History and Theory* (London 1979), and James E. Cronin, *Labour and Society in Britain, 1918–1979* (London 1984), 146–172.

Antonio Gramsci's theory of cultural hegemony applied to mass culture is more complex. If defined narrowly, it comes close to embourgeoisement in suggesting that, by participating in mass culture, workers come to share values with the ruling elite and thereby reinforce its control. If defined more broadly, however, the theory allows for more diversity in responses to mass culture, but nonetheless argues that if the experience does not make workers into revolutionaries, it still serves to legitimate elite rule. For a useful discussion of the strengths and weaknesses of Gramsci's theory of cultural hegemony, see T. J. Jackson Lears, "The Concept of Cultural Hegemony: Problems and Possibilities," *American Historical Review* 90 (June 1985), 567–593.

4. On the wages of unemployment of Chicago's factory workers, see my dissertation, "Learning to Live in the Welfare State: Industrial Workers in Chicago Between the Wars, 1919–1939" (Ph.D. diss., University of California, Berkeley, 1986), ch. 4, "Contested Loyalty at the Workplace."

5. Wilbur C. Plummer, "Social and Economic Consequences of Buying on the Installment Plan," "Supplement," *Annals of the American Academy of Political and Social Sciences* 129 (Jan. 1927), 2; Edwin R. A. Seligman, *The Economics of Installment Selling: A Study in Consumers' Credit with Special Reference to the Automobile* (New York 1927) cited in "Economics of Installment Selling," *Monthly Labor Review* 26 (Feb. 1928), 233.

6. Leila Houghteling, *The Income and Standard of Living of Unskilled Laborers in Chicago* (Chicago 1927); Chicago Tribune, *Chicago Tribune Fact Book*, 1928 (Chicago 1928), 46; Frank Stricker, "Affluence for Whom?—Another Look at Prosperity and the Working Classes in the 1920's," *Labor History* 24 (Winter 1983), 30–32. Stricker estimates that even by 1929, a working-class family had no more than a thirty percent chance of owning a car.

7. John Dollard, "The Changing Functions of the American Family" (Ph.D. diss., University of Chicago, 1931), 137–138.

8. See the following transcripts of interviews from Italians in Chicago Project (IC), University of Illinois Chicago Circle (UICC): Rena Domke, Apr. 28, 1980, Chicago, 3; Mario Avignone, July 12, 1979, Chicago, 24; Thomas Perpoli, June 26, 1980, Chicago, 34; Theresa DeFalco, Apr. 28, 1980, Downers Grove, Ill., 17; Leonard Giuleano, Jan. 2, 1980, Chicago, 19; Rena Morandin, July 22, 1980, Chicago, 18; Ernest Dalle-Molle, Apr. 30, 1980, Downers Grove, Ill., 76; Edward Baldacci, Apr. 29, 1980, Chicago Heights, Ill., 17. For additional evidence of how Italians valued the phonograph as a way to enjoy their native culture, see Gaetano DeFilippis, "Social Life in an Immigrant Community" (c. 1930), box 130, folder 2, 42, Burgess Papers, University of Chicago Special Collections (UCSC); C. W. Jenkins, "Chicago's Pageant of Nations: Italians and Their Contribution," *Chicago Evening Post*, Nov. 16, 1929, Chicago Foreign Language Press Survey (CFLPS), box 22, UCSC; Autobiography of an Italian Immigrant, n.d., box 64, folder 24, 18, Chicago Area Project Papers (CAP), Chicago Historical Society (CHS). Chicago.

9. Pekka Gronow, "Ethnic Recordings: An Introduction"; Richard K. Spottswood, "Commercial Ethnic Recordings in the United States," and his "The Sajewski Story: Eighty Years of Polish Music in Chicago," in *Ethnic Recordings in America: A Neglected Heritage,* American Folklife Center, Studies in American Folklife, no. 1 (Washington, D.C. 1982), 1–66, 133–173; Robert C. Jones and Louis R. Wilson, *The Mexican in Chicago* (Chicago 1931), 7. I am grateful to an anonymous reviewer for *American Quarterly* for pointing out how similarly Southerners used phonograph recordings.

10. "Supreme Court of the District of Columbia in Equity No. 37623, United States of America Petitioner vs. Swift & Company, Armour & Company, Morris & Company, Wilson & Co., Inc., and The Cudahy Packing Co., et al., Defendants, On Petitions of Swift & Company, and Its Associate Defendants, and Armour & Company, and Its Associate Defendants, for Modification of Decree of February 27, 1920, Petitioning Defendants Statement of the Case," 1930, 14. For more on chain stores as a way of streamlining distribution to make it equal in efficiency to mass production see, *Chain Store Progress* 1 (Nov.-Dec. 1929), and 2 (Jan. 1930).

For basic information on the development of chain stores, see James L. Palmer, "Economic and Social Aspects of Chain Stores," *Journal of Business of the University of Chicago* 2 (1929): 172–290;

14. *Dziennik Zjednoczenia*, Nov. 28, 1932, quoted in Joseph Chalasinski, "Polish and Parochial School Among Polish Immigrants in America: A Study of a Polish Neighborhood in South Chicago," n.d., box 33, folder 2, 20, CAP Papers.

Among Mexican immigrants, who came to Chicago in increasing numbers during the 1920s, loyalty to Mexico entered into the selection of stores to patronize. It was not enough that a merchant be Mexican, but he had to also remain a Mexican citizen. One storekeeper complained. "I have a store in the Mexican district. If I become a citizen of the United States the Mexicans won't trade with me, because they wouldn't think I was fair to them or loyal to my country. I read the papers and I would like to vote, but I must not become a citizen. I have to have the Mexican trade to make a living." Quoted in Edward Hayden, "Immigration, the Second Generation, and Juvenile Delinquency," n.d., box 131, folder 3, 10, Burgess Papers.

On a practical level, patrons felt that they could best trust their own merchants; butchers of other "races" would certainly put a heavier thumb on the scale. R. D. McCleary, "General Survey of Attitudes Involved in the Formation of a Youth Council on the Near-West Side," n.d., box 101, folder 10, 2, CAP Papers.

15. Paul Penio, June 30, 1980, Itasca, Ill., IC, UICC, 17.

16. Sidney Sorkin, "A Ride Down Roosevelt Road, 1920–1940," *Chicago Jewish Historical Society News*, Oct. 1979, 6; The Chicago Tribune, "Consumer Survey: An Investigation into the Shopping Habits of 2205 Chicago Housewives, October 1929," mimeographed. A study of one hundred working class Chicagoans found that in 1927 "curiously enough, canned goods and American inventions—the cheaper ways of filling an empty stomach . . . —seem to have invaded the ranks but little." Laura Friedman, "A Study of One Hundred Unemployed Families in Chicago, January 1927 to June 1932" (M.A. thesis, University of Chicago, 1933), 112.

Sophonisba Breckinridge spoke with a Croatian woman who pointed out that in her neighborhood store she could ask the grocer about new things she saw but did not know how to use, whereas elsewhere she could not ask and so would not buy. Sophonisba Breckinridge, *New Homes for Old* (New York 1921), 123.

17. JoEllen Goodman and Barbara Marsh, "The Goldblatt's Story: From Poverty to Retailing Riches to Ch. 11 Disgrace," *Crain's Chicago Business* 4 (Oct. 19–25, 1981): 17–27; "Four Boys and a Store," June 30, 1960, mimeographed press release.

Paul H. Nystrom, *Economic Principles of Consumption* (New Y
1929), 518–522, and his *Chain Stores* (Washington, D.C. 193
Walter S. Hayward, "The Chain Store and Distribution," *Soci
Science Review* 115 (Sept. 1924): 220–225.

For details on Chicago's chain stores, see Ernest Hug
Shideler, "The Chain Store: A Study of the Ecological Organizatioi
of a Modern City" (Ph.D. diss., University of Chicago, 1927); Com
mittee on Business Research, "Study Sales of Groceries in Chi
cago," *Chicago Commerce,* Apr. 14, 1928, 15: "Analyze Variety
Store Sales Here," *Chicago Commerce,* Sept. 1, 1928, 23; Einer
Bjorkland and James L. Palmer, *A Study of the Prices of Chain
and Independent Grocers in Chicago* (Chicago 1930); Ernest Frederic Witte, "Organization, Management, and Control of Chain
Drug Stores" (Ph.D. diss., University of Chicago, 1932); Robert
Greenwell Knight, "A Study of the Organization and Control
Methods of Walgreen Company's Chain of Drug Stores" (M.A. the-
sis, University of Chicago, 1925).

11. "How Strong Are the Chain Groceries in the Leading Cities?" *J. Walter Thompson News Bulletin,* no. 122 (June 1926), 14–
21, RG 11, JWT; United States Department of Commerce, Bureau
of the Census, *Fifteenth Census of the United States: 1930, Vol. 1;
Retail Distribution* (Washington, D.C. 1934), 662.

12. Ling Me Chen, "The Development of Chain Stores in the
United States" (M.A. thesis, University of Chicago, 1929), 12, 102;
William J. Baxter, "The Future of the Chain Store," *Chicago Com-
merce,* Oct. 29, 1928, 24; "The Science of Chain Store Locations,"
Chain Store Progress 1 (Mar. 1929), 5; Stanley Resor, "What Do
These Changes Mean?" *J. Walter Thompson News Bulletin,* no. 104
(Dec. 1923), 12–13, JWT.

A 1927–28 study of chain store locations in Atlanta found a
situation much like Chicago's. Forty-five chain stores served the
8,634 families in the "best" areas of town—one store for every 191
families—while in the "third-best" and "poorest" areas combined,
the same number of chains served 33,323 families, one store for
every 740 families. Guy C. Smith, "Selective Selling Decreases
Costs: Market Analysis Enables Seller to Choose His Customer,
Saving Costly Distribution Wastes," *Chicago Commerce,* Apr. 14,
1928, 24.

13. Quoted in Paul S. Taylor, *Mexican Labor in the United
States, Chicago and the Calumet Region,* University of California
Publications in Economics 7 (Berkeley 1932), 169.

18. Betty Wright, Paper for Sociology 264, Mar. 1931, box 156, folder 2, 4–6, Burgess Papers. William Ireland noted that the Wieboldt's Store on Milwaukee Avenue lost its lower class customers to Iverson's—across the street—when it changed its merchandising techniques to attract middle class customers. " 'The lower-class' Poles will only trade where the store puts out on the sidewalk baskets of wares through which customers can rummage." William Rutherford Ireland, "Young American Poles" (written as M.A. thesis, University of Chicago, 1932, but not submitted), 26.

19. Louis E. Boone, *Classics in Consumer Behavior: Selected Readings Together with the Authors' Own Retrospective Comments* (Tulsa 1977).

20. Alice Miller Mitchell, *Children and Movies* (Chicago 1929), 66.

21. "Cost of Living in the United States—Clothing and Miscellaneous Expenditures," *Monthly Labor Review* 9 (Nov. 1919), 16.

22. Mary F. Bogue, *Administration of Mothers' Aid in Ten Localities with Special Reference to Health, Housing, Education and Recreation,* Children's Bureau Publication no. 184 (Washington, D.C. 1928), 90.
At the end of the decade, one study showed wage-earner families spending a greater percentage of income on picture shows than families of either clerks or professionals: The $22.56 a year they put toward movies equalled that expended by clerks with a third more income and was twice as much as professionals spent who were earning salaries almost four times higher. President's Research Committee, *Recent Social Trends in the United States* 2 (New York 1933; reprinted Westport, Conn. 1970), 895.

23. For a study that analyzes film content for insight into audience response, see Lary May's fascinating *Screening Out the Past: The Birth of Mass Culture and the Motion Picture Industry, with a New Preface* (Chicago 1983).

24. "Trip to Calumet Theatre Brings Back Memories," *Daily Calumet,* Nov. 23, 1981; "South Chicago Was Home to Many Theaters," *Daily Calumet,* Apr. 25, 1983; Felipe Salazar and Rodolfo Camacho, "The Gayety: A Theatre's Struggle for Survival," Project for Metro History Fair, n.d., manuscript; "Southeast Chicago Theatres Filled Entertainment Need," *Daily Calumet,* Jan. 3, 1983; "Theaters Plentiful on the Southeast Side," *Daily Calumet,* Jan. 10, 1983.

25. Douglas Gomery, "Movie Audiences, Urban Geography, and the History of the American Film," *The Velvet Light Trap Review of Cinema* 19 (Spring 1982), 23–29.

26. Interview with Jim Fitzgibbon, July 16, 1981, Chicago, Oral History Collection, Southeast Chicago Historical Project (SECHP), 14.

27. Interview with Ernest Dalle-Molle, Apr. 30, 1980, Chicago, IC, UICC, 76.

28. Robert A. Slayton, " 'Our Own Destiny': The Development of Community in Back of the Yards" (Ph.D. diss., Northwestern University, 1982), 59–60.

29. For a description of amateur night, see "Fitzgibbons Was Important Part of Southeast Historical Project," *Daily Calumet*, June 13, 1983. On the "Garlic Opera House," see Harvey Warren Zorbaugh, *The Gold Coast and the Slum: A Sociological Study of Chicago's Near North Side* (Chicago 1929), 164–165.

30. Student paper, n.a., n.t., n.d. but c. 1930, box 154, folder 5, 26, Burgess Papers; for more evidence of the discrimination blacks encountered at movie theaters, see The Chicago Commission on Race Relations, *The Negro in Chicago: A Study of Race Relations and a Race Riot* (Chicago 1922), 318–320.

31. Quoted in Taylor, 232.

32. Barney Balaban and Sam Katz, *The Fundamental Principles of Balaban and Katz Theatre Management* (Chicago 1926), 15, 17–20.

33. Hiram L. Jome, *Economics of the Radio Industry* (Chicago 1925), 116–117. For more on home assembly of radios by workers, see Provenzano, Mar. 17, 1980, Brookfield, Ill., IC, UICC, 24–25; Thomas Perpoli, June 26, 1980, Chicago, IC, UICC, 59; Anita Edgar Jones, "Conditions Surrounding Mexicans in Chicago" (Ph.D. diss., University of Chicago, 1928), 85. On abundance of aerials, see *Radio Broadcast*, Oct. 1922, quoted in Erik Barnouw, *A Tower in Babel: A History of Broadcasting in the United States* 1 (New York 1966), 88. Also, Paul F. Cressey, "Survey of McKinley Park Community," Oct. 20, 1925, box 129, folder 7, 1, Burgess Papers.

34. For an amusing picture of "DX fishing," see Bruce Bliven, "The Legion Family and the Radio: What We Hear When We Tune

In," *Century Magazine* 108 (Oct. 1924): 811–818; on Chicago's "silent night," see Barnouw, 93; on technical challenges, see "Merry Jests and Songs Mark Radio Party," *Chicago Commerce*, Apr. 5, 1924, 17; "Radio Marvels Will Be Seen at Show," *Chicago Commerce*, Oct. 2, 1926, 9.

35. Daniel Starch, "A Study of Radio Broadcasting Made for the National Broadcasting Company, Inc.," 1928, box 8, folder 4, 23, Edgar James Papers, Wisconsin State Historical Society (WSHS); American Telephone and Telegraph Company, "The Use of Radio Broadcasting as a Publicity Medium," 1926, mimeographed, box 1, folder 8, 4, Edgar James Papers, WSHS; Clifford Kirkpatrick, *Report of a Research into the Attitudes and Habits of Radio Listeners* (St. Paul 1933), 26; Malcolm Willey and Stuart A. Rice, *Communication Agencies and Social Life* (President's Research Committee on Social Trends) (New York 1933), 202; Provenzano, 25.

36. For more discussion of youths' attraction to mass culture, see my "Learning to Live in the Welfare State," 190–195. For vivid descriptions of club life, see Isadore Zelig. "A Study of the 'Basement' Social Clubs of Lawndale District," Paper for Sociology 270, 1928, box 142, folder 3, Burgess Papers; S. Kerson Weinberg, "Jewish Youth in the Lawndale Community: A Sociological Study," Paper for Sociology 269, n.d., box 139, folder 3, 50–79, Burgess Papers; Meyer Levin, *The Old Bunch* (New York 1937), 3–9, 18–26, 121–139; Ireland, 72–75; "The Regan's Colts and the Sherman Park District" and "The Neighborhood," 1924, box 2, folder 10, McDowell Papers, CHS; Guy DeFillipis, "Club Dances," 1935, box 191, folder 7, CAP Papers; Robert Sayler, "A Study of Behavior Problems of Boys in Lower North Community," n.d., box 135, folder 4, 24–27, Burgess Papers; William J. Demsey, "Gangs in the Calumet Park District," Paper for Sociology 270, c. 1928, box 148, folder 5, Burgess Papers; Donald Pierson, "Autobiographies of Teenagers of Czechoslovakian Backgrounds from Cicero and Berwyn," 1931, box 134, folder 5, Burgess Papers.

37. Willey and Rice, 196, 200.

38. Bruce Linton, "A History of Chicago Radio Station Programming, 1921–1931, with Emphasis on Stations WMAQ and WGN" (Ph.D. diss., Northwestern University, 1953), 155; Mark Newman, "On the Air with Jack L. Cooper: The Beginnings of Black-Appeal Radio," *Chicago History* 12 (Summer 1983), 53–54; *Chicago Tribune Picture Book of Radio* (Chicago 1928), 75–86;

WGN: A Pictorial History (Chicago 1961), 28; *Poles of Chicago, 1837–1937: A History of One Century of Polish Contribution to the City of Chicago* (Chicago 1937), 240; Martha E. Gross, "The 'Jolly Girls' Club: Report and Diary," Mar. 1933, box 158, folder 5, 28, Burgess Papers; Joseph Kisciunas, "Lithuanian Chicago" (M.A. thesis, DePaul University, 1935), 40; Interview with Margaret Sabella, Mar. 29, 1980, Chicago, IC, UICC, 8; from the CFLPS, UCSC: "Colonial Activities," *Chicago Italian Chamber of Commerce*, May 1929, 17, and "Radio Concert of Polish Songstress," *Dziennik Zjednoczenia*, Aug. 5, 1922; *Immaculate Conception, B.V.M. Parish, South Chicago, Diamond Jubilee: 1882–1957*, n.p.; Peter C. Marzio, ed., *A Nation of Nations: The People Who Came to America as Seen Through Objects and Documents Exhibited at the Smithsonian Institution* (New York 1976), 443.

39. Edward Nockels to Trade Union Secretaries, Dec. 23, 1926, box 15, folder 106, Fitzpatrick Papers, CHS; William J. H. Strong, "Report on Radiocasting for the Special Committee, Mssrs. Fitzpatrick, Nockels and Olander, of the Chicago Federation of Labor and the Illinois Federation of Labor, November 5th, 1925," box 14, folder 100, 1, Fitzpatrick Papers; "The Aims, Objects and History of WCFL," *WCFL Radio Magazine* 1 (Spring 1928), 58–59; Erlign Sejr Jorgensen, "Radio Station WCFL: A Study in Labor Union Broadcasting" (M.A. thesis, University of Wisconsin, 1949).

40. Starch, 28.

41. Willey and Rice, 195–199; Linton, 61–62, 121; Barnouw, 99–101; Arthur Frank Wertheim, *Radio Comedy* (New York 1979); Christopher H. Sterling and John M. Kittross, *Stay Tuned: A Concise History of American Broadcasting* (Belmont, Calif. 1978), 71–78.

42. N. Goldsmith and Austin C. Lescarboura. *This Thing Called Broadcasting* (New York 1930), 296.

43. On the philosophy of a separate black economy, see Allan Spear, *Black Chicago: The Making of a Negro Ghetto, 1890–1920* (Chicago 1967), 111–118, 192–200 and M. S. Stuart, *An Economic Detour: A History of Insurance in the Lives of American Negroes* (New York 1940), xvii–xxv, 101. P. W. Chavers devoted his life to the establishment of a viable black economy in Chicago. Madrue Chavers-Wright, *The Guarantee—P. W. Chavers: Banker, Entrepreneur, Philanthropist in Chicago's Black Belt of the Twenties* (New York 1985).

44. Quoted in St. Clair Drake and Horace R. Cayton, *Black Metropolis: A Study of Negro Life in a Northern City* (New York 1945), 430.

45. Edmund David Cronon, *Black Moses: The Story of Marcus Garvey and the Universal Negro Improvement Association* (Madison 1968), 50–61, 174–175.

46. On Black businesses that flourished in Chicago and in the nation in general, with special attention to successful trades like undertaking, barber, and beauty shops, cosmetics and newspapers, see Drake and Cayton, 433–436, 456–462; Spear, 112–115, 184–185; Chicago Commission on Race Relations, 140–141; Thomas E. Hunter, "Problems of Colored Chicago," 1930, box 154, folder 4, Burgess Papers; Camille Cohen-Jones, "Your Cab Company: How a Colored Man Organized a Cab Company in Chicago," *The Crisis* 34 (Mar. 1927), 5–6; Abram L. Harris, *The Negro as Capitalist: A Study of Banking and Business Among American Negroes* (Philadelphia 1936), 170–172; J. H. Harmon, Jr., "The Negro as a Local Business Man," *The Journal of Negro History* 14 (Apr. 1929): 137–138, 140–141, 144–151; Gunnar Myrdal, *American Dilemma: The Negro Problem and Modern Democracy* 1 (New York 1944), 309–310, 317; Jervis Anderson, *This Was Harlem 1900–1950* (New York 1981), 92–98.

47. Although black companies faced aggressive competition from mainline insurance companies, they exploited the fact that white firms charged blacks higher premiums and rarely hired black agents. Leo M. Bryant, "Negro Insurance Companies in Chicago" (M.A. thesis, University of Chicago, 1934), 1–80; Hylan Garnet Lewis, "Social Differentiation in the Negro Community" (M.A. thesis, University of Chicago, 1936), 98–101; Robert C. Puth, "Supreme Life: The History of a Negro Life Insurance Company" (Ph.D. diss., Northwestern University, 1967), 1–93; Spear, 181–183; C. G. Woodson, "The Insurance Business Among Negroes," *The Journal of Negro History* 14 (Apr. 1929), 202–226; Harry H. Pace, "The Possibilities of Negro Insurance," *Opportunity* 8 (Sept. 1930): 266–269; Stuart, 35–62, 72–108.

48. For discussion of the difficulties that black businessmen faced, see Drake and Cayton, 438–456; Hunter, 12; Spear, 183–184; Paul K. Edwards, *The Southern Urban Negro as a Consumer* (New York 1932), 126, 135–139; Harris, 54–55, 172; Myrdal, 1, 307–312; Harmon, 131, 140, 142, 144–145, 147, 152–155.

49. Edwards, 153–166, 209–213. Several years after this study was published, Edwards expanded his investigation into urban black consumption habits to include the North. He concluded that Northern Negroes showed the same predisposition toward brand names as Southern urbanites. Also see Raymond A. Bauer and Scott M. Cunningham, *Studies in the Negro Market* (Cambridge, Mass. 1970), 11–14, and Raymond A. Bauer, Scott M. Cunningham, and Lawrence H. Wortzel, "The Marketing Dilemma of Negroes," *Journal of Marketing* 29 (July 1965), reprinted in Boone, 353–364.

50. St. Clair Drake, "Churches and Voluntary Associations in the Chicago Negro Community," Report of Official Project 465–54–3–386 Conducted Under the Auspices of the Works Projects Administration, 1940, mimeographed, 247; Oliver Cromwell Cox, "The Negroes Use of Their Buying Power in Chicago as a Means of Securing Employment," Prepared for Professor Millis, University of Chicago, 1933, cited extensively in Drake, "Churches and Voluntary Associations," 230, 247–251; T. Arnold Hill, "Picketing for Jobs," *Opportunity* 8 (July 1930), 216; Stephen Breszka, "And Lo! It Worked: A Tale of Color Harmony," *Opportunity* 11 (Nov. 1933), 242–244, 350; "Butler Stores Cheat," *The Messenger* 7 (Apr. 1925), 156; Wright, Paper for Sociology 264, Mar. 1931, 7, Burgess Papers; Elizabeth Balanoff, "A History of the Black Community of Gary, Indiana, 1906–1940" (Ph.D. diss., University of Chicago, 1974), 200–202; John L. Tilley, *A Brief History of the Negro in Chicago, 1779–1933 (From Jean Baptiste DeSaible–To "A Century of Progress")* (Chicago 1933), 16–18, 25–26; Hunter, "Problems of Colored Chicago," 10, Burgess Papers.

51. Of course the Afro-American influence on American popular music did not begin in the 1920s, but in this decade its impact on mainstream music was particularly formative. The sources on jazz are voluminous. On black jazz in Chicago, see particularly Thomas Joseph Hennessey, "From Jazz to Swing: Black Jazz Musicians and Their Music, 1917–1935" (Ph.D. diss., Northwestern University, 1973); Robert L. Brubacker, *Making Music Chicago Style* (Chicago 1985), 16–25, 148–155; Louis Armstrong, *Swing That Music* (New York 1936); Demsey J. Travis, *An Autobiography of Black Jazz* (Chicago 1983).

52. Marshall W. Stearns, *The Story of Jazz* (New York 1956), 167–168.

53. A survey of a 1929 out-of-town edition of the *Chicago Defender* revealed that 18.7 percent of the 1,070 advertisements were

27. Lichtenstein, "Life at the Rouge," 248ff.; and his "Auto Worker Militancy and the Structure of Factory Life, 1937–1955," *Journal of American History* 67, no. 2, Sept. 1980, 348ff.

28. Zabala, esp. 115ff.

29. Serrin, ch. 1; Rothschild, *Paradise Lost: The Decline of the Auto-Industrial Age* (New York 1973), 125–131; Barnard, 202–203.

30. Quoted in Serrin, 16. Also see Barnard, 204–212.

31. Rothschild, 97–125; and B. J. Widick, ed., *Auto Work and Its Discontents* (Baltimore 1976), 91–93.

32. Twenty-third UAW Convention Proceedings, 1972, 81.

33. Jefferies, 168.

34. Katz, 51–53; Jefferies, ch. 10; Robert Reich and John Donahue, *New Deals: The Chrysler Revival and the American System* (New York 1985), 23–46.

35. "Walter Reuther," 293–294. Lichtenstein makes this UAW model the centerpiece of his essay, "From Corporatism to Collective Bargaining."

36. Quoted in Halpern, 218.

37. Barnard, 117.

38. Dubofsky, 221–223.

39. Edsforth, 215–219.

40. "Our Fear of Abundance," in Henry Christman, ed., *Walter P. Reuther: Selected Papers* (New York 1961), 13–21.

41. "This is Your Fight," *The Nation* 162, no. 2, January 12, 1946, 35–36.

42. Barnard, 212.

43. Christman 22. See also Aronowitz, 75ff.

Chapter Seven. "If a Body Catch a Body": *The Catcher in the Rye* Censorship Debate.

1. Respectively: Harrison Smith, "Manhattan Ulysses, Junior," *The Saturday Review of Literature* 34, July 14, 1951, 12; T. Morris Longstreth, "Review of *The Catcher in the Rye*," *The Christian Science Monitor*, July 19, 1951, 7.

for race records. Edwards, 185. For information on race records, see Lawrence W. Levine, *Black Culture and Black Consciousness: Afro-American Folk Thought from Slavery to Freedom* (New York 1977), 224, 231; LeRoi Jones, *Blues People: The Negro Experience in White America and the Music That Developed from It* (New York 1963), 99–103, 128–129; Stearns, 167–168, 190; Barnouw, 128–131.

54. Steve Nelson, James R. Barrett and Rob Ruck, *Steve Nelson: American Radical* (Pittsburgh 1981), 68.

Chapter Six. Affluence, Anti-Communism, and the Transformation of Industrial Unionism Among Automobile Workers, 1933–1973.

1. For recent examples of radical revision of New Deal labor history, see Mike Davis, *Prisoners of the American Dream: Politics and Economy in the History of the American Working Class* (London 1986); Christopher Tomlins, *The State and the Unions: Labor Relations, Law, and the Organized Labor Movement* (Cambridge 1985); and Stanley Vittoz, *New Deal Labor Policy and the American Industrial Economy* (Chapel Hill 1987). See Howell Harris, "The Snares of Liberalism? Politicians, Bureaucrats, and the Shaping of Federal Labour Relations Policy in the United States," in Steven Tolliday and Jonathan Zeitlin, eds., *Shop Floor Bargaining and the State: Historical and Comparative Perspectives* (Cambridge 1985) for an eloquent and sophisticated response to the radical revisionists.

2. For examples see Davis, 102–124; Stanley Aronowitz, *Working Class Hero: A New Strategy for Labor* (New York 1983), 81–89; Gabriel Kolko, *Main Currents in American History* (New York 1984), 188–194; George Lipsitz, "Labor and the Cold War," in Paul Buhle and Alan Dawley, eds., *Working for Democracy: American Workers from the Revolution to the Present* (Urbana 1985).

3. Lawrence T. McDonnell, "You Are Too Sentimental: Problems and Suggestions for a New Labor History," *Journal of Social History*, Summer 1984, identifies the work of Herbert Gutman and David Montgomery as the source of these trends.

4. I argue that the failures of both the Old Left and New Left can be traced in large part to a failure to accurately describe and comprehend the power and appeal of the ideology of "consumer-oriented Americanism"; see section VI below.

5. Labor's role in 1936 is nicely summarized in Robert Zieger, *American Workers, American Unions, 1920–1985* (Baltimore 1986), 45–46. My own understanding of this Roosevelt revolution is elaborated in *Class Conflict and Cultural Consensus: The Making of a Mass Consumer Society in Flint, Michigan* (New Brunswick 1987), esp. 149–155.

6. See especially David Brody, *Workers in Industrial America: Essays on the Twentieth-Century Struggle* (New York 1980, chs. 5–6; Melvyn Dubofsky, "Not so Turbulent Years: A New Look at the 1930s," in Charles Stephenson and Robert Asher, eds., *Life and Labor: Dimensions of American Working Class History* (Albany 1986); Aronowitz, *Working Class Hero*, 106ff; Kolko, chapters 3 and 5.

7. Aronowitz, 90.

8. These measurable changes are conveniently compiled in Clair Brown, "Consumption Norms, Work Roles, and Economic Growth, 1918–1980," in Clair Brown and Joseph Pechman, eds., *Gender in the Workplace* (Brookings Institute 1987).

9. Except where noted, all expenditure figures are from Brown, 24–25.

10. Brown, 30; and Ruth Schwartz Cowan, *More Work for Mother: The Ironies of Household Technology from the Open Hearth to the Microwave* (New York 1983), 195–196.

11. *Advertising the American Dream: Making Way for Modernity, 1920–1940* (Berkeley and Los Angeles 1985), 363.

12. Nelson Lichtenstein, "From Corporatism to Collective Bargaining: Organized Labor and the Eclipse of Social Democracy in the Postwar Era," in Steve Fraser and Gary Gerstle, eds., *The Rise and Fall of the New Deal Order* (Princeton 1989), 145ff. Except where noted, all statistics in this section are from the above source.

13. Raucher, "Employee Relations at General Motors: The 'My Job' Contest, 1947," *Labor History* 28, no. 2, Spring 1987.

14. Raucher, 225.

15. The Harris survey may be found in the Ken Bannon Collection, box 10, Archives of Labor and Urban History, Walter P. Reuther Library, Wayne State University (hereafter WSU). The Quayle survey is located in the Walter P. Reuther Collection, boxes 147 and 148, WSU.

16. Oliver Quayle and Company, "A Study in Dep Rank and File of the United Automobile Workers" May 1, 71–83.

17. Frank J. Bellafatto and Carolyn San Phillip Nanfel tomobile Workers—How Dissatisfied Are They?," M.S. thes sachusetts Institute of Technology, 1975, 33.

18. Bellafatto and Nanfeldt, 35, 58–60.

19. The films are titled *Talking About ... Women Wo Talking About ... Younger Workers—Older Workers,* and *Ta About ... Dreams and Aspirations.* Many Hours of partly e soundtapes not included in the films are located at the Archive Labor and Urban History, WSU.

20. Especially in the interviews made for *Talking About . Younger Workers—Older Workers.*

21. Richard Feldman and Michael Betzold, eds. (New Yor 1988).

22. Nelson Lichtenstein, "Walter Reuther and the Rise of La bor Liberalism," in Melvyn Dubofsky and Warren Van Tine, eds., *Labor Leaders in America* (Urbana 1987), 288–290; John Barnard, *Walter Reuther and the Rise of the Auto Workers* (Boston 1983), ch. 6; Barton Bernstein, "Walter Reuther and the General Motors Strike of 1945–46," *Michigan History* 49, no. 3, Sept. 1965.

23. Martin Halpern, "Taft-Hartley and the Defeat of the Progressive Alternative in the United Auto Workers," *Labor History* 27, no. 2, Spring 1986. The Foreman's Association lockout is described in Nelson Lichtenstein, "Life at the Rouge: A cycle of Workers' Control," in Stephenson and Asher, 247–252.

24. Steve Jefferies, *Management and Managed: Fifty Years of Crisis at Chrysler* (Cambridge Mass. 1986), 6–11.; William Serrin, *The Company and the Union: The 'Civilized Relationship' of the General Motors Corporation and the United Automobile Workers* (New York 1973).

25. Jefferies, 33–46; Craig Zabala, "Collective Bargaining at UAW Local 645, General Motors Assembly Division, Van Nuys, California 1976–1982," Ph.D. dissertation, University of California at Los Angeles 1983, 318–323.

26. Henry Katz, *Shifting Gears: Changing Labor Relations in the U.S. Automobile Industry* (Cambridge, Mass. 1985), 42–44.

2. Adam Moss, "Catcher Comes of Age," *Esquire* 96 (Dec. 1981), 56. See also "Footnotes" in *The Chronicle of Higher Education*, Sept. 29, 1982, 21 for a summary of two studies (California, 1962, and national, 1982) in which American Literature professors were asked which American novels published after 1941 should be considered "classics" and which novels should be taught to college students. *Catcher* was the number one response to both questions in 1962 and number three in 1982. *Catcher* was further identified as the foremost novel on the censor's list in Tracy Metz, "The New Crusader's of the USA," *Index on Censorship*, Jan. 1982, 20, and in the editorial essay, "Survey Reports Rise in School Library Censorship," *Newsletter on Intellectual Freedom* 32, no. 1 (Jan. 1983), 1, 18.

3. *Catcher* is referred to, for example, in Eric Segal's *Oliver's Story* (New York 1977) and W. P. Kinsella's *Shoeless Joe* (Boston 1982). Television references to *Catcher* range from the CBS *Sixty Minutes* (Nov. 1, 1981) and *Archie Bunker's Place* (Feb. 21, 1982) to the ABC game show, *Family Feud* (Oct. 19, 1983).

4. For extended discussion of reader loyalty, see Edward Corbett, "Raise High the Barriers, Censors," *America 104, Jan. 7, 1961, 441; Joan Didion, "Finally (Fashionably) Spurious," National Review 11*, Nov. 18, 1961, 341; Robert Gutwillig, "Everybody's Caught *The Catcher in the Rye*," *New York Times Book Review: Paperback Section*, Jan. 15, 1961, 38–39; Granville Hicks, "J. D. Salinger: Search for Wisdom," *Saturday Review* 42, July 25, 1959, 13; Marvin Laser and Norman Fruman, *Studies in J. D. Salinger* (New York 1963); Arthur Mizener, "The Love Song of J. D. Salinger," *Harper's Magazine* 218, Feb. 1959, 83; Sanford Pinsker, "*The Catcher in the Rye* and All: Is the Age of Formative Books Over?", *Georgia Review* 40 (Spring 1986), 953–967; Richard Stayton, "Required Reading: Why Holden Caulfield Still Catches You," *Los Angeles Herald Examiner*, Oct. 12, 1985, 35.

5. Gutwillig, 38.

6. Corbett, 441.

7. Pinsker, 953.

8. Stayton.

9. J. D. Salinger, *The Catcher in the Rye* (New York, Bantam Books ed. 1964 [1951]), 173.

10. I first reviewed the *Newsletter on Intellectual Freedom*, which in each issue identifies censorship controversies across the nation (initially erratic in its publication, it has been published monthly since 1965). I then followed all controversies identified as continuing for three months or longer and/or involving fifty or more participants as they appeared in local and national newspapers. Interviews were conducted in 1983 in four states. The communities and the year of controversy were: Calhoun County, Alabama (1982); Marin County, California (1960–61); Albuquerque, New Mexico (1968) and Hanover County, Virginia (1963). These four communities were selected on the basis of a fairly-high level of participation in both number of participants and length of controversy, with an attempt to provide regional and time frame variation.

11. "Issaquah, Washington," *Newsletter on Intellectual Freedom* 27, no. 6 (Nov. 1978), 138.

12. In the 1960-61 California controversy, the school district Director of Instruction suffered his first heart attack: His participation in the controversy was believed to be the precipitating strain; however, he continued to participate even while recovering in the hospital. Another school board member felt his personal reputation in the same community suffered due to his support of the book and he recounted neighborhood gossip as evidence. Similarly, a minister in the Albuquerque controversy felt the reputation of his high-school-age daughter suffered, as well as his own, for his criticism of *Catcher*, and an Alabama mother provided documentation of her elementary-school-age son's harassment by teachers and administrators, which she believed was in response to her pro-*Catcher* stance. Finally, as columnist Dorothy Simpers closed her "I–J Reporter's Notebook" in the *San Rafael Independent Journal* (Dec. 29, 1960, 1c.) in regard to the California controversy: "The book controversy apparently produced its share of family squabbles, too. The board received two letters on the subject from a man and wife. One was for banning the books; the other was opposing."

13. Interview Aug. 19, 1983, Anniston, Ala.

14. Robert N. Bellah, Richard Madsen, William M. Sullivan, Ann Swidler, Steven M. Tipton, *Habits of the Heart: Individualism and Commitment in American Life* (Berkeley and Los Angeles 1985).

15. Interview Apr. 28, 1983, San Rafael, Calif.

16. Edward Gordon, "Freedom to Teach and to Learn," *PTA Magazine* 58, no. 2 (Oct. 1963), 5.

17. As quoted in Dorothy Simpers, "Tam Trustees Again Refuse to Ban Books," *San Rafael Independent Journal*, Jan. 10, 1961, 4A.

18. Letter to the Board of Trustees of Tamalpais Unified High School District, Dec. 16, 1960, 1–2.

19. See particularly Frederick L. Gwynn and Joseph L. Blotner, *The Fiction of J. D. Salinger* (Pittsburgh 1958); Warren French, *J. D. Salinger* (Boston 1963); Marvin Laser and Norman Fruman, *Studies in J. D. Salinger* (New York 1963); James Lundquist, *J. D. Salinger* (New York 1979).

20. The archetypal character isolated by R. W. B. Lewis in his review of nineteenth-century American literature was "the image of a radically new personality, the hero of the new adventure: an individual emancipated from history, happily bereft of ancestry . . . an individual standing alone, self-reliant and self-propelling, ready to confront whatever awaited him with the aid of his own unique and inherent resources" where society is deemed "the element which provides experience." *The American Adam* (Chicago 1955), 111.

21. Salinger, 204.

22. Salinger, 141.

23. Interview Apr. 28, 1983, San Rafael, Calif.

24. Interview Aug. 18, 1983, Anniston, Ala.

25. Board of Trustees Meeting Minutes, Tamalpais Union High School District, Marin County, Calif., Feb. 6, 1961.

26. *Newsletter on Intellectual Freedom* 30, no. 6 (Nov. 1981), 150.

27. Marcus Klein, *After Alienation: American Novels in Mid-Century* (Cleveland 1965), 295. See also Ihab Hassan, *Radical Innocence: Studies in the Contemporary American Novel* (Princeton 1961).

28. Sandra Christenson, "On *The Catcher in the Rye*," student essay published in Fred B. Myers, ed., *The Range of Literature: Nonfiction Prose* (Boston 1969), 37–39.

29. John E. Mack, "Psychosocial Trauma," In Ruth Adams and Susan Cullen, eds., *The Final Epidemic: Physicians and Social Scientists on Nuclear War* (Chicago: Educational Foundation for Nuclear Science, 1981), 21.

30. Mack, 26.

31. Peter Goldman, "Living with the Bomb: The First Generation of the Atomic Age," *Newsweek*, July 29, 1985, 28.

32. See "Depression," *Newsweek*, May 4, 1987, 48, which documents the drop in the age of onset of clinical depression from late middle age (50s) to mid-20s and early 30s in the Post–World War II period. Several sources document the rise in adolescent suicide. I found Herbert Hendin's *Suicide in America* (New York 1984) particularly accessible.

33. Phyllis La Farge, "Learning to Live with the Bomb," *Parent's Magazine*, March 1987, 125.

34. La Farge, 125.

35. Mack, 25.

36. La Farge, 125.

Chapter Eight. The Domestication of Rock and Roll.

1. In the summer of 1989, The Who made a "silver anniversary tour" of the United States, but only after Townshend rethought his determination to put his years in the band behind him. John Milward, "The Who and the Why," *Chicago Tribune*, Apr. 30, 1989, sec. 13, 6–7.

2. Allan Bloom, *The Closing of the American Mind* (New York 1987), 76.

3. Simon Frith, *Sound Effects: Youth, Leisure and the Politics of Rock'n'Roll* (New York 1981), 12–38; Charlie Gillett, *The Sound of the City: The Rise of Rock and Roll* (New York 1984), 23–35.

4. See Dick Hebdige's account of the punk movement in England, *Subculture: The Meaning of Style* (New York 1979); also, Frith, 218–224.

5. George Lipsitz, *Class and Culture in Cold War America* (South Hadley, Mass. 1981), 219.

6. Theodor W. Adorno, *Introduction to the Sociology of Music*, E. B. Ashton, trans. (New York 1976), 29, 26–27.

7. Gillett, 17; "Rock-and-Roll Called 'Communicable' Disease," *New York Times*, Mar. 28, 1956, 33.

8. "Segregationist Wants Ban on 'Rock and Roll'," *New York Times*, Mar. 30, 1956, 39.

9. Albert Goldman, *Elvis* (New York 1981).

10. Gillett, 25.

11. Tom Smucker, "The Politics of Rock: Movement vs. Groovement," in Jonathan Eisen, ed., *The Age of Rock 2: Sights and Sounds of the American Cultural Revolution* (New York 1970), 83.

12. Gillett, 350.

13. Stanley Booth, *Dance with the Devil: The Rolling Stones and Their Times* (New York 1984), 110–111, 142–154, 200–204.

14. Benjamin DeMott, "Rock as Salvation," *New York Times Magazine*, Aug. 25, 1968, 30–52.

15. "Return of Satan's Jesters," *Time*, May 17, 1971, 60.

16. Hebdige; Dave Laing, *One Chord Wonders: Power and Meaning in Punk Rock* (Philadelphia 1985), pictures.

17. Simon Frith, "Beyond the Dole Queue: The Politics of Punk," *Village Voice*, Oct. 24, 1977, 78.

18. Robert Christgau, "Funkentelechy vs. the Placebo Syndrome," *Village Voice*, Feb. 22, 1983, 43–47.

19. Irvin Molotsky, "Hearing on Rock Lyrics," *New York Times*, Sept. 20, 1985, C8.

20. Dave Marsh and Phyllis Pollack, "Wanted for Attitude," *Village Voice*, Oct. 10, 1989, 33–37.

21. In the United States, accounts of the "cooptation" of rock and roll usually indict greedy performers in collusion with greedy recording company executives, and leave the story at that. More sophisticated analyses, which take account of the industry and then try to work through its relationships with rock and roll fans, include Lawrence Grossberg, "The Politics of Youth Culture: Some Observations on Rock and Roll in American Culture," *Social Text* 8

(Winter 1983/84), 104–126, and the set of essays in Simon Frith, ed., *Facing the Music* (New York 1988).

22. Frith, *Sound Effects*, 167.

23. David Riesman, "Listening to Popular Music," in Bernard Rosenberg and David Manning White, eds., *Mass Culture: The Popular Arts in America*, (New York 1957) 412; Frith, *Sound Effects*, 205–212; Deena Weinstein, "Rock: Youth and Its Music," *Popular Music and Society* 9 (1983), 11–12.

24. See S. I. Hayakawa, "Popular Songs vs. the Facts of Life," 393–403 in Rosenberg and White, for a contrast of pop fantasy and blues realism. Hayakawa, like Adorno, was not an admirer of the comparatively literate and carefully crafted show tune. Among the pop composers he excoriated were George and Ira Gershwin, Irving Berlin, and Rodgers and Hart.

25. Gillett, 3–7.

26. Laing, 82.

27. Laing, 90.

28. George Melly, *Revolt into Style* (Garden City, N.Y. 1971), 99.

29. Regarding the notorious Monkees, see Gillett, 331–332. The rise of New Kids on the Block is the subject of Peter Watrous, "White Singers + Black Style = Pop Bonanza," *New York Times*, Mar. 11, 1990, H1, H34.

30. For a discussion of the connotations of crossing over, in this instance by transcending racially defined audiences, see Steve Perry, "Ain't No Mountain High Enough," in Frith, *Facing the Music*, 51–87.

31. "Human League," in Phil Hardy, Dave Laing, Stephen Barnard, and Don Perretta, eds., *Encyclopedia of Rock* (London 1987), 222.

32. Jack Kroll, "Beatles vs. Stones," *Newsweek*, Jan. 1, 1968, 62.

33. Jann Wenner, *Lennon Remembers: The Rolling Stone Interviews* (San Francisco 1971), 45–46.

34. "Fleetwood Mac," in Hardy et al., 171.

35. Michael Lydon, "Rock for Sale," in Eisen, 59.

36. Wenner, 67–69, 144–160; Albert Goldman, *The Lives of John Lennon* (New York 1988), 322–326.

37. Quoted in "The Clash," in Hardy et al., 103.

38. Greil Marcus, "Anarchy in the U.K.," in Jim Miller, ed., *The Rolling Stone Illustrated History of Rock & Roll* (New York 1980), 460.

39. Don McCleese, "Shrieking Crowd at Pavilion Just Can't Get Enough of INXS," *Chicago Sun-Times*, Mar. 14, 1988, 33.

40. Goldman, *Elvis,* 431-448.

41. Chuck Berry, *Chuck Berry: The Autobiography* (New York 1987), 270.

42. Tom Popson, "Growing Up with Buster," *Chicago Tribune*, June 17, 1988, sec. 7, H-1.

43. Mary Harron argues that the success of David Bowie and Madonna is attributable to the their skillful manipulation of self-consciously artificial, disposable personas. In essence, this is another route around the typical stages of the rock and roll career. See Harron, "McRock," in Frith, *Facing the Music*, 207–219.

44. Simon Frith, "Art Ideology and Pop Practice," in Cary Nelson and Lawrence Grossberg, eds., *Marxism and the Interpretation of Culture* (Urbana 1988), 463.

Chapter Nine. Closing Thoughts: Popular Culture and National Anxiety.

1. William J. Bennett, *Our Children and Our Country: Improving America's Schools and Affirming the Common Culture* (New York 1988); Allan Bloom, *The Closing of the American Mind: How Higher Education Has Failed Democracy and Impoverished the Souls of Today's Students* (New York 1987); E. D. Hirsch, Jr., *Cultural Literacy: What Every American Needs to Know* (Boston 1987).

2. Maria Margaronis, "Waiting for the Barbarians," *Voice Literary Supplement*, Jan./Feb. 1989, 12–17.

3. Dwight MacDonald, "A Theory of Mass Culture," 59–73 in Bernard Rosenberg and David Maning White, eds., *Mass Culture: The Popular Arts in America* (Glencoe, Ill. 1957).

4. Martin Jay, *The Dialectical Imagination: A History of the Frankfurt School and the Institute for Social Research 1923–1950* (Boston 1973), 173–218.

5. Stuart Ewen, *Captains of Consciousness: Advertising and the Social Roots of the Consumer Culture* (New York 1977); Dolores Hayden, *Redesigning the American Dream: The Future of Housing, Work, and Family Life* (New York 1984), especially 17–38; Neil Postman, *Amusing Ourselves to Death: Public Discourse in the Age of Television* (New York 1985). For a concise summary of contemporary leftist cultural criticism in the United States, see Donald Lazere, "Introduction: Entertainment as Social Control," in Lazere, ed., *American Media and Mass Culture: Left Perspectives* (Berkeley and Los Angeles 1987), 1–26.

6. Jonathan Rauch, "Is the Deficit Really Bad?" *Atlantic Monthly*, Feb. 1989, 38.

7. Christopher Lasch, *The Culture of Narcissism: American Life in an Age of Diminishing Expectations* (New York 1979); Robert N. Bellah, Richard Madsen, William M. Sullivan, Ann Swidler, and Steven M. Tipton, *Habits of the Heart: Individualism and Commitment in American Life* (Berkeley and Los Angeles 1985); Frances Fitzgerald, *Cities on a Hill* (New York 1987).

8. Fitzgerald, 412–413.

9. Andrew Goodwin, "The Cultural Crash of '89," *The Reader* (Chicago), Nov. 11, 1988, 32.

10. For instance, see Richard Sennett's discussion of the fifteenth-century Florentine priest Savonarola in *The Fall of Public Man* (New York 1978), 232–235.

11. Postman, 125–141.

12. Andrew Ross, *No Respect: Intellectuals and Popular Culture* (New York 1989), 209.

13. Among the more interesting analyses of the film are Stanley Crouch, "Do the Race Thing," *Village Voice*, June 20, 1989, 73–74, 76; Joe Klein, "Spiked?" *New York*, June 26, 1989, 14–15; and Jonathan Rosenbaum, "Say the Right Thing," *The Reader* (Chicago), Aug. 4, 1989, 10, 28–30. Also see the forum " 'Do the Right Thing': Issues and Images," *New York Times*, July 9, 1989, H1, H23.

14. David Denby, "He's Gotta Have It," *New York*, June 26, 1989, 54; Jack Kroll, "The Fuse Has Been Lit," *Newsweek*, July 3, 1989, 65.

15. For example, Terrence Rafferty, "Open and Shut," *The New Yorker*, July 24, 1989, 80.

16. Dick Hebdige, *Subculture: The Meaning of Style* (New York 1979), 88.

17. In the film's final, post-riot encounter between Mookie and Sal, Lee makes it clear that Mookie, at least, has not even derived any greater understanding in the wake of the torching of Sal's pizzeria.

18. Klein, 15.

CONTRIBUTORS

Howard Abramowitz taught in the Department of Sociology, Anthropology, and Social Work at Skidmore College from 1964 to 1990. His publications included articles in the *American Sociological Review* and *Science and Society*.

Michael Barkun is a Professor of Political Science in the Maxwell School of Syracuse University. His books include *Disaster and the Millennium*, and *Law Without Sanctions*. He serves as the Editor of *Communal Societies*, the journal of the Communal Studies Association. He is presently writing a book on the religious roots of white supremacist ideology.

Larry Bennett teaches in the Political Science Department and directs the Urban Studies Program at DePaul University. He is the author of *Fragments of Cities: Downtowns and Neighborhoods* and co-author of *Chicago: Race, Class, and Response to Urban Decline*.

Lizabeth Cohen is an Assistant Professor of History at Carnegie Mellon University. She received her PhD. from the University of California, Berkely in 1986, and is the author of *Making a New Deal: Industrial Workers in Chicago, 1919–1939*.

Ronald Edsforth has taught American history at the Massachusetts Institute of Technology, Skidmore College, the University of Wisconsin-Parkside, and Michigan State University. He is the author of *Class Conflict and Cultural Consensus: The Making of a Mass Consumer Society in Flint, Michigan*, and co-editor of the forthcoming *Auto Work*, a collection of essays and documents to be published by SUNY Press.

Nancy J. Rosenbloom is an Associate Professor of History at Canisius College. She received her PhD. in History from the University of Rochester in 1981. She has published in the journal *Film History*, and is currently working on a book on the politics of film censorship in the Progressive era.

Pamela Steinle is an Assistant Professor of American Studies at California State University-Fullerton. She received her PhD. in Comparative Cultures from the University of California-Irvine. Her dissertation, "If a Body Catch a Body: J. D. Salinger's *The Catcher in the Rye* and Post-World War II American Culture," was a finalist for the 1988 Ralph Henry Gabriel Prize in American Studies.

INDEX